UK
Government
& Politics

UK
Government
& Politics

Second Edition

ANDY WILLIAMS

Heinemann Educational Publishers
Halley Court, Jordan Hill, Oxford OX2 8EJ
a division of Reed Educational & Professional Publishing Ltd

OXFORD MELBOURNE AUCKLAND
JOHANNESBURG BLANTYRE GABORONE
IBADAN PORTSMOUTH (NH) USA CHICAGO

Heinemann is a registered trademark of Reed Educational & Professional Publishing Ltd

First published in 1995
This edition published in 1998

04 03
10 9 8 7 6

British Library Cataloguing in Publication Data
A catalogue record for this book is available from the British Library

ISBN 0 435 33158 2

Designed by Jackie Hill at 320 Design, Kent
Typeset and illustrated by Wyvern 21 Ltd, Bristol
Cover illustration by Debbie Hinks
Cover design by Aricot Vert Design
Printed and bound in Great Britain by CPI Bath

Acknowledgements

The publishers would like to thank the following for permission to reproduce copyright material.

Philip Allan Publishers Ltd for the extract from 'The Fall of a Prime Minister', by J Benyon, *Social Studies Review* 6 (3) (January 1991), on pp. 65–6; Rt Hon. Paddy Ashdown, MP, for the extract on pp. 75–6; The Associated Examining Board for the questions on pp. 38, 75–6, 103, 211 and 237; Blackwell Publishers for the extracts on pp. 72–3, 82; Curtis Brown Group Ltd. for the extracts from *Whitehall*, by Peter Hennessey, on pp. 119, 144, 148–9, 151, 152; Causeway Press for the extract from 'Recent Parliamentary Developments', by M Rush, in *Developments in Politics*, vol.2, 1991, on pp. 103–4; © *The Economist*, London, for the extracts on pp. 17–18, 44, 100, 168–9, 187, 223, 230, 232; Prentice Hall Europe for the extracts from *Politics UK*, by Bill Jones et al., 1998, on pp. 35, 140; HarperCollins for the extract from RHS Crossman's introduction to *The English Constitution*, Collins, 1963, © RHS Crossman, on pp. 117, 134; Her Majesty's Stationery Office for the extract from the Royal Institution of Public Administration Report (1985) on p. 151; Hodder and Stoughton for the extract from *The Essential Anatomy of Britain*, by Anthony Sampson, 1993: reproduced by permission of Hodder and Stoughton Limited on p. 101; The Institute of Contemporary British History for the extract from *Contemporary Record*, by Peter Hennessy, 1988, on pp. 161–2; London Examinations, A division of Edexel Foundation, for the questions on pp. 17, 36–7, 64–6, 75, 102–4, 133–4, 160–2, 191–2, 209–10, 222–3 and 236–7; The London School of Economics and Political Science for the table on p. 29, from *Replaying the 1992 General Election*, by Dunleavy, Margetts and Weir, The Public Policy Group, 1992; Manchester University Press for the extracts from *British Politics Today*, by Bill Jones and Dennis Kavanagh, and the quotation from *Parliament Today*, by Andrew Adonis, 1993, on pp. 37 and 93; The Daily Mirror for the headline on p. 139; Penguin Books for the extract from *Freedom, the Individual and the Law*, by Geoffrey Robertson, © Geoffrey Robertson 1993, on p. 16; Random House for the extracts from *Arguments for Democracy*, by Tony Benn, Jonathan Cape, 1979, on pp. 143, 150; The Joseph Rowntree Foundation for the extract from *Local Government Since Widdicombe*, November 1990, on p. 210; Sage Publications for the extract from 'The Federal Constitutional Court in the German Political System', by Donald P Kommers, in Comparative Political Studies, January 1994, copyright © 1994 by Donald P Kommers, reprinted by Permission of Sage Publications on p. 183; The Sun for the headlines on p. 139; Hugo Young for the extract from *The Judges* on p. 176; The questions on pp. 37, 65, 103, 161, 168, 210 and 237 are reproduced by permission of the University of Cambridge Local Examinations Syndicate; UODLE material is reproduced by permission of the University of Cambridge Local Examinations Syndicate on pp. 17, 37, 103, 133, 161, 168, 192, 210, 222 and 237.

The publishers have made every effort to contact copyright holders. However, if any material has been incorrectly acknowledged, the publishers would be pleased to correct this at the earliest opportunity.

Contents

Introduction   ix

1   Concepts and constitutions   1

Politics   1
Political power   2
Constitutions   5
Written and unwritten constitutions   11
Flexible and rigid constitutions   13
Constitutional reform   14

2   Elections   19

Introduction   19
Democracy   19
Elections and democracy   20
The British electoral system   21
The first-past-the-post system   23
Proportional representation (PR)   28
Constitutional effects of PR   32
Voting behaviour   33

3   Political parties   39

Introduction   39
A definition of party politics   40
The development of parties in Britain   40
Functions of political parties   40
The party system   50
Party organization and structure   55

4   Political ideologies   67

Introduction   67
What is ideology?   67
Liberalism   68
Conservatism   70
Socialism   73

5   Parliament   77

Introduction   77
The composition of Parliament   77

Parliamentary sovereignty 82
The functions of Parliament 85
Factors affecting Parliament's performance 91

6   The Prime Minister and the Cabinet   105

Introduction 105
Cabinet government 106
Prime ministerial government 113
The decline of Cabinet decision-making 123
The Prime Minister's personality 126
Internal constraints on the Prime Minister 127
External constraints on the Prime Minister 128
Conclusion 132

7   The civil service   135

Introduction 135
The executive branch of government 135
Functions of higher civil servants 136
Characteristics of the civil service 141
The civil service's power and influence 144
Potential civil service bias 149
Challenges to the constitutional position 150
Efficiency and reforms 153
The impact of reform 156
The civil service and 'New Labour' 158
Further perspectives on the civil service 159

8   The monarchy   163

Introduction 163
The development of the constitutional monarchy 163
The power of the monarch 165
The authority of the monarch 166
Arguments for and against the monarchy 166

9   The judiciary   170

Introduction 170
Judges and the constitution 171
The judiciary and politics 173
Judicial power 182
Civil liberties 184
Civil rights in Britain 185
The courts and civil liberties 189
The European Convention on Human Rights 190
A bill of rights 190

10 Local and regional government   193

LOCAL GOVERNMENT
Introduction 193

Why have local government? 194
The role of local councillors 194
The structure of local government 195
The central–local relationship 197
Centralization under Margaret Thatcher 199
Financial reform 204
The status of local government today 206

REGIONAL GOVERNMENT
Introduction 206
States and nations 207
The historical composition of the United Kingdom 208
The governance of the United Kingdom 208
Progress towards devolution 208
Constitutional issues surrounding devolution 209

11 The European Union 212

Introduction 212
The history of the European Union 212
The institutions of the EU 217
The European debate 219

12 Pressure groups 224

Introduction 224
What are pressure groups? 224
Determinants of the power of the individual groups 227
Targets of pressure group activity 229
Perspectives on pressure group activity 234

Sources 238

Index 240

Introduction

In the past, many politics textbooks have been written in an attempt to help both A level students and undergraduates. As a result, A level students have been forced to wade through a mass of material, some of which is relevant to their course and some of which is not. While teachers provide a valuable guide inside the classroom, outside it, students have had little help in deciding whether material is fundamental, useful or merely interesting.

UK Government & Politics has been updated to take into account the rapid changes in British politics over recent years and particularly since the general election of 1997. It has been written with you, the A level student, in mind. It offers a complete grounding in the processes, institutions and policy areas of the British political system, as well as an introduction to the European dimension of British politics. Every opportunity has been taken to update the text in the light of the changes which have taken place. For example the chapter on local government has been expanded to take into account the move towards devolution for Scotland and Wales.

The book combines description, explanation and analysis – the three levels of understanding required of A level students. The basic workings of the institutions and processes are described to ensure that you understand how, for example, the British electoral system works and how a bill passes through Parliament, but simple description has been kept to a minimum.

The quality of written work at A level will depend on your ability to explain and to analyse the British political system, so this book looks closely at the political institutions and processes and analyses their effectiveness.

While it is designed to introduce you to the analysis of British politics, rather than its historical development, the elements of the system are to some extent the products of historical events and so each chapter puts its subject into historical context. For example, important political developments from medieval England are covered when considering the role of the monarchy. If you choose to read this book from beginning to end, rather than dipping into selected chapters, you will find that certain historical events are referred to many times; for example, electoral reform in the nineteenth century. This is deliberate as the events explain turning points in British political history and it is important that you understand their relevance to the development of today's politics.

As essential as the historical context are up-to-date examples. Every effort has been made to include as many of these as possible, but since political textbooks can soon date, it is recommended that you keep in touch with the day-to-day developments in British politics through newspapers, television and radio.

In some cases it has only been possible to hint at changes in the political system that are likely to come in the next few years. Tony Blair's leadership style, reform of the House of Lords, reform of the electoral system, unrest within the ranks of the Labour Party and the future of the Conservative Party are all on the agenda so students will need to keep abreast of the developments in UK politics through the media.

Where the book describes the institutions of British politics, these are set in their historical context and then their position in the constitutional framework is considered. Therefore, many chapters include an outline of the traditional position of an institution in the British constitution. Parliamentary sovereignty, Cabinet government, civil service permanence, neutrality and anonymity are all covered at some length in order to establish the traditional foundations of British political institutions. However, the analysis then examines how far it can be argued that the reality conforms to the constitutional pattern.

In line with the recommendations for the A level Government and Politics syllabuses, the performance of British political institutions and the effectivness of political processes are compared not only to constitutional theory but also to their counterparts overseas. Therefore, throughout the book you will find references to the political system in the USA and, in some cases, to the political systems of Europe. The use of comparative politics is not intended to give an in-depth knowledge of other political systems but rather to enhance understanding of the British system through comparison.

The aim has been to make the material easily accessible, leaving you with a clear understanding of the British political system. However, politics, like chemistry, physics or economics, has its own technical terminology. Concepts like sovereignty, authority and legitimacy, as well as descriptive terms such as bicameral, access points and 'backwoodsmen', are not merely jargon designed to make the subject more complicated! The terminology forms the language of politics which you will need to understand and to use in your written work. To emphasize the importance of these terms and to help you become familiar with them, key words are listed at the beginning of each chapter and then highlighted in the text.

The scope of *UK Government & Politics* has been reduced for this new edition. The first edition attempted to cover the fundamentals of UK politics whilst also encompassing contemporary issues. This new edition is more focused on the fundamentals thus giving the opportunity to expand the key areas.

1 Concepts and constitutions

Questions to be answered in this chapter

- What is politics?
- What is power and where does it lie?
- What are states and governments?
- What are constitutions and why do states have them?
- How is the British constitution made up, and should it be changed?

Terms to know

- Amendments
- Adversarial politics
- Authority
- Bicameral
- Bill of rights
- Cabinet
- Civil rights
- Codified
- Collective Cabinet responsibility
- Common law
- Consensus politics
- Constitution
- Conventions
- Devolution
- Executive
- Federal
- Flexible
- Independent judiciary
- Individual ministerial responsibility
- Influence
- Judiciary
- Legislature
- Legitimate
- Limited government
- Overall majority
- Parliamentary executive
- Parliamentary sovereignty
- Politics
- Power
- Rule of law
- Separation of powers
- Sovereignty
- Unitary

Politics

When most people think about what is meant by **politics,** they usually define it as political parties, Parliament and the Prime Minister, but all of these terms confine politics to the British system of government. Politics appears in a variety of forms in every country in the world and is not confined to the institutions of government. The trade union member is participating in politics just like the government minister and, in some countries, the priest is as involved as the army general.

Politics is about conflict. It is the disagreement between groups or individuals about the way in which their lives should be governed. In Britain the Conservative and Labour parties embody the disagreements between conservatives and socialists. In the USA,

Conflict

political divisions are between the Republican and Democratic parties. But even in undemocratic countries politics is present. Military leaders who stage a coup in order to wrest a country from the control of politicians might ban political parties, but they are not abolishing politics; they are merely changing the context of politics and the divisions will now occur between the army and the navy or within the army.

In the former Soviet Union, many observers saw the Communist party as a monolithic thing in which there was no disagreement. No other parties were allowed to exist, so they concluded that there was no political competition. Of course there was, but it took place behind closed doors, within the party.

So, politics will be with us so long as people continue to disagree. Many dictators have tried to remove disagreement by banning the symptoms of politics, such as freedom of speech, a free press and the freedom of association, but none has succeeded in extinguishing the human spirit to such an extent that all resistance, debate and feeling were destroyed.

Political power

In any conflict the winner is the player with the most **power**. That power could be derived from, among other things, supporters, money or skill. Politics is no exception, and the political players compete for power as energetically as a business executive, a footballer or a general. In politics the individual or party with the greatest power will be able to make decisions, according to their ideas and principles, about how the country is governed – the conflict will have been won.

Definition It is relatively easy to see why politicians desire power. It is a much more difficult matter to define power or to observe it. The political scientist, Robert Dahl, described his intuitive idea of power:

'*A has power over B to the extent that he can get B to do something that B would otherwise not do.*' ('The concept of power', in *Behavioural Science*, 1957)

This definition contains two important elements of any definition of power – a relationship and the removal of coincidence.

Relationship Power is a relationship. A person sitting alone on a desert island has no power because there is no one over whom to wield that power – there is no 'B'. The ancient Greeks were no more powerful than the Chinese because they did not know of each other's existence, and so the issue of which country was more powerful was irrelevant. The issue of 'coincidence' raises the problem of observation. The effort to remove any coincidences is to ensure that if A *does* get B to do something B would not have done it anyway. If the power of Prime Ministers is assessed by observing how many of their proposals are approved by Cabinet, it is possible to be misled because the Cabinet might be expected to agree with the Prime Minister anyway. Therefore, observations say little about the power of the Prime Minister.

Observation Even in seemingly innocuous situations, power can be difficult to observe. For example, if the population of a country is given the opportunity to depose a dictator via the ballot box, it might be observed that power lies with the electorate. Given the situation, it might be expected that the voters would elect to oust the dictator. However, if they vote to retain the dictator, it is possible to imagine that power really lies with the dictator and the voters made their decision with the dictator's possible reprisals in mind. Therefore, despite the power to vote, the real power lies with the ruler.

Types of power

Robert Dahl's definition of power is extremely broad. It is helpful to divide power into three different types: coercion, **influence** and **authority** (see Figure 1.1).

Figure 1.1 Types of power

Coercion

Coercion is based on force. A is able to get B to do something that B would otherwise not do because of some explicit or implicit threat. Some commentators argue that the South African government was encouraged to release Nelson Mandela and to relinquish power to the African National Congress as a result of the sanctions imposed on South Africa by the rest of the world. This illustrates the negative aspects of coercive power. However, there are positive aspects to coercion. 'If you do not … we will impose sanctions' can become 'If you do … we will lift the sanctions'. In the latter, the end of coercion becomes a reward.

Sanctions

Influence

Influence is based on persuasion. A has influence over B if A can persuade B to do something B otherwise would not do. Influence is most commonly associated with pressure groups such as trade unions, the Confederation of British Industry (CBI) and the British Medical Association (BMA). Pressure groups seek to persuade government to adopt policies that suit the needs of the pressure group, its members or society as a whole.

Persuasion

Authority

Authority is based on the right to wield power. A can get B to do something B otherwise would not have done because B believes A has the right to tell them what to do. A parent, a teacher, a priest or a government are all believed to have the right to tell their children, students, etc. what to do.

Right

The German sociologist Max Weber believed that authority could be divided into three types: traditional, legal and charismatic. Traditional authority includes the monarch, the Pope and a parent. Their authority is customary, well established and comes from

Weber

experience as much as their position. Legal authority encompasses those who gain their authority from their office – for example, the Prime Minister and the US President. The final category is perhaps the most problematic – charisma. An individual is considered charismatic when the strength of his or her personality is so great that people will follow their lead. Charismatic leaders have included Winston Churchill, Adolf Hitler and Margaret Thatcher.

Weber's typology should be handled with care because it is difficult to separate clearly different types of authority as there is considerable overlap. Similarly, there is a degree of blurring between the different types of power. Most governments, for example, rely on people to obey the law due to the government's authority, however, they must also be able to turn to coercion to threaten those who do not respect the laws or the government's authority.

Consent and legitimacy

Elections and consent

In democratic countries a government's authority is based on elections. Provided those elections are free and competitive (freedom of speech, a number of parties from which to choose, a secret ballot, etc.) they allow the people to give their consent to government. This means that the people are governed in a manner, and by a government, of which they approve. However, consent need not be achieved solely through elections. Many regimes that would not be considered democratic have tried to show that they have the consent of the people through demonstrations, marches and public shows of support. The Nazis in Germany in the 1930s tried to show their public support through mass rallies, and public support in Cuba for Fidel Castro has been shown by 'spontaneous' public demonstrations.

Legitimacy

However, in Western states, elections are the usual means of gaining consent. An elected government is considered to be **legitimate**, in that it is the rightful government. From its legitimacy comes its authority.

Public order

Governments lay down laws in order to create predictable patterns of behaviour. These laws reflect the ideology and morals of the society. The fact that people abide by these laws is known as public order.

It is achieved by the legitimacy of the government making the laws. In Britain the House of Commons is elected and so makes law on behalf of the people. As a result the people obey the law made in their name.

Public order is necessary to create a stable society in which art, science and commerce can flourish. However, some degree of disorder is also necessary to allow progress. Absolute order implies no disagreement. Without disagreement ideas are not challenged and there is no progress.

The link between legitimacy and authority is extremely important in representative democracies. The fact that the people elect representatives makes the government legitimate. Those representatives then make the laws that will govern people's lives. People obey those laws because they believe that their elected representatives have the right or the authority to make law. Therefore, most people obey the laws not because they fear the sanctions that would follow from a breach of the law but because they believe the law was made in their name and that it should be obeyed. The result is public order.

Legitimacy can also be bestowed by the international community, usually represented by the United Nations. If a government is considered to be the rightful government of a country, it will achieve recognition from other governments and will take up its seat at the United Nations. For many years the Communist government of the Peoples' Republic of China was not recognized by Western states, firstly because it came to power via a revolution rather than democratic elections, and secondly because it joined the Communist bloc during the Cold War.

International legitimacy

Constitutions

Given that politicians compete fiercely for political power, rules are needed to regulate this competition. These rules are included in a **constitution**. They are intended to ensure that competition takes place within limits. In Britain the conflict between the Conservative and Labour parties is fervent, but takes place through parliamentary debate, elections and in the media. It does not spill over into armed conflict or civil war. This is because Britain has a constitution by which all, or most, politicians are prepared to abide.

Rules

Formally, a constitution is a broad set of rules and principles by which a state is governed. It is important that the rules should be broad because a constitution must allow a political system to develop over time. If rules are very precise, they will date quickly and the constitution will break rather than bend with changes in circumstances.

> **Unconstitutional and anti-constitutional**
>
> *Unconstitutional* behaviour breaches the principles of the constitution. For example, if the government acts beyond the power given to it by Parliament it is said to have acted *ultra vires* (beyond its powers) – this is unconstitutional behaviour.
>
> *Anti-constitutional* behaviour involves opposition to the constitution with a view to its overthrow. In the UK the Anarchist movement and the IRA might be considered anti-constitutional.

A constitution should contain rules regarding the three main elements of a political system: the relationship between central and local government; the relationship between the institutions of central government; and the relationship between the government and the governed.

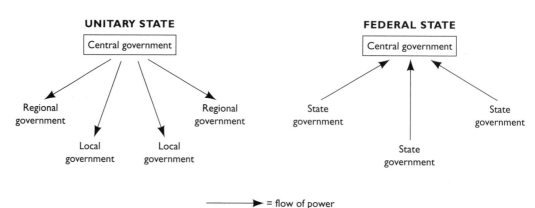

Figure 1.2 Central–local relationships in unitary and federal states

The central–local relationship

All states have a central government that takes responsibility for national policy-making, but they also have smaller units of government that are responsible for policy at a regional or local level. The relationship between the centre and the local units varies considerably from state to state (see Figure 1.2).

Unitary state

In Britain the state is **unitary**. This means that constitutionally power lies with central government, and units of local government are given a degree of power by the central government. In Britain, local government is responsible for education, housing, police, fire services, etc. Depending on the government in power at Westminster, local government power has varied from freedom of action in these areas to acting merely as an agency for central government policies. It can be argued that the latter was particularly true under Margaret Thatcher's Conservative administrations.

State and government

A *state* is a legal, political and geographical entity.

- Legal because states have an identity under international law and so can act illegally in the eyes of the international community.

- Political because within a state all citizens are subject to a system of laws and are under the authority of a government.

- Geographical because all of this takes place within a recognized geographical boundary. The boundary of a state does not necessarily coincide with the boundaries of a nation. Nation refers to an historical, linguistic and cultural identity.

Government can mean the system of government by which a state is governed, for example, parliamentary or presidential. More usually, it refers to the executive branch that governs the state on a day-to-day basis. The personnel of government may change while the state remains constant.

Britain has also experimented with regional government. In 1921 it set up a Parliament in Northern Ireland at Stormont Castle. This had the power to make policy for the province. However, as the 'troubles' in Northern Ireland escalated, the Parliament at Westminster decided that the province should be ruled directly from London, and in 1972 it revoked Stormont's powers and returned them to Westminster (see page 208). At no time did Westminster give up its **sovereignty** over the regional government.

Comparison

Such a system is in stark contrast to a **federal** system such as that which exists in the USA. It began life in 1776 as a loose grouping of independent states, the former British colonies. However, in 1787 each state decided to give up some of its independence in order to create a central government that could make policy for the USA as a whole. In this case, the power flowed from the peripheral states into the central government, not the other way round as in the UK. As a result, individual states in the USA have the power to make their own laws on some areas of policy. Hence the differences between states on the use of the death penalty, the availability of abortions, and laws relating to alcohol.

Federalism

The institutions of central government

All systems of government need to be able to perform three functions: to make law, to implement law, and to apply law. In modern states these functions are carried out by the **legislature**, **executive** and **judiciary** respectively, and according to the doctrine of the **separation of powers**, as outlined by Baron Montesquieu in the eighteenth century, each unit of government should be independent of the others. Splitting up the powers of government between different institutions is intended to prevent the concentration of power in the hands of one individual, or institution, who would then have the power to remove the liberties of the citizens.

Separation of powers

In Britain the legislative function is carried out by Parliament (see Chapter 5); the executive by the Prime Minister and the Cabinet (Chapter 6), supported by junior ministers and the civil service (Chapter 7); and the judicial function by the courts (Chapter 9).

Comparison

In the USA, Congress is responsible for the legislative function; the President heads the executive branch; and the Supreme Court sits at the head of the judiciary.

Having outlined the institutions of central government, we now look at the way in which they are arranged – the relationships between them. Britain has a parliamentary system (see Figure 1.3). Any parliamentary system has three key components:
- an elected assembly
- an executive branch that is drawn from the assembly
- an executive branch that is accountable to the assembly.

Parliamentary government

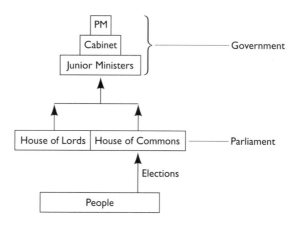

Figure 1.3 Parliamentary government

Britain's Parliament is **bicameral** (made up of two houses): the House of Commons and the House of Lords. Only the former is elected; the latter is currently based on an hereditary system and, more recently, a system of appointment. The two houses are often referred to simply as the Commons and the Lords.

Parliamentary executive

The composition of the Commons determines the party of government, or the executive branch. In the 1997 general election the Labour party won more seats in the Commons than all of the other political parties put together and is, therefore, said to have an **overall majority** in the House. Assuming that the party's MPs work and vote together, the party will have the support of the Commons to form a government. The leader of the party becomes Prime Minister and has the power to appoint colleagues to sit with him or her in the **Cabinet**. So, the executive branch of government is drawn from Parliament, giving Britain a **parliamentary executive**. Therefore, in Britain the executive is not elected directly.

Governmental functions

If we look at the example of a new education policy as it goes through the governmental process, we can see the role that each branch of government plays.

- The executive usually initiates policy. It is formulated by ministers and their civil servants.

- The policy is presented to the legislature in the form of a written document, called a 'bill'. It is then debated and a vote follows.

- If the bill is approved by the legislature, the responsibility for implementing the policy returns to the executive. The civil service informs schools of the policy change.

The judiciary may be called upon if a school fails to implement the policy correctly. The judges will apply the law to the specific case.

Finally, the executive is held accountable to Parliament by the concepts of **collective Cabinet responsibility** and **individual ministerial responsibility**. The former means that the whole Cabinet should take part in decision-making, should publicly support decisions once made, and should collectively stand or fall by those decisions. Individually, ministers are also responsible for the work of their civil service departments and might have to resign if a major error occurs.

Ministerial responsibility

The parliamentary structure of British government infringes upon Montesquieu's concept of the separation of powers between the three institutions of central government. Far from being separate, the executive branch is actually a part of the legislature with all members of the executive branch also holding seats in either the House of Lords or the House of Commons.

An added element to the relationship between the legislature and the other branches of government in Britain is the idea of **parliamentary sovereignty**. In other words, Parliament is the most powerful institution in the UK. According to A V Dicey, writing in the nineteenth century, this meant:

Parliamentary sovereignty

'*Parliament ... has, under the English constitution, the right to make or unmake any law whatever; and, further, that no person or body is recognized by the law of England as having the right to override or set aside the legislation of Parliament.*'

Comparison

The USA's political institutions are arranged not in a parliamentary structure but as a presidential system in which the head of the executive branch, the President, and the legislature, Congress, are elected separately (see Figure 1.4). The people choose the legislature and the head of the executive branch, and so whoever becomes President has nothing whatsoever to do with the majorities in either house of Congress.

Presidential government

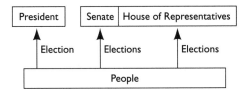

Figure 1.4 Presidential government in the USA

The separation of powers is more strictly adhered to with members of the executive prohibited from holding seats in the legislature.

In addition, no single institution in the USA is sovereign. The President needs the support of Congress, and vice versa. Therefore, a system of checks and balances is in place which is intended to create a **limited government**, no institution of which has unlimited power. Britain also has checks and balances, but they are much weaker because only the judiciary and the executive can be checked – not Parliament because it is sovereign.

Limited government

In terms of the relationships between the institutions of government, parliamentary sovereignty is probably the most important principle of the British constitution. Parliament can make, amend or repeal any law. It can create or bring down a government and no Parliament can bind a future Parliament, meaning that the Parliament of today is always supreme and cannot be tied down by anything a Parliament has done in the past. Thus the executive, the judiciary and local government are all subordinate to Parliament.

Britain and the USA have one principle of central government organization in common – an **independent judiciary**. A fundamental tenet of Western democracies is that judges should be free to apply the law without political interference (see page 171). This is intended to ensure that laws are applied equally to all citizens regardless of their standing in society, their wealth or their political beliefs. Law should be implemented according to a predictable and equitable pattern rather than on the whim of politicians. Thus is created a government of laws not of people.

Rule of law
This is the basis for A V Dicey's **rule of law**. According to this theory everyone is equally subject to the law – citizen and government; everyone is equal before the law and is entitled to a fair trial presided over by a non-partisan judge (see page 172). In order to achieve this, judges should be free from political interference and so the political branches of government should be separate from the judicial. Even so, in both Britain and the USA there are infringements of this separation; for example, judges are appointed by the executive branch (see page 173).

The government and the governed

Bill of rights
A constitution should outline the relationship between the government of the state and the citizens of the state. Essentially, this concerns the rights and liberties that citizens can expect within a state. This is most clearly illustrated in those states that have a **bill of rights** incorporated into their constitutions.

Comparison

The first ten **amendments** to the American constitution are collectively known as the Bill of Rights – here are enshrined freedom of speech, religion and assembly (1st Amendment); the right to bear arms (2nd Amendment); and the right not to incriminate oneself (5th Amendment).

The British constitution contains a Bill of Rights which established the rights of Parliament over the monarchy in 1689. However, there is no bill establishing the rights of citizens in relation to the government. The main responsibility for upholding the rights of citizens lies with Parliament and the judiciary. Parliament should pass laws that uphold rights and liberties, while the judiciary should apply these laws in a fair and just manner to preserve rights and liberties.

Written and unwritten constitutions

As well as in their contents, constitutions may also vary in the manner in which they are compiled. The British constitution is **unwritten** or **uncodified** – there is no single document in which the British constitution can be found. Instead it is made up of a variety of different elements, some of which are written down, some of which are not.

Codified and uncodified

> **Comparison**
>
> The American constitution is a written constitution. More precisely, it is **codified**, written in a systematic way in a single document. At the end of most American politics textbooks you will find the American constitution and its amendments.

The British constitution is one of the last remaining unwritten constitutions in the world. This is largely because most other nation states have undergone significant upheavals during their recent political history and this has given an opportunity (or a need) to formulate a written constitution. The American Revolution, the French Revolution, independence from colonial rule for India, Kenya, etc., defeat in war for Germany and Japan, and a civil war in Spain have all given opportunities to write or rewrite constitutions.

Britain has not, of course, been free from major upheavals. The Civil War and the subsequent restoration of the monarchy (1642–60) and the Glorious Revolution (1688) were both significant turning points in British political history, but they came at the very beginning of talk of written contracts between government and citizens and so did not present an opportunity to codify the constitution.

Therefore, the British constitution has evolved as political, economic and social circumstances have changed. In medieval England the king was absolute ruler until the barons began to resent his power; hence King John was forced to sign the Magna Carta in 1215. The power of the monarch – and particularly King Charles I's relationship with Parliament – became a further source of conflict in the mid-seventeenth century, resulting in first the Civil War and then the Glorious Revolution. As a result, the power of the monarch was curbed and Parliament began to take the upper hand.

In the nineteenth century the electoral franchise was gradually extended in 1832, 1867 and 1884. This process continued into the twentieth century, until 1969 when the voting age was reduced from 21 to 18. The extension of the franchise made the House of Commons more democratic, so the power of the unelected House of Lords seemed hard to justify. Therefore, in 1911 and 1949 the power of the Lords was reduced.

Since then it is the power of the executive branch of government that has been on the increase. The Prime Minister and Cabinet, backed by departments of civil servants, have come to dominate the policy-making process. The size and influence of the civil service has been particularly noticeable in the second half of the twentieth century. Its responsibility has grown to such an extent that ministers are increasingly willing to ignore the doctrine of individual ministerial responsibility and refuse to resign in the wake of major departmental errors.

Sources This outline of some important political developments in British history shows how the British constitution has been added to, reinterpreted and modified to suit the changing environment. The ways in which it may be adjusted can be examined by looking at the sources of the British constitution.

Historical documents

We have already seen that the Magna Carta and the Bill of Rights laid down important rules concerning the power of the monarch. They are stages in the development of the British constitution and so are part of it.

Statute law

Parliament Statute law is law made by Parliament. Any law that involves constitutional relationships becomes part of the constitution. The 1911 Parliament Act, for example, removed the House of Lords' power of veto and replaced it with the power to delay legislation for two years. It also prevented the Lords from examining financial legislation. Therefore, it is part of the constitution.

Common law

Judges **Common law** is sometimes referred to as 'judge-made law'. It concerns judicial interpretations of statute law. No law is so precise that it needs no interpretation, and as judges interpret the law they are deciding what Parliament intended it should mean and so are contributing to making that law work in practice (see page 175).

International treaties and agreements

Treaties In recent years the signing of treaties and agreements has been one of the most significant sources of the British constitution, largely owing to Britain's membership of the European Union (EU) (see Chapter 11).

Europe In 1972, Britain signed the Treaty of Rome and Parliament passed the European Communities Act to allow Britain to become a member of what was then the European Community (EC) in 1973. The British constitution was thus fundamentally changed. Britain accepted the superiority of European law, and for the first time Parliament was subject to an authority greater than its own. In other words, Parliament was no longer sovereign. Today British courts have the power to review Acts of Parliament in the light of EU legislation and can suspend statute law if necessary. British courts did this in 1991 when the 1988 Merchant Shipping Act was suspended as part of the so-called Factortame case (see page 182).

Britain is also a signatory of other international agreements and treaties, all of which reduce its ability to act totally independently. For example, Britain is a member of the

United Nations (UN) and the North Atlantic Treaty Organization (NATO) and is a signatory of the European Convention on Human Rights.

Conventions

As their name suggests, **conventions** are habitual or normal patterns of behaviour. They are an important part of the British constitution, but are also perhaps the most difficult to understand. They are considered binding on those who should abide by the constitution, but they are not legally enforceable.

Examples of constitutional conventions include the relationship between the Prime Minister and the Cabinet, the royal prerogative (see page 165), and the conventions of individual and collective ministerial responsibility (see pages 106 and 137). Theoretically, the monarch retains the power to dissolve Parliament, appoint the Prime Minister and to grant the Royal Assent to bills. However, in reality the monarch dissolves Parliament on the advice of the Prime Minister – no monarch has declined to give the Royal Assent since 1708.

Legally, there is no punishment for the breach of a constitutional convention. Therefore, if a minister decides not to resign in the light of mistakes made by their civil service department, there is no recourse to any legal action. However, there might be political repercussions to such decisions, including a weakening of the minister's position, parliamentary and media criticism, and perhaps the undermining of prime ministerial authority.

Patterns of behaviour

Academic opinion

Some famous commentators on the British constitution have been so influential with regard to its interpretation that their work has become part of the constitution itself. Perhaps most famous are Walter Bagehot (1826–77) and A V Dicey (1835–1922). Again, such work is only interpretation and is not legally binding.

Bagehot and Dicey

Flexible and rigid constitutions

As the British constitution is unwritten, or uncodified, it is often considered a **flexible** constitution. All that is needed to change it is a new law through a majority in Parliament, a change in an habitual pattern of behaviour, or even a change in interpretation. It is this flexibility that has allowed the constitution to evolve with political circumstances.

Some observers have suggested that flexibility seriously weakens a constitution because it should be a set of broad rules which lay down the structure of the system, against which the branches of government should be judged. It should not be a set of rules that bend and contort to suit any political circumstance. In fact, Alexis de Tocqueville, the French eighteenth-century statesman and historian, even claimed that Britain had no constitution at all. It certainly does have a constitution, but perhaps it is best described as descriptive, outlining relationships as they are, rather than as they should be.

Descriptive

> **Comparison**
>
> Prescriptive
>
> The constitution of the USA is codified and prescriptive with a rigorous amendment procedure. In order to amend the constitution a two-thirds majority in both the House of Representatives and the Senate is required, followed by the approval of three-quarters of the legislatures in the individual states. Since 1787 this has been achieved only 27 times – the first ten of which were all passed together in 1791.
>
> However, even the seemingly most rigid of constitutions can be kept up to date by the courts. In the USA the Supreme Court's interpretations of the document have changed dramatically as circumstances and attitudes have changed. The issue of **civil rights** illustrates this very clearly. In 1896 (*Plessy v Ferguson*) the Supreme Court declared racial segregation constitutional, so long as the provision for both races was equal. In 1954 (*Brown v Board of Education, Topeka, Kansas*) the court used the same document to declare racial segregation unconstitutional.

Constitutional reform

Evolution or revolution

Britain is faced with two possible routes to constitutional reform. The first is, in fact, a continuation of the evolutionary track followed to date. Reforms could be adopted on a piecemeal basis as and when it is seen fit. Examples of possible reforms might include the introduction of an electoral system based on proportional representation, fixed terms for Parliament, and reform of the House of Lords and the monarchy. Such an approach favours the gradual evolution of institutions rather than radical reform or revolution.

Charter 88

An alternative, and perhaps more radical, approach is that suggested by Charter 88, a pressure group which seeks a written constitution for Britain. Many of the proposals for piecemeal reform and for inclusion in a written constitution might well be similar; the radical element is in the demand for a codified document. The Liberal Democrat party has been a long-term supporter of such proposals, and more recently the Labour party too. In the 1997 general election the Labour party campaigned on a series of constitutional issues: a referendum on electoral reform; referendums on devolution for Scotland and Wales; reform of the House of Lords; the incorporation of the European Convention on Human Rights into domestic law – effectively becoming a bill of rights; and the creation of a new metropolitan authority for London. By the beginning of 1998 the referendums on devolution had taken place and discussion of House of Lords reform was under way. Other constitutional reform might take a back seat as the Labour government moves through the priorities on its policy agenda.

Arguments for a written constitution

Limit Parliament

A major concern about Britain's unwritten constitution is the fact that Parliament is unrestrained. Its sovereignty, as we have seen, means that it can make or unmake any laws without restriction. The danger of this is that one branch of government has ultimate power and cannot be checked by any other branch. With the workload of

Parliament being very heavy, there is the threat that Parliament will pass bad or ill-considered laws.

This is particularly worrying when parliamentary sovereignty is combined with the federal system. Parliament can make laws which affect all areas of the state and might not be particularly sensitive to local conditions. This is why many groups – including the Liberal Democrat and Labour parties – have sought greater **devolution** of power to national and regional Parliaments.

Devolution

Under the present constitutional arrangement, the executive branch of government can be checked by Parliament and by the courts. If it acts beyond the powers given to it by Parliament, it is acting *ultra vires* (outside the law). However, parliamentary majorities, backed by strong party discipline, mean that the executive is able to dominate the legislature. This has led former Lord Chancellor Lord Hailsham to argue that Britain is an 'elective dictatorship'. In 1976 Lord Hailsham stated in a Guildhall lecture:

Limit government

Elective dictatorship

'*The sovereignty of Parliament has increasingly become, in practice, the sovereignty of the Commons, and the sovereignty of the Commons has increasingly become the sovereignty of the government which, in addition to its influence in Parliament, controls the party whips, the party machine, and the civil service. This means that what has always been an elective dictatorship in theory, but one in which the component parts operated in practice to control one another, has become a machine in which one of those parts has come to exercise a predominant influence over the rest.*' (*Quoted in The Search for Justice*, Hodder and Stoughton, 1994)

Since 1976 the Commons has been less subservient than Lord Hailsham might have expected. The Select Committee system was reformed in 1979 and backbench revolts have become more frequent, but a written constitution would limit the power of Parliament and in turn that of the executive.

Many observers are keen to restrict the power of the government because they question the mandate to govern. Every government since 1945 has been elected with less than 50 per cent of the vote and so cannot claim to be representative of the majority of all voters. This has been of particular concern since the mid-1970s, when Britain moved away from **consensus politics** towards **adversarial politics** with the two main parties becoming more polarized in the policies they sought to implement when in government. Supporters of the centre of British politics, such as Roy Jenkins and Shirley Williams, have been keen to remove the exaggerated mandate by reforming the electoral system.

Electoral mandate

A further concern is that Britain does not have a bill of rights which outlines the rights of citizens. Therefore, nowhere are the rights and liberties of citizens clearly laid down. It is Parliament's duty to preserve those liberties, but it can remove them at any time. The Prevention of Terrorism Act was first imposed in 1974 in the wake of the Birmingham pub bombings and has been reimposed annually by every government since then. The Act allows a suspected terrorist to be held, upon the issue of a warrant by the Home Secretary, for two days without access to any adviser, and for a further five days with access to a solicitor. This is an infringement of the traditional right to see an adviser without unreasonable delay and to be released after 24 hours unless charged with an offence.

Bill of rights

The fear that civil liberties might be removed is of particular concern to minority groups. Parliament is elected and so is likely to be in tune with the majority of voters because the well-being of the majority is likely to determine the future of a political party. Minority groups are far less influential in the outcome of general election results. Therefore, the minority groups in society are in danger of having their rights removed by the 'tyranny of the majority'. Geoffrey Robertson QC has said:

'*Majority rule resulting from free and fair elections does make most of us safe most of the time, and there is little likelihood that any government would risk electoral reprisals by passing laws which deprive the majority of any right which they value. But it is minorities who are at risk – immigrants, homosexuals, persons suspected of crime, demonstrators, parents of children taken into care, mental patients and other classes of persons insufficiently numerous to wield electoral power but large enough to attract obloquy or resentment.*' (*Freedom, the Individual and the Law*, Penguin, 1993)

Arguments against a written constitution

Evolution

Many of the arguments against a written constitution rest on the desirability of tradition. The Conservative party, in particular, is keen to avoid radical change to the constitutional arrangement unless absolutely necessary. Britain's unwritten constitution has served us well to date, the argument goes, so why change it now? Furthermore, if it does need to be changed it could be done on a piecemeal basis to suit the circumstances – in other words, the constitution should continue to evolve.

Judicial interpretation

However, other arguments against a written constitution concentrate on the role that judges would play in the interpretation of a written constitution. If it is to survive, a written constitution must be relatively vague, in order to allow it to develop over time. Responsibility for interpreting and reinterpreting the constitution to suit the time would be the responsibility of the judiciary. This raises a number of difficulties.

Unelected judges

Judges are not elected, whereas the House of Commons is. Nevertheless, they would have the power to overrule the elected representatives of the people. If Parliament passed a law that was considered unconstitutional, the judges on a 'supreme court' would be able to veto it.

Unaccountable judges

Judges are also unaccountable. They do not have to answer to the electorate or even to Parliament for the decisions they make. This is to protect them from political influence, but if they were given the power to interpret a constitution, such freedom from accountability might be a cause for concern.

Unrepresentative judges

In addition, they are unrepresentative of the people at large. John Griffith of the London School of Economics has argued that judges are biased in their attitudes against racial minorities, demonstrators and trade unionists. If this were true, the value of a bill of rights would be undermined if it were interpreted in a biased way and the groups most in need of protection might not receive it. (The role of judges in the preservation of civil liberties is discussed more fully on pages 184–190.)

Content

There is also controversy about what should be included in a written constitution and a bill of rights. Socialists and conservatives, for example, emphasize different rights. A socialist might wish to emphasize a positive role for the state, giving people the right to work, to welfare and to some degree of economic equality. A conservative is more likely to highlight a limited role for the state with individuals being free to develop without governmental interference. These divisions have led critics of the idea of a bill of rights to argue that it might confuse, rather than clarify people's rights and liberties.

Finally, a written constitution and a bill of rights are only as good as the willingness of politicians to abide by both documents. The courts, with their limited powers, would be unable to force a government to conform to constitutional requirements. Therefore, ultimately, rights and liberties rest on the constitutionalism of politicians.

Exercises

Short questions

1   a   Why is British government described as constitutional?
     b   Outline a case against such a description.
     (ULEAC, June 1993)

2   a   Define public order.
     b   To what extent is it an issue in British politics?
     (ULEAC, June 1994)

3   Distinguish between unconstitutional and anti-constitutional behaviour. Give an example of each.

4   Distinguish between a written and an unwritten constitution.

5   Distinguish between a flexible and a rigid constitution.

Essay questions

1   The British constitution is what happens. Discuss.
     (ULEAC, January 1993)

2   Has the time come to draw up a written constitution for Britain?
     (ULEAC, January 1991)

3   What aspects of constitutional reform are most needed in Britain and why?
     (Oxford & Cambridge, June 1994)

4   Would a bill of rights make the British political system more democratic?
     (ULEAC, January 1994)

Data response question

The following is taken from *The Economist*, 17 December 1994.

'*Outside Westminster the constitution has precious little authority. The public sees a government that does not hear its grievances, a House of Commons discredited by sleaze, an unaccountable quangocracy and a philandering monarchy. Only isolated ministers, advised by obsequious civil servants, could believe otherwise.*

… The "efficient secret" of the British constitution, according to Walter Bagehot … was the omnipotence of Parliament. Yet this is changing before our very eyes. Power flows up from Westminster to European institutions. As judges lose faith in the state, it flows out, to the courts …

Meanwhile ministers are quite happy to change the constitution, sacred though it may be, whenever it suits them. Power flows from Westminster to Whitehall as the government waters down parliamentary accountability by establishing quangos and semi-autonomous agencies. It flows to the centre, in the form of a determined assault on the powers of local government. It flows out again as some of the powers local government has lost are handed to local schools. If and when peace is established in Northern Ireland, power will flow from Westminster back to Stormont – yet another in the myriad constitutional changes that have transformed the province's government over the century.

The "efficient secret" of the British constitution is not the one that Bagehot thought he had discovered. Its real secret lies in its adaptability to circumstances. And that, in turn, has been sustained by the ability of Britain's rulers, with good or ill grace, themselves to change the constitution in good time before its anachronisms destroy what remains sound and relevant.'

1   What factors have diminished the power of Parliament over recent years?

2   Explain the phrase, 'Its real secret lies in its adaptability to circumstances'.

3   Outline the case in favour of drawing up a written constitution in Britain.

2 Elections

Questions to be answered in this chapter

- What is democracy?
- Why are elections so important?
- How does the UK electoral system work?
- Should the electoral system be reformed?
- What would be the effects of reform?

Terms to know

- Additional member system (AMS)
- Alternative vote system
- Class
- Coalition government
- Democracy
- Deviant voting
- Embourgeoisement
- Expressive voting
- First-past-the-post (FPTP)
- Hung parliament
- Instrumental voting
- Minority government
- Opinion polls
- Party identifiers
- Petit bourgeoisie
- Proportional representation (PR)
- Regency approach
- Representation
- Representative democracy
- Responsibility
- Salariat
- Single transferable vote (STV)
- Socialization
- Tactical voting
- Wasted votes
- Winner-take-all system

Introduction

In a representative democracy elections are a vital means of popular participation. Few people will choose to join political parties or pressure groups, so elections remain the single most important means for individuals to influence the manner in which they are governed for the next five years. Therefore it is crucial to our democracy that the mechanism by which people make their choices works fairly. Unfortunately there is no single idea of what would constitute a 'fair' electoral system. Opinion is divided between those who favour a winner-take-all system such as first-past-the-post used in the United Kingdom and the United States of America, and those who prefer some form of proportional representation, used in most European countries.

Democracy

The word **democracy** comes from the Greek word *demokratia* meaning *demos* (people)   Origins
and *kratos* (rule). From understanding the derivation of 'democracy', it is a short step

to the words of American president Abraham Lincoln at Gettysburg in 1863 in which he described democracy as 'Government of the people, by the people, for the people'. However, this does not explain exactly how democracy can be put into practice in a political system.

Representative democracy

The city states of Ancient Greece had a 'pure' democracy which allowed citizens to participate directly in political decision making (women and slaves were not considered to be citizens and so could not take part). However, in modern societies direct participation is not practical. Britain's 58 million citizens cannot be regularly involved in political decision making. Therefore, liberal democrats in the eighteenth century introduced the idea of **representative democracy** to political theory.

In a representative democracy the citizens recognize that they cannot all participate directly and so they choose a smaller group of representatives to act on their behalf. The mechanisms by which we choose these representatives are elections. Therefore the adequacy of the system of elections is fundamental to the functioning of a country's democracy.

Elections and democracy

In Western democracies the term 'election' tends to conjure up images of political parties, campaigns, speeches, media interviews, the secret ballot and late-night declarations of results. We therefore have a tendency to believe that all elections are automatically characterized by these things. This is not true.

Who votes?

In 1832, 5 per cent of the adult population were allowed to vote. In 1867 this increased to 13 per cent and reached 25 per cent in 1884. Women were not given the vote until 1918 and 1928 when the percentage reached 99 per cent of adults. In 1969 the 'adult' age was reduced from 21 to 18.

In order to vote an individual must be registered in a constituency and must be a British subject.

Peers, those certified insane and certain categories of criminal are not allowed to vote.

Democracy

In many countries elections take place in difficult circumstances, in which one party rules the country and will not tolerate opposition; the press is controlled by the government; voters are subjected to intimidation and corruption; and the election result is always in danger of being overturned if it does not suit the ruling bodies. Therefore elections alone do not make a democracy. Political toleration, multi-party competition, a free press, a constitutional commitment to abide by the results, and of course the ability to vote for representatives to fill offices that actually have some power, are all basic requirements of a true representative democracy.

If, for the moment, we lay aside arguments about the power of Parliament and the bias of the press, we can say that – broadly speaking – the British democracy satisfies these requirements. Nevertheless a great deal of controversy does surround British general elections. The Liberal Democrats, in particular, argue that the electoral system is biased against them and exaggerates the support of the two larger parties. Hence, they argue, it is fundamentally unfair.

Before examining these claims we need to understand how the British system of elections works.

The British electoral system

Since the 1911 Parliament Act the lifetime of a British Parliament has been limited to no more than five years. Within this period the Prime Minister must ask the monarch for a dissolution of Parliament – in other words a general election must be called. British elections are not held on a fixed-term basis, and so the timing of the general election is at the discretion of the Prime Minister. Usually, Prime Ministers call an election when they believe that their party has the best chance of victory, although occasionally they may be forced into one by the loss of a vote of confidence in the House of Commons – as happened in 1979 when the minority Labour government lost such a vote and went on to lose the general election.

Life of Parliament

In a general election all adults over the age of 18 are, with very few exceptions, allowed to vote. This was not always the case. The male franchise was gradually widened throughout the nineteenth century by the Reform Acts of 1832, 1867 and 1884. Women did not receive the vote until 1918 and 1928. The voting age was lowered from 21 to 18 in 1969.

Electorate

The secret ballot was introduced in Britain in 1872. This was an important advance because for the first time voters could complete their ballot without the knowledge of their landlord, employer or any officials. As a result, they could cast their vote freely, without any interference from outsiders.

Secret ballot

Electoral boundaries

There is a Boundary Commission responsible for England, Scotland, Wales and Northern Ireland. It reviews the distribution of parliamentary seats every 10–15 years and redraws boundaries in an effort to keep pace with movements in the population.

The ideal of constituencies of equal size is an important aspect of a representative democracy. It ensures that every person's vote is of equal worth. Nevertheless, there are significant divergences between constituencies.

The Boundary Commission revisions implemented in 1983 have benefited the Conservative party as they have taken into account the growth of the population in suburbs and in the south – i.e. traditional Conservative strongholds. It was expected that the changes implemented prior to the 1997 general election would benefit the Conservatives. However, their defeat was so resounding that any benefits were wiped out.

Constituencies The UK is divided into 659 electoral constituencies each one sending one Member of Parliament (MP) to the House of Commons. To ensure that each citizen is equally represented by their MP, the constituencies should all be of approximately the same size – around 65,000 people.

By-elections

By-elections are held whenever a seat falls vacant in the House of Commons.

They tend to attract a great deal of media and political attention, which in itself makes them unrepresentative of a normal constituency contest in a general election.

Governments often perform badly in by-elections as the electorate pass judgement on their performance in office. Sensible governments take by-election results as a jab in the ribs from the electorate.

The Liberal Democrats have often performed well in by-elections as the electorate use the opportunity to protest against the two main parties.

The reliability of by-election results as a means of predicting a general election result is further undermined by the low turnout, which is often less than 50 per cent – compared with 70 per cent in general elections.

First-past-the-post The British method of election is known as **first-past-the-post** (**FPTP**). This means that voters choose their MP by placing an 'X' against their preferred candidate. The candidate in each constituency with the most votes wins the election. The winning candidate need only poll more votes than their nearest rival – they do *not* need more than all of the other candidates put together, nor do they need more than 50 per cent of the votes.

Election of government The British electoral system does not, however, merely elect individual MPs to represent their constituents in Parliament. As Britain is a parliamentary system, by voting for individual MPs the electorate are indirectly determining the nature of the government. The British government is drawn from the House of Commons and relies on the support of the Commons. Therefore, the party with the majority of seats in the Commons is usually asked by the monarch to form the government after a general election.

In Britain the parliamentary system means that voters are seeking not only an MP who

Assessing an electoral system

Representation An electoral system should give the electorate the opportunity to select the people whom they would like to act on their behalf in the country's assembly, and then it should give them the opportunity to remove those individuals at the next election if they are unhappy with their performance. These twin ideas are formalized in the concepts of **representation** and **responsibility**.

represents them but, indirectly, a representative government. Similarly they need the ability to de-elect a government by de-electing their MP. So the electoral system is operating at two levels: assembly (made up of MPs) and government (drawn from the assembly). It needs to be assessed using the criteria of representation and responsibility at both of these levels. This task is made difficult by the fact that the supporters and critics of first-past-the-post are often using different definitions of these criteria.

The first-past-the-post system

Support for first-past-the-post

According to supporters of the British electoral system, first-past-the-post does give fair representation. The majority of the adults over the age of 18 do have the right to vote for an MP to act on their behalf. They do so in constituencies that the Boundary Commission makes every effort to ensure are, as far as is feasible, of equal size.

> **Representatives and delegates**
>
> The nineteenth-century philosopher and MP, Edmund Burke, distinguished between delegates and representatives.
>
> Delegates make decisions according to the instructions of others. They refer to those whom they represent whenever a decision is to be made. Representatives make decisions on the basis of their own judgement. Although they might consider their constituents' views when making a decision, they do not have to abide by their wishes.
>
> Traditionally a British MP is a representative, acting on behalf of his or her whole constituency. However, the advent of strong political parties has pushed the MP nearer to being a party delegate. Most MPs will follow the party whip in the House of Commons.

Once elected the MP should adhere to the view of philosopher Edmund Burke (see the box), who believed that MPs are representatives and they should act on behalf of all their constituents, not merely those who voted for them. They are not delegates and they should use their own judgement when deciding how to vote in the Commons.

Edmund Burke

In the Commons the views of that MP, along with 658 others, allow a government to be formed with the support of the majority of the electorate's representatives. Therefore the government must, surely, represent the electorate as well and is said to have a mandate to govern.

Usually the government has a clear, overall, majority in the House of Commons, so not only is it representative, it is *responsible*. This can be used in two ways. Firstly, its overall majority leaves it free to act responsibly and to do the 'right thing' whilst in government. Thus it is not tied to taking the most popular course solely to preserve a Commons majority. It can follow a strong policy line, even though it might be unpopular in the short term.

Responsibility

Secondly the government is easily held accountable for its 'responsible' policy line. At the time of the next election the electorate can assess the quality of its performance and can vote for one of the opposition candidates in their constituencies in order to displace their MP and the sitting government.

Responsibility is often seen as the predominant characteristic of the British electoral system. Therefore we may conclude that the supporters of first-past-the-post tend to concentrate on the benefits it brings to the workings of government rather than the 'fairness' of the House of Commons – they argue that FPTP produces a government that takes a responsible course for which it is then held accountable.

Opposition to first-past-the-post

Public opinion

Opponents of first-past-the-post hold that representation should extend beyond every constituency having an MP to act on its behalf. They argue that the composition of the House of Commons should reflect public opinion and that the electoral system should not distort the result. In other words the result should be proportional – if the Conservatives receive 42 per cent of the votes cast they should win 42 per cent of the seats in the Commons.

The results of the 1983 general election show clearly that the composition of the House of Commons does not reflect the votes cast in the country (see Table 2.1).

Table 2.1 Results of the 1983 general election

Votes cast (% votes)				No. of seats (% of seats)			
Con	Lab	Lib	Other	Con	Lab	Lib	Other
13.0m	8.5m	7.8m	1.4m	397	209	23	21
(42.2)	(27.6)	(25.4)	(4.6)	(61.1)	(32.2)	(3.5)	(3.2)

On the basis of only 42.2 per cent of the popular vote the Conservative party gained 61.1 per cent of the seats; whilst the Liberal–Social Democrat Alliance gained 25.4 per cent of the vote but won only 3.5 per cent of the seats in the assembly. In terms of reflecting opinion, the Conservative party was vastly over-represented in the Commons whilst the Alliance were even more seriously under-represented.

Winner take all

This is possible because first-past-the-post is a **winner-take-all system** under which parties are rewarded only if they win a constituency. It does not matter how many votes are accumulated across the country, only that enough votes are amassed in certain areas in order to win constituencies.

Concentrated support

Traditionally the Conservative and Labour parties have had their support concentrated in the south and the north respectively, so the Labour party tends to win seats in the north and the Conservatives win in the south. The Liberal Democrats do not have concentrated support, except in the south-west of England. Their support is considerable but it is spread evenly across the country. Therefore they can amass enough votes to beat the two leading parties into second and third place only in very few constituencies. In fact, in 1987 the Alliance came second in 261 constituencies. As a result of these anomolies, in the 1983 general election, 300,144 votes were needed to elect an Alliance MP compared with the 41,811 needed to elect a Conservative (see Table 2.2).

Table 2.2 Results of general elections, 1945–92

Year	Votes cast (% of votes)				No. of seats (% of seats)			
	Con	Lab	Lib	Other	Con	Lab	Lib	Other
1945	9.6m (39.8)	11.6m (48.3)	2.2m (9.1)	0.7m (2.8)	213 (33.3)	393 (61.4)	12 (1.9)	22 (3.4)
1950	12.5m (43.5)	13.3m (46.1)	2.6m (9.1)	0.4m (1.3)	299 (47.9)	315 (50.4)	9 (1.4)	2 (0.3)
1951	13.7m (48.0)	13.9m (48.8)	0.7m (2.5)	0.2m (0.7)	321 (51.4)	295 (47.2)	6 (1.0)	3 (0.5)
1955	13.3m (49.7)	12.4m (46.4)	0.7m (2.7)	0.3m (1.2)	345 (54.8)	277 (44.0)	6 (1.0)	2 (0.3)
1959	13.7m (49.4)	12.2m (43.8)	1.6m (5.9)	0.3m (0.9)	365 (57.9)	258 (41.0)	6 (1.0)	1 (0.2)
1964	12.0m (43.4)	12.2m (44.1)	3.1m (11.2)	0.3m (1.3)	304 (48.3)	317 (50.3)	9 (1.4)	– (–)
1966	11.4m (41.9)	13.1m (47.9)	2.3m (8.5)	0.5m (1.7)	253 (40.2)	363 (57.6)	12 (1.9)	2 (0.3)
1970	13.1m (46.4)	12.2m (43.0)	2.1m (7.5)	0.9m (3.1)	330 (52.4)	287 (45.6)	6 (1.0)	7 (1.1)
1974 Feb	11.9m (37.8)	11.6m (37.1)	6.1m (19.3)	1.8m (5.8)	297 (46.8)	301 (47.4)	14 (2.2)	23 (3.6)
1974 Oct	10.5m (35.8)	11.5m (39.2)	6.3m (18.3)	1.9m (6.7)	277 (43.6)	319 (50.2)	13 (2.0)	26 (4.1)
1979	13.7m (43.9)	11.5m (36.9)	4.3m (13.8)	1.7m (5.4)	339 (53.4)	269 (42.4)	11 (1.7)	16 (2.5)
1983	13.0m (42.2)	8.5m (27.6)	7.8m (25.4)	1.4m (4.6)	397 (61.1)	209 (32.2)	23 (3.5)	21 (3.2)
1987	13.8m (42.3)	10.0m (30.8)	7.3m (22.6)	1.4m (4.3)	376 (57.8)	229 (35.2)	22 (3.4)	23 (3.5)
1992	14.2m (42.9)	11.6m (35.0)	6.1m (18.4)	1.2m (3.6)	336 (51.6)	271 (41.6)	20 (3.1)	24 (3.7)

Note: In 1983 and 1987 the Liberal Party contested elections in partnership with the Social Democratic party, and together they were known as the Alliance. In 1988 the two parties merged to become the Social and Liberal Democratic party. This became the Liberal Democrats in 1989.

The 1997 general election

The 1997 general election was a ground-breaking election if for no other reason than the fact that it brought to an end 18 years of Conservative government. However, the result was more dramatic than that. The election shocks were:

- Tony Blair's 'New Labour' gained the largest parliamentary majority of any government since 1945 and the largest number of Labour MPs ever elected in a single Parliament.

- The Conservative party gained its lowest proportion of the vote since 1832.

- The Liberal Democrats gained the highest number of seats (46) for a third party since 1929.

Table 2.3 Results of the 1997 general election

	Total votes	Total seats	Percentage of vote	Percentage of seats
Labour	13,516,632	418	43.2	63.4
Conservative	9,592,999	165	30.7	25.0
Liberal Democrat	5,242,894	46	16.8	7.0
Northern Ireland parties	790,778	18	2.5	2.7
Welsh and Scottish Nationalists	782,570	10	2.5	1.5
Others	524,928	1	1.7	0.2
Speaker	23,969	1	0.1	0.2
Referendum	811,827	0	2.6	–
Totals	31,286,597	659	–	–

The obvious conclusions to be drawn from these results are that the Labour party had a phenomenal success, the Conservative party had a disastrous election, and the Liberal Democrats finally broke through the restrictions of the winner-take-all system to double their number of MPs. On the surface all of these conclusions are correct, but behind the headlines the story is far more complex.

The Labour party won an incredible number of seats but did so with a smaller *proportion* of the vote than they gained in any election between 1945 and 1966 – and, of course, they lost three of those elections.

In terms of MPs elected, the Conservative party suffered the biggest rout of any party since 1945 – but still gained a higher proportion of the *votes* than the Labour party did in 1983 when *it* was routed by the Conservatives.

The Liberal Democrats gained the greatest number of seats since 1945 with the lowest proportion of votes since 1970 – with the exception of 1979. Furthermore, the Welsh Nationalists (Plaid Cymru) won 9.9 per cent of the vote in Wales and won 10 per cent of the seats. The Scottish Nationalist party won 13.0 per cent of the Scottish vote and 13.9 per cent of the Scottish seats in the Commons.

These details would seem to suggest that the electoral system does indeed exaggerate the support of the largest, winning party. In fact the 'bonus' in 1997 was greater than might normally be expected. This was due to the concentration of votes. The Conservatives lost most heavily in those constituencies in which they had a majority in 1992 – particularly in the south-east of England and London. The Conservative vote held up best in the north of England, Wales and Scotland – where they were already weak – but even in these areas Conservative support fell most heavily when they were defending seats. As a result, Conservative support was now too evenly concentrated across the UK to allow them to win sufficient seats to make an impact in the Commons.

Labour and the Liberal Democrats, on the other hand, benefited from an opposite tendency. The Labour party's greatest swings of voters to them (+13 per cent) were in the constituencies that they targeted, whilst the Liberal Democrat's support fell by the greatest amount (–3 per cent) in these seats. The Liberal Democrats on average only experienced positive swings (+2 per cent) in their targetted constituencies.

Put very simply, this final point would suggest a pincer movement against the Conservative party. It suggests that in key constituencies voters selected the party with the best chance of beating the Conservatives. This is known as **tactical voting**. Had the swing been uniform across the country, rather than targeted, the Labour majority would have been 131 seats and the Liberal Democrats would have won only 28 seats.

The result of the 1997 general election is shown pictorially in Figure 2.1.

Figure 2.1 The result of the 1997 general election

Under a winner-take-all system the size of a candidate's majority in a constituency is ignored. If a candidate wins by 20,000 votes or only 2000 the reward is still one seat in the Commons. This results in **wasted votes** because the large majorities are votes that could have been better used in other constituencies where they would have gained more seats. In other words, all votes other than those required to secure a simple majority do not contribute to the election of an MP.

Wasted votes

Obviously, the ability to place voters strategically around the country is every party's desire. However, wasted votes can lead to serious electoral anomalies. In 1951 the

Labour party polled 13.9 million votes compared with the Conservative's 13.7 million, but Labour lost the election because the Conservatives won 26 seats more than Labour.

These electoral anomalies also affect the extent to which a British government can be held accountable for its actions. It is true that under a winner-take-all system one party is likely to control government, with an overall majority in the Commons, and is therefore in a position to act 'responsibly'. However, that government is not always held accountable for its actions.

In 1979 the Conservative party gained 13.7 million votes (43.9 per cent of votes cast) and as a result won 339 (53.4 per cent) of the seats in the Commons. In 1983 it polled only 13.0 million votes (42.2 per cent) and so might be considered less popular than four years earlier. However, their reward was 397 (61.1 per cent) of the seats. The increase in the seats won by the Conservatives was largely due to the revision of constituency boundaries by the Boundaries Commission. However, it seems surprising that a party that had lost support in the country should be able to form a government with an increased majority of seats in the Commons.

Proportional representation (PR)

While first-past-the-post embodies the winner-take-all principle, an alternative system would be based on **proportional representation**. PR is not a system in itself but a characteristic of a number of different systems, all of which will give an election result in which the composition of the assembly will reflect, to a greater or lesser extent, the way the votes were cast.

For those who favour an assembly that reflects public opinion, PR is obviously a preferred method of election. Table 2.4 (opposite) shows clearly how a different system of election would have affected the result of the 1992 election (the results from Northern Ireland have been excluded).

The **alternative vote system** is not founded on the principle of proportional representation; rather it tries to ensure that a winning candidate gains at least 50 per cent of the vote in the constituency. Therefore, it would change the election result relatively little. However, either of the two systems of PR that have been considered for Britain – the **additional member system** (AMS) and the **single tranferable vote** (STV) – would dramatically reduce Conservative seats and redistribute most of

The additional member system (AMS)

The additional member system has two different types of MP – those elected under the FPTP system, and an additional 'top-up' member chosen from lists of party nominees. The former MPs are the constituency representatives. The second top-up MPs are used to build up each party's representation to reflect fully the proportion of votes cast for that party. Usually a 5 per cent threshold operates and parties are not given top-up MPs until they have reached this level of voter support. This is the basis of the system used in Germany. Its great advantage is that it combines the assets of PR with those of FPTP.

Table 2.4 Number of seats won by the parties in the 1992 general election, according to proportional representation

System	Con	Lab	Lib–Dem	Nationalist	Greens
FPTP	336	271	20	7	0
PR systems:					
Alternative vote	325	270	30	9	0
Additional member	268	232	116	18	0
Single tranferable vote	256	250	102	20	6

Source: Dunleavy, Margetts and Weir, *LSE Public Policy Paper 3*, London School of Economics, 1992: quoted in Conley, *General Elections Today*, Manchester University Press, 1994

them to the Liberal Democrats, the nationalists and, in the case of STV, to the Green party.

Under a system of PR, the distribution of seats would certainly reflect the votes cast and in that sense would be fairer. However, Table 2.4 also highlights a criticism of PR – it would allow a multi-party system of government to develop.

The single transferable vote system (STV)

The STV system is employed in the Republic of Ireland. Voters are divided into multi-member constituencies and they register their preferences for candidates 1, 2, 3, 4, etc. Candidates are elected when they receive a certain quota of the votes. The quota is determined by the so-called Droop formula:

$$\frac{\text{Number of votes cast}}{\text{Number of seats} + 1} + 1$$

Any candidate receiving the quota on first preferences is elected. If not all of the seats are filled in this way, the candidate with the least votes is eliminated and their second preferences redistributed. Any candidate receiving in excess of the quota has his or her surplus redistributed also. Ultimately the required number of candidates will be elected.

Multi-party politics and coalitions

Traditionally the British party system has been viewed as a two-party system, with the House of Commons dominated by the Conservative and Labour parties. A system of PR would reduce the representation of the two largest parties and increase the number of seats held by smaller parties. Therefore seats would be more evenly distributed between the parties, to such an extent that no single party would have an overall majority in the Commons. This is known as a **'hung' parliament**.

Hung Parliament

The problem of a hung parliament can be solved in two ways – either by a minority government or a by a **coalition government**. The former happens when the largest

Minority government

single party decides to govern alone, despite the fact that if all the other parties in the Commons combined against the government it would lose every vote. To achieve any success in the assembly the government needs to win the support of individuals or parties on the floor of the House of Commons. Therefore it needs to form a coalition of support around each proposal.

Minority and coalition governments

Minority and coalition governments both stem from 'hung' parliaments, in which no single party has an overall majority of seats. **Minority governments** are formed when the largest single party decides to govern alone. The Labour governments of February–October 1974 and in 1978 were minorities. In the latter case, Prime Minister James Callaghan governed with the support of the Liberals through the Lib–Lab Pact. A coalition government involves two or more parties forming the government together and sharing seats in Cabinet, forming policy jointly and sharing responsibilities for policy. Coalition governments are common in Germany, Italy and Sweden.

James Callaghan's government of 1976–79 became a minority government as its small overall majority was gradually whittled away by a series of by-election defeats. In order to maintain a majority in the Commons the Labour government formed a pact with the Liberals, known as the Lib–Lab Pact. Both parties were keen to make such a pact because each wished to avoid a general election. It gave the Labour government time for the state of the economy to improve and the Liberal party a voice in the determination of government policy.

The Lib–Lab Pact did not give the Liberal party any seats in Cabinet. A government in

The electoral mandate

A mandate is an instruction to carry out a proposal or a set of proposals. An electoral mandate comes from the people to a political party through a general election. When people cast their votes they are assumed to be endorsing the policies of a particular party. If that party then gains an overall majority in the House of Commons they are regarded as having a 'mandate' to carry out the policies in their manifesto.

The type of electoral system in Britain has caused some commentators to question the existence of an electoral mandate. FPTP exaggerates the support of large parties, taking a minority of the vote and turning it into a majority of the seats. The current government has the approval of 42 per cent of voters but only around 30 per cent of electors. Also, most voters do not read manifestos but vote on the basis of their *perception* of the policies. Finally, governments often depart from their manifestos during their term of office, introducing policies for which it can be said to have no mandate, although it may refer to the 'Doctor's Mandate' which allows it to take any steps it considers necessary.

which two or more parties share seats in Cabinet is known as a coalition government. Under these circumstances the coalition partners jointly determine policy and take responsibility for those policies. During World War II, Britain was governed by a coalition of the Conservative and Labour parties, under the leadership of Winston Churchill. Given the special circumstances, this was called a government of 'national unity'. The period between World Wars I and II saw coalitions led by Lloyd George and Ramsay MacDonald, but coalitions have never been considered 'normal' under the British system. They would be much more likely to be so if Britain adopted a system of proportional representation.

Coalitions and representation

Coalition governments have a number of implications for representation and responsibility. Usually parties do not announce their intentions to form coalitions prior to a general election in the hope that they might win an overall majority. Therefore the voters do not have an opportunity to approve or disapprove of the idea of a coalition.

Once the need for a coalition has been established by the election result, the voters are once again excluded from the process as politicians negotiate, behind closed doors, to find a bargain that will suit both parties. Therefore, whilst proportional representation gives an assembly that reflects public opinion, the government is determined without any reference to public opinion. As a result, some commentators argue that the coalition has not been given a mandate to govern by the electorate.

If two or more parties combine to form a government, a significant proportion of the voters ought to be satisfied. For example, if the Labour party had formed a coalition with the Liberal Democrats after the 1992 election, 17.7 million voters would have been satisfied that their party was in government – as opposed to the 14.2 million who were happy with a Conservative victory. However, this assumes that people vote for a party solely to see it enter government. Perhaps it is more likely that people vote for a party in order to see its policies implemented. Participation in a coalition government is by no means a guarantee of this.

When two or more parties join together in a coalition, the policies that result are likely to be compromises between those of all the players. In the example above, they would be neither Labour nor Liberal Democrat but a third set of hybrid policies that were never presented to voters and so could not be representative of public opinion. It is also possible that the junior partner wielding influence over policy-making is a small party representing a tiny proportion of voters. Their influence in government would be far beyond their popularity in the country and in no way a reflection of public opinion.

Compromise

In Britain, coalition government is often considered to be a coalition of the 'centre' with either the Conservative or Labour parties joining with the Liberal Democrats. In this case the junior partner in the coalition is seen to be a moderating, and so perhaps a desirable, influence. This need not be so, however. Voters might not feel comfortable with a coalition of the right which might include the Conservative party and the Ulster Unionists or even the British National party. Similarly, an extreme coalition of the left might include the Labour and Communist parties.

Coalitions and responsibility

Coalitions can also be difficult to hold accountable. With only one party in government it is clear who should be to blame. In a coalition the question of which party should take responsibility might arise.

Small parties

This is particularly the case when one party holds the balance of power in a parliament. In Germany, for example, the Freie Demokratische Partei (FDP) has held the balance of power between the right-wing Christlich-Demokratische Union (CDU) and the left-wing Sozialdemokratische Partei Deutschlands (SPD). As a result it has been a party in government since 1961, with the exception of 1969 when the CDU and SPD formed a coalition between themselves. Therefore, the SPD or CDU win or lose elections while the FDP remains in office whatever happens and so is not being held responsible.

When the second definition of responsibility – strong leadership – is considered, coalition government can again be criticized. Policies must always be based on compromises, so the government does not have the strength to undertake the policies it might consider necessary.

Instability

Coalition governments can also be affected by instability. The senior partner of the coalition can live in fear of the junior partner withdrawing from the relationship. In Italy governments have been made and unmade with alarming regularity. Between 1945 and 1994 Italy had more than 50 governments. To an extent, this instability has contributed to the Italian government's decision to reform the electoral system along the lines of a winner-take-all system.

However, the appearance of instability can be deceptive. While Italian governments have come and gone, the personnel of government has largely remained the same. Democrazia Cristiana (DC) dominated government from 1946 to 1994 with many of its senior officials circulating between high offices.

Adversary politics

On the other hand, the apparent stability of British government has, at times, also been illusory. Professor Samuel Finer coined the term 'adversary politics' to describe the dramatic swings of policy as a 'strong' Labour government was replaced by an equally 'strong' Conservative government. Perhaps this concept is more useful to describe the situation in the 1970s when the two main parties moved to extremes of the political spectrum and seemed likely to alternate regularly in government.

Constitutional effects of PR

The introduction of a system of proportional representation would not only have effects on representation and responsibility. It would also have a significant impact on many of the institutional relationships of the governmental system.

The monarch

The monarch has two roles concerning elections: the dissolution of Parliament prior to an election, and the appointment of a Prime Minister after the election (see page 165). Both roles have been considered largely ceremonial given the relative simplicity of the first-past-the-post electoral system: the leader of the party with the overall majority becomes Prime Minister and then has the power to call a general election at a time most suitable to his or her own party within the next five years.

The introduction of a system of proportional representation could offer a significantly different scenario. For example, suppose that Tony Blair were to lead the largest party in the House of Commons but lack an overall majority. Reluctant to form a coalition, he decides that the Labour party should govern alone, forming a minority government. The opposition parties unite against the Labour government, and in a vote of confidence the government is defeated. Tony Blair asks the monarch to dissolve parliament, to allow another general election to be held. At this point the monarch would have two key decisions to make:

Dissolution of Parliament

- Should the Prime Minister be given a dissolution?

- If not, who should be asked to form an alternative government?

The second question is perhaps easier to answer than the first. Presumably the alternative Prime Minister would be the leader of the Opposition who would be asked if he or she could form a minority or coalition government that could retain the confidence of the Commons. To turn down a Prime Minister's request for a dissolution of Parliament might be a little more controversial.

Appointment of Prime Minister

These issues are more likely to arise under a system of proportional representation and would involve the monarch – an unelected and non-partisan figure – in a politically controversial situation.

The Prime Minister

Prime Ministers who lead a government made up of their own loyal party supporters with a guaranteed majority in the Commons are in a very powerful position. The introduction of proportional representation could change this. A coalition government would be highly likely and a Prime Minister would have to consider the feelings not only of their own party but also those of the coalition partners. The need for compromise would be paramount and the scope for prime ministerial government would be severely reduced.

Prime ministerial power

The House of Commons

If, as seems likely, proportional representation were to lead to a hung parliament, the power of the Commons would increase. No longer would governments be able to take the support of the House for granted, and like a US President they would have to work to build a secure coalition of support around every piece of legislation. The threat of a vote of no confidence would always hang over them.

Voting behaviour

For much of the post-war period explanations of voting behaviour in Britain were relatively uncomplicated. The way people voted was largely explained by **class**

Party identifiers

allegiances. Very simply, the Conservative party was seen as the party of the middle class and the Labour party that of the working class. Ninety per cent of voters supported one of the two main parties, so third parties and nationalist parties were largely ignored. In addition, the way people cast their votes was relatively predictable because 80 per cent of voters were loyal to their party – in other words, were **party identifiers**.

In the 1970s, analysis became rather more complicated as society underwent fundamental changes. Today the level of party identifiers has fallen; the Liberal Democrats and the nationalist parties have become more popular, and the nature of class has changed.

Class voting

Socialization

Class voting is typical of what sociologists refer to as **expressive voting**. We all tend to identify ourselves as part of a particular group in society which is made up of family, friends and colleagues. As we grow up within this group we are **socialized** to behave in particular ways, and the way we vote in elections is one aspect of this. If we see ourselves as a member of the working class and believe that the Labour party best represents the interests of our class, then we are likely to vote Labour in a general election. Such trends are reinforced by peripheral factors such as membership of a trade union, living in an industrial community and perhaps living in local authority accommodation.

Deviant voting

As the working class once accounted for 60 per cent of the population it would seem likely that if individuals voted by class, the Labour party would be the 'natural' party of government, never being out of office. However, in the post-war period this was not the case because, even in the 1950s, voting along class lines did not always occur: approximately 67 per cent of the working class voted Labour; while 80 per cent of the middle class voted Conservative. The willingness of one-third of the working class to desert their class loyalties allowed the Conservative party to dominate government for 13 years in the 1950s and 1960s. As a result, much analysis of voting behaviour during this period concentrated on the reasons for this pattern of **deviant voting**.

Embourgeoise-ment

The 'working-class Tory', as this deviant voter became known, was explained in a number of ways. The term **embourgeoisement** was coined to explain the tendency of the working class to vote Conservative as their standard of living improved. Also some political scientists sought to explain working-class behaviour via deference. According to this view, members of the working class viewed members of the Conservative party as their 'betters' who were well suited to governing the country.

Partisanship

Since the 1970s, explanations of deviant voting have been more than ever called for. Voters are no longer so tied to the two-party model of party competition. The level of partisanship (those voters who are loyal to a particular party) declined dramatically from 81 per cent in 1964 to 70 per cent in 1983, with only 23 per cent identifying strongly with a particular party (down from 38 per cent in 1964). Labour's claim to 67 per cent of the working-class vote fell to only 38 per cent in 1983, while the Conservative party's hold over 80 per cent of the middle class had fallen to 60 per cent.

Some political scientists have attempted to explain the recent changes in voting

Definitions of social class

Social class categories (Heath et al.)

Salariat	27%
Routine non-manuals	24%
Petit bourgeoisie	8%
Foreman, technicians	7%
Working class	34%

Social class categories (Dunleavy and Husbands)

Manual workers	45%
Non-manual	25%
Controllers of labour	22%
Employees/petit bourgeoisie	8%

Social class categories (British Market Research Society)

A	Upper middle	2%
B	Middle	13%
C1	Lower middle	24%
C2	Skilled workers	31%
D	Semi-skilled and unskilled workers	18%
E	Poor	2%

Source: Bill Jones et al., *Politics UK*, Harvester Wheatsheaf, 1994

behaviour by claiming that the traditional methods of stratifying British society have become outdated.

Most traditional analysis has relied on the classification used by the British Market Research Society which uses categories A, B, C1, C2, D and E. This has been considered inadequate because its categories are largely based on occupation. A teacher would fall into category B – professional and managerial – and would, therefore, be expected to vote Conservative. However, many teachers in state schools have in the past felt insecure with Conservative policies towards education.

Classification

Anthony Heath, Roger Jowell and John Curtice (*How Britain Votes*, Pergamon, 1985) have created a new middle-class category, the **salariat**, to take account of the growing number of salaried members of the middle class who might well vote Labour. Erik Ohlin Wright ('Class crisis and the state', *New Left Review*, 1975) has referred to these voters as 'contradictory' because their status suggests they should vote Conservative, but their occupational circumstances encourage them to support Labour.

Heath and colleagues use a category called the **petit bourgeoisie**, including owners of small businesses. In the British Market Research Society classification these are included in the C1 category with the skilled working class, with whom traditionally they share little in terms of ideals and objectives.

Patrick Dunleavy and Chris Husbands (*British Democracy at the Crossroads*, Longman, 1985) have also redefined class boundaries by including a Marxist perspective. Individuals are classified according to their relationship to their means of production. This system takes into account not only the traditional divisions between working class and middle class, but also an individual's position in 'the system of production and exchange'. In other words, the working class can be further subdivided into those who own their own home or rent from the local authority, work in the public or private sector, are members of trade unions or not, etc. According to this view, those who deal mostly with the private sector are more likely to vote Conservative.

Instrumental voting

Regency approach

Instrumental voting behaviour concentrates on the short-term factors that influence behaviour, rather than the long-term factors such as class loyalty. This is sometimes known as the **regency approach**. Issues that might affect voting habits, according to this, might include policy issues, leadership, media coverage and the election campaign. Naturally, as short-term factors, these points can be used to explain the volatility of voting behaviour, particularly in the light of the rise of the independent, or floating, voter.

Such an approach might explain the great swings in popularity of parties and governments as leaders and circumstances change. One of the factors leading to Margaret Thatcher's downfall was her poor standing in **opinion polls** compared with Michael Heseltine and John Major. Also, prior to each of the Conservative party's general election victories of 1979, 1983, 1987 and 1992, the Conservative government had gone through periods of considerable unpopularity, including the loss of by-elections, before recovering to win the general election.

Opinion polls

The difficulty of assessing the importance of such issues in determining electoral behaviour is that research relies on opinion poll data. Polling companies, such as MORI and Gallup, have designed scientific methods to ascertain the way a sample of people feel about particular issues, leaders and parties. They then extrapolate from the sample to predict the way in which the country as a whole will react. Given a margin of error of approximately plus or minus 3 per cent, opinion polls are quite reliable. However, pollsters consistently predicted a hung parliament in 1992 with Labour as the largest party, so an overall majority for the Conservatives was a great surprise. The misleading poll information may have been due to a poor sample or to voters being able to separate their replies to opinion poll questions from their voting intentions. For example, some commentators believe that a number of voters stated a preference for more funding for the health service and education but, when faced with a ballot box decision, voted for the lower taxes offered by the Conservative party.

Exercises

Short questions

1   What importance may be attached to by-election campaigns and their results? (ULEAC, June 1992)

2   Briefly describe:
    a   the single transferable vote
    b   the additional member system.
    c   Which do you prefer and why?
    (ULEAC, January 1991)

3   a   Define the concept of the electoral mandate.
    b   Assess its validity as a principle of representative government.
    (ULEAC, June 1991)

4   a   Briefly describe one alternative electoral system to first-past-the-post.
    b   Outline its advantages and disadvantages.
    (EdExcel, January 1996)

Essay questions

1   State (a) the case for, and (b) the case against electoral reform.
    (ULEAC, January 1993)

2   'Social class remains the significant indicator of voting behaviour.' Discuss.
    (Oxford & Cambridge, 1992)

3   Did the 1992 general election demonstrate once again that the first-past-the-post system is undemocratic?
    (Cambridge, June 1994)

4   Why do some voters 'float'?
    (Oxford, June 1992)

5   Assess the arguments for and against electoral reform.
    (EdExcel, June 1996)

6   'What we regard as the most desirable form of electoral reform will depend on the view we have about the nature of representative government.' Discuss.
    (EdExcel, January 1995)

Data response question

The 1987 general election (1983 figures in brackets)

Party	Percentage of votes	Seats	Percentage of seats
Conservative	42.3 (42.4)	375 (397)	57.7 (61.0)
Labour	30.8 (27.6)	229 (209)	35.2 (32.0)
Liberal/SDP	22.6 (25.4)	22 (23)	3.4 (3.5)
Others	4.3 (4.6)	23 (21)	3.5 (3.2)

Overall Conservative majority: 101 (144)
(Speaker not included)

Turnout: 75.4% (72.2%)

From Bill Jones and Dennis Kavanagh, *British Politics Today*, Manchester University Press.

Imagine that a general election is to be held tomorrow. The latest opinion polls suggest the result will be: Conservatives 38 per cent; Labour 34 per cent; Liberal Democrats 21 per cent; Others 7 per cent. Big swings seem likely in some constituencies and regions. 80 per cent say they are 'certain' or 'very likely' to vote.

What assumptions would you make in estimating the number or proportion of seats each party is likely to win? Suggest the number of seats you would expect each party to hold when the votes have been counted, and indicate the factors which influence your prediction.

(AEB, June 1993)

3 Political parties

Questions to be answered in this chapter

- What are political parties?
- What roles do they perform and how powerful are they in Britain?
- What is a party system?
- To what extent can the British party system be considered a two-party system?
- How are British political parties organized and where does the power lie within the parties?

Terms to know

- Adversarial politics
- 'Bottom-up'
- Consensus politics
- Electoral role
- Extra-parliamentary
- Fabians
- Governing role
- Labour Reform Group
- Manifesto
- Manifesto Group
- Militant Tendency
- The Monday Club
- Multi-party system
- Neo-liberal
- 1922 Committee
- One member, one vote (OMOV)
- One-nation Toryism
- Party discipline
- Party whip
- Political consensus
- 'Top-down'
- Tribune Group
- Two-party system
- 'Wets'

Introduction

Political parties can be analysed as entities in their own right or as elements of the wider party system. In both cases, the 1980s and 1990s have seen considerable changes for political parties in the UK. In terms of the UK party system, analysis has moved through a **two-party system**, a **multi-party system** (with the rise of the Social Democrat–Liberal Alliance party), a dominant party system with the pre-eminence of the Conservative party for 18 years, and now into a new era of party politics with the Labour party holding the largest parliamentary majority of any government since 1945.

Within each party there have also been radical changes. First it was the Labour party that underwent reforms initiated by Tony Benn and the Labour Left to give more power to the grassroots. This was followed by a growing centralization of the party under Neil Kinnock, John Smith and now Tony Blair. The Liberal party has been through a number of emanations: the Liberal party, the Liberal–Social Democratic Alliance, and now the Liberal Democrats. Finally, in the wake of its worst electoral defeat since World War II, the Conservative party has begun a programme of reform and renewal under the leadership of William Hague.

A definition of party politics

A political party is a group of like-minded people organized as a single unit in order to gain the power necessary to govern the country. The group considers a wide range of issues and seeks to implement its solutions when in government. In a democracy, parties seek power by proposing candidates for election.

The development of parties in Britain

Electoral reform

Prior to the extension of the electoral franchise in the nineteenth century, political parties were merely loose formations of MPs, bound together by anything from political beliefs to friendship and family. However, as the right to vote was extended in 1832, 1867 and 1884 parties began to formalize their organizations in an effort to gain the support of voters and to organize the House of Commons. The parties set up bureaucracies to manage party affairs from the centre, as well as constituency bodies to organize local support.

Organization

This trend towards formal party organization was given an additional boost by the rise of the Labour party in the twentieth century. As the representatives of the working class, which had been excluded from British politics for so long, the Labour party felt that it would need to be highly organized in order to make an impression on the status quo as represented by the Conservative and Liberal parties.

Functions of political parties

Electoral and governing roles

Parties perform a wide range of functions, but a definition of what they are varies from one textbook to another. Suggestions include representation, communication and recruitment. All of these tend to concentrate on the participative aspect of party functions. By this, we mean political parties allow citizens to take part in the political process, either by becoming a member, a candidate or even a leader of a political party. This aspect of the role of parties is undoubtedly important; in fact, parties are often identified as one of only three ways to take part in politics – voting, parties and pressure groups. However, the role, or the power, that political parties have in any political system can best be seen by examining their functions under two broad headings: **electoral** and **governing** roles.

In the former Soviet Union the electoral role of the Communist party of the Soviet Union was minimal, but its role in government was commanding. In the USA the Republican and Democratic parties play a limited role in elections because campaigns and voting tend to be centred on the candidates rather than the parties themselves – and as a result the role they play in congressional politics is also narrow. In Britain political parties dominate both elections and the processes of government.

The electoral role

The electoral role that political parties play in elections can be divided into:
- nomination of candidates
- organization of campaigns
- finance of campaigns
- provision of policy
- organization of voters.

Nomination of candidates

Parties in Britain put forward candidates for election at national and local levels. The main unit of party organization away from the centre is the constituency party and in both the Conservative and Labour parties this unit carries the prime responsibility for the selection of parliamentary candidates.

In the Conservative party the constituency party selection committee usually puts forward one or two candidates for consideration by the constituency association as a whole. However, the chosen candidate must be on the list of 'approved candidates' put together by Conservative party Central Office (see page 56). Therefore, the central party keeps a firm grip on who is chosen as a prospective candidate. Nevertheless, Central Office is reluctant to interfere in the choice of candidates by overruling a constituency choice. For example, in 1997 one constituency persisted with the candidacy of Neil Hamilton, despite the allegations of the 'cash-for-questions' scandal hanging over him. This was obviously bad for a party struggling with allegations of sleaze – but the national party could not overrule the constituency association.

Conservative method

The Labour party, too, has a number of 'approved lists'; these are trade union sponsored, constituency party nominated, Co-operative Society nominated and those recommended by the Women's Section. A shortlist is drawn up by the general management committee of the constituency party and the list must include a female candidate. The Labour party has committed itself to increasing the number of women in Parliament. In 1993 it agreed to the selection of women candidates for all safe Labour seats falling vacant at the time of the next general election. In these constituencies the shortlists were to be made up of women candidates only. Whilst this proved a controversial policy, it did result in the election of 101 female MPs to the new Parliament in 1997.

Labour method

Comparison

Political parties in the USA have lost control of the nomination process. Candidates for both presidential and congressional elections are selected through mini elections called 'primaries'. These allow the voters to choose who the final candidates will be, and they were introduced in an effort to bring the parties back in line with public opinion.

The breadth of participation in primaries varies. In 'open' primaries all voters can participate in the primary of either the Republican or the Democratic party – but not both. In 'closed' primaries only registerd party supporters may vote.

OMOV Traditionally, the final choice was made by an electoral college made up of all the elements of the constituency party, including individual members, trade unions and other affiliated organizations. However, since 1993 the selection has been on a **one member, one vote (OMOV)** basis.

Reselection Until 1992 the Labour party had an additional part to its selection process, i.e. the mandatory reselection of parliamentary candidates prior to a general election. Adopted in 1980, this requirement meant that all sitting MPs were required to go through the reselection process within the lifetime of a parliament. They did not have an automatic right to stand as the party's candidate in the next election. This had the effect of encouraging candidates to pay attention to the wishes of their local party as well as to the national leadership. Today reselection occurs only if requested by the constituency party.

Liberal Democrat method The Liberal Democrats also have a list of 'approved candidates', but allow the local party to make the final choice by a ballot of all constituency party members.

These slightly varying methods of selecting candidates have in common the importance of the party in the choice of candidates. Unlike in the USA, the voters have no voice in the matter at all and so the party, whether local or national, becomes the focus of loyalty.

Organization of campaigns

Once the candidates have been appointed, the election campaign needs to be organized. The pattern of campaigning for much of the twentieth century was set at the end of the nineteenth century – at constituency level. In the Midlothian campaign of 1879 and 1880, former Liberal leader William Gladstone toured his constituency denouncing the Conservative government. At about the same time the Conservative party was setting up its constituency organizations with local members and party agents.

Local activists Since then local party activists have organized party events, raised money, recruited members and campaigned for their candidates. At election time a small army of party members can be seen in every constituency carrying out the ritual of door-to-door campaigning. They spend hours cajoling, chatting and arguing with voters trying to get them to vote for their party.

National campaigns However, since the late 1950s elections have been increasingly dominated by the national campaign. Initially, this meant the party leaders would travel all over the country meeting and addressing the voters. In 1959, for example, Conservative Prime Minister Harold Macmillan travelled 2500 miles and spoke at 70 public meetings. More recently, party leaders have used the media to gain access to the electorate.

Media Party political broadcasts, television and radio interviews, stage-managed media events, 'photo opportunities' and 'sound bites' now dominate election campaigns. Highlights of recent campaigns have included Labour leader Neil Kinnock's broadcast of 1987 and the Conservative party leader John Major's 'soap box' in 1992. These events are elements of the national party campaign, not constituency activism. Therefore, the national parties have a very firm grip on the organization of campaigns.

The 1997 general election campaign was certainly no exception to the trend for the national parties to dominate. Tony Blair's grip on the Labour party was firm, and the campaign was highly stage-managed and choreographed along the lines of an election campaign in the USA. In contrast, the Conservative party – so renowned for being led from the top – actually proved more difficult to control at a national level. Approximately 150 Conservative backbench MPs stated their opposition to joining the single European currency in their election addressses to constituents – this was contrary to stated party policy at national level.

Finance of campaigns

As the campaign is dominated by national party activity, it follows that much of the money for the campaign is raised and spent at a national level. In 1987 the Conservative party spent over £17 million on its election campaign (not including 'benefits in kind', such as free postage and television broadcasts). Of this total, £9 million was spent at national level (£5 million on national advertising). In fact, British campaign finance law encourages expenditure to be controlled from the centre because there are no limits on the level of election spending at national level. In the 1987 general election individual candidates were restricted to a campaign budget of £5000–£6000.

Thirty-three per cent of the Conservative party's national election spending in 1987 was financed by a levy on local parties. The remainder came from donations to the party's Central Office, mainly from industry.

In 1992 Conservative candidates spent the most, on average £5840, with Labour candidates following with £5090 and the Liberal Democrats with £3169. Centrally the Conservative party estimates that it spent £10 million, with Labour spending only £7 million. Advertising by organizations such as trade unions on behalf of the Labour party brings their figure up to one almost comparable with their main rivals.

In fact, following the 1992 general election campaign the Conservative party was left with a deficit of approximately £19 million. Prior to the 1997 general election campaign the party chairman, Brian Mawhinney, appointed in 1995, worked hard to put the finances on an even keel with the help of a newly appointed Director General and Board of Directors. *The Guardian* has estimated that the party's 1997 election campaign cost approximately £40 million at central and local levels.

In 1994 the Parliamentary Home Affairs Select Committee reported on political funding. The eleven-member committee was split along party lines, with Labour members submitting a minority report that was highly critical of Conservative party funding, which was described as 'one of the great mysteries of British politics'. Between 1987 and 1991 half of the £38 million donated to the party could not be traced to any source, although a former chairman of the Conservative Board of Finance confirmed that about £7 million came from abroad before the 1992 election. It is believed that Polly Peck, owned by Asil Nadir who fled Britain to avoid fraud charges, donated £440,000 without declaring it, as is required by law.

More recently, the Labour party has fallen foul of public sensibilities regarding campaign and party funding in connection with the donation of £1 million from the head of Formula One motor racing, Bernie Eckleston. This donation, it is alleged,

Election spending

Conservative funds

Election funding

Odd man out

'Britain is unusual among Western democracies in not providing large-scale funding for political parties. It is also unusual in fixing no limit to what parties may spend at national level in general elections, and having no requirement at all for party accounts to be meaningful to outsiders.

In the USA, taxpayers can tick a box on their tax forms to opt to pay $1 towards federal funding for presidential elections. This provides payments to match money raised privately by candidates in primaries, as well as grants for presidential candidates and party conventions. Candidates are required to disclose any contribution over $200.

In **Japan**, political parties receive a monthly subsidy of about £47,000 per member of parliament. Under current rules, donations to individual politicians are theoretically limited to £9735 a year, but this has not prevented widespread corruption.

In **Germany**, about £100m a year is paid to parties represented in the Bundestag, according to a formula based on their electoral success. Parties must publish accounts including the names of anyone giving them £8000 or more.

In **Spain**, parties receive £8000 for every seat they hold in the Cortes plus 31p for every vote they win. Details of private donations – which must not exceed £50,000 – have to be published and party funds audited.

In **Italy**, generous state financing of political parties was introduced in 1974. But a national referendum last year ended it. Italian parties are required by law to publish details of donations.

In **Sweden, Finland, Denmark** and **Norway**, state subsidies relate to numbers of votes or MPs. Parties are required to publish accounts and list large donors.

In **Belgium**, each party receives an annual subsidy of £100,000, plus £1 for every vote it won in the previous election. Accounts must be submitted to an independent audit commission. Political donations by companies or trade unions are illegal.

In **Canada**, voters are entitled to a tax credit for political donations. The scale of the credit is geared to encourage small donations. There are strict limits on electoral spending. Parties are reimbursed 22.5 per cent of their electoral expenses, individual candidates up to 50 per cent.

Should Britain follow suit? Already the so-called short money, £2m a year, is provided to opposition parties for their work in Parliament. But sceptics will note that neither state funding nor regulation stops abuse – as the examples of Italy, Spain and Japan demonstrate.'

Source: *The Economist*, 16 April 1994

Table 3.1 Selections from the 1997 election manifestos

Issue	Conservative	Labour	Liberal Democrat
Economy policy	Continue to target inflation. Bring unemployment down through training and general economic growth	Maintain low inflation rate but seek to bring down unemployment through extensive training programmes, eg Welfare to Work	Maintain low inflation but make efforts to reduce unemployment through training
Public spending	Seek to reduce public sector spending as a proportion of GDP	Maintain Conservative spending proposals	Increase spending on education and health
Taxation	Seek long term reductions in levels of direct taxation	No new direct taxation except the 'windfall tax' on privatized utilities	Increase taxation to pay for increased social welfare spending
Education	Retain league tables, grant maintained schools and nursery vouchers to increase parental choice. Introduce fees for higher education	Use 'windfall tax' to increase education spending. Make education a top priority	Increase spending in order to reduce class sizes
Health	Continue with drive for greater efficiency	Use 'windfall tax' to increase spending with aim of reducing waiting lists	Increase spending to reduce waiting lists
EU	'Wait and see' regarding single European currency and a referendum. Extend EU membership and oppose federal power of Brussels bureacracy	Sign up to 'Social Chapter' of Maastricht Treaty. Make Britain a leading player at the heart of the EU. Referendum on single European currency	Central role in the EU. Yes to Social Chapter. Yes to single European currency
Constitutional reform	Oppose changes to the Union, reform of the House of Lords, voting system and bill of rights	Referendum on devolution in Scotland and Wales. Reform of Lords. Consider reform of the electoral system. Incorporate the European Convention on Human Rights into domestic law	Devolution for Scotland and Wales. Reform of the Electoral system. Increased powers for local government

gained Formula One the ear of the Prime Minister in order to put its case for exemption from a proposed ban on advertising in sport by cigarette companies.

Provision of policy

Manifesto Immediately prior to a general election, each party publishes its election **manifesto** which outlines the policies it will seek to enact if elected to government. As well as giving voters a choice, the manifesto also fulfils an educational function as the electorate learns more about the political, economic and social issues of the day and alternative approaches to them (see Table 3.1).

Comparison

In the USA when the candidate is selected they simply take over the party for the duration of that election campaign. To an extent the party, and party policy, is whatever the candidate proclaims it to be. Therefore the party is less the judge of the contest and rather more the prize.

The policy themes of a British election are all determined by the national parties with little room for local variations or freedom of expression for candidates. Certainly, national media coverage, national advertising and party political broadcasts are all focused on national party policy. Therefore, individual candidates and even constituency parties have little or no voice in the making of party policy, but they are expected to follow the party manifesto during the election campaign.

Organization of voters

By offering candidates for election who are grouped around sets of policies, parties allow the electorate to make a choice between different approaches to the governing of the country. Their freedom to do this is a fundamental characteristic of truly democratic elections.

However, 55 million individual voters could have 55 million attitudes to each issue confronting the country. It is impossible in a representative democracy to give all of these views a fair hearing. Therefore, they need to be consolidated into a smaller, more manageable range of views. Parties do this by uniting voters behind their respective banners as people vote for the party that most closely suits their own attitudes.

Comparison

The USA has seen a rise in the proportion of independent, or 'floating', voters. In 1940 approximately 20 per cent of voters were independent, but by 1986 this had risen to 36 per cent. It is this decline in partisanship that is the root of the parties' declining electoral role. As parties have become less popular the focus has turned increasingly to the candidates, and the result is the highly candidate-orientated campaigns of American politics.

Between 1945 and 1965, once voters had decided on a party affiliation they were unlikely to lose it. In fact, it was likely to grow stronger as they grew older. Since 1965 the level of voters identifying themselves with a particular party has declined from 81 per cent to 70 per cent. Over the same period those voters *strongly* identifying themselves with a political party has fallen from 38 per cent to 23 per cent. This means that there are more floating voters to be captured by the parties at general elections and that they can no longer take the votes of many of the electorate for granted.

In Britain, individual candidates have not been able to base campaigns on their own appeal. The campaign at the constituency level is relatively insignificant because general elections are so dominated by the campaign at national level. Most voters will decide whether to switch their vote according to the appeal of a national party leader, a particular set of national issues, or even a national advertising campaign. They do not do so according to the personality of their local candidate or their policies. Therefore, elections in Britain remain party-orientated rather than candidate-orientated.

Party identification

Comparison

In the USA the decline of partisanship has meant that individual candidates have taken control of their own campaigns, promoting *themselves* more than the party. As a result, the party tends to be a label to hang on a particular candidate. However, it does not mean that the influence of political parties has disappeared. The party label continues to be important as a foundation on which to build one's personal appeal.

American campaigns

The governing role

Once elections are over, parties move into office, whether as the government or as one of the opposition parties in the House of Commons. When installed, parties perform three further functions:
- provision of policy
- allocation of office
- organization of the assembly.

Provision of policy

We have already seen that provision of an election manifesto is the responsibility of the party. According to the concept of the mandate, the next step is to carry through these

---

Comparison

We have already seen that in the USA candidates determine the policy, rather than the party doing so. This is continued through into government, where national party lines are relatively weak. This permits members of Congress to adjust policy to suit the needs of their consistuents. Therefore the aims of the parties is to win as many seats as possible rather than holding up a strong national manifesto and a set of ideological beliefs.

policies in government, having received the permission of the electorate to do so. However, political, economic and social circumstances change during the lifetime of a parliament and so governments have always reserved the right to depart from manifestos if necessary. On these occasions, decisions are taken by the party leadership in the Cabinet rather than by the party as a whole.

Conservative party

Within the Conservative party such a decision-making process is expected and even demanded because the party looks for strong leadership and gives decision-making power to its leaders. This reflects the origins of the party – a collection of constituency organizations designed to support the party in the Commons.

Conservative divisions

Nevertheless, in the 1992–97 Parliament the Conservative party was more divided than at any time since 1945. The issue of Europe lay at the heart of ideological differences, but divisions spilt over into economic management and John Major's style of leadership. This apparent lack of discipline whilst in government undoubtedly contributed to the Conservative party's 1997 general election defeat. As a result there has been a move under its new leader, William Hague, to give the grassroots of the party a greater voice in the determination of policy and the general direction of the party.

Labour party

The Labour party originated outside Parliament in order to gain parliamentary representation for the Labour movement as a whole, led by the trade union movement. This is most clearly illustrated by the original title of the modern Labour party – the Labour Representation Committee – which was abandoned in 1906. As a result, decisions regarding Labour party policy are, according to the party's constitution, the responsibility of the annual conference or, when the conference is not in session, the responsibility lies with the National Executive Committee. Therefore, the focus of decision-making in the Labour party is at odds with the focus of decision-making in the British political system as, theoretically, a Labour government and Labour MPs would be required to consult with **extra-parliamentary** bodies before departing from stated party policy.

In fact, Labour leaders in government have paid more attention to the British Constitution than to that of their party. In 1928, Ramsay MacDonald told the Labour party Conference: 'As long as I hold any position in the parliamentary party – and I know I can speak for my colleagues also – we are not going to take instructions from any outside body unless we agree with them.' In recent years, Harold Wilson and James Callaghan both ignored conference decisions by claiming a greater responsibility to the country than to the party.

Labour party conference

When the Labour party is in opposition its leaders have found it more difficult to ignore the extra-parliamentary elements of the party. Hugh Gaitskell, James Callaghan, Neil Kinnock and John Smith all had battles with the Labour party conference over issues such as unilateral disarmament (Hugh Gaitskell), the expulsion of **Militant Tendency** (Neil Kinnock), internal democracy (James Callaghan, Neil Kinnock and John Smith), and rewriting Clause 4 (Tony Blair). Unable to resort to the argument of government – that they must consider the interests of the nation as a whole – party leaders have tended to use the carrot of electoral success as the means to restrain the extra-parliamentary party.

Tony Blair has played this card particularly effectively since he became Labour leader. He took up the baton from John Smith and before him Neil Kinnock and has continued to 'modernize' the party. Ironically his tactics have been, to some extent, an extension of the Labour party reforms of 1981. These reforms (see page 62) were initiated by the Left of the party under the leadership of Tony Benn. The intention was to give greater power to the grassroots by extending Labour democracy. This was extended by John Smith who introduced one member one vote (OMOV), thus diminishing the power of trade unions. Blair, in turn, has used plebiscites (referendums) to achieve his aims. The rewrite of Clause 4 and the 1997 election manifesto were approved by plebiscites, and it is his intention to contine this trend by allowing the grassroots a greater voice in policy-making. By doing so Tony Blair has marginalized the trade unions, home of the traditional Left of the party, and has gone over the heads of the annual conference and the National Executive Committee.

In government and opposition, therefore, most policy is party policy – but the focus of the decision-making power within the party varies between the Conservatives and Labour.

Allocation of office

In a parliamentary system the party that commands a majority in the assembly is usually asked to form the government because it has the confidence of the Commons. Once installed, the party leader – the Prime Minister – has the power to allocate around 120 ministerial offices, from Cabinet ministers to a range of junior ministers.

Ministerial positions

The power of patronage lies solely with the Prime Minister and so is not the responsibility of the wider party, in terms of MPs or the extra-parliamentary party. However, the Prime Minister usually bears in mind the wishes of the party when making appointments. Therefore in the British system of government the rewards of office are within the gift of the party and its leader, and so there is a great incentive for members of the parliamentary parties to 'toe the party line' in the hope of achieving promotion into the executive branch of government.

Patronage

Again, the situation differs slightly between the Conservative and Labour leaders. In the Conservative party the leader has the power to appoint ministers, when in government, or shadow spokespeople, when in opposition. In the Labour party the members of the shadow Cabinet are elected by MPs as a whole and the leader must

Shadow cabinets

Comparison

In the USA, promotion from the legislature to the executive lies in the hands of the President, not the party. He or she has the power to appoint anyone to the executive regardless of party affiliation or political background.

Within Congress, promotion to the chair of a committee used to be based on the Seniority Rule. This meant that the longest serving member of a committee from the majority party automatically became its chairperson. Recently this has begun to lapse and the party leadership has had a greater voice in selection.

create the shadow Cabinet from those chosen. When in government, however, the Labour leader has the freedom to choose the Cabinet.

Organization of the assembly

Party discipline

The House of Commons and, to a lesser extent, the House of Lords are organized along party lines. The vast majority of the members of the Commons are members of a political party. Currently, the only exception is Martin Bell who was elected as an independent candidate. This was something of a special case because he stood against a Conservative, with Labour and the Liberal Democrats agreeing to allow the independent candidate a clear passage to victory.

In the House of Lords most peers are affiliated to one party or another. However, some choose to be 'crossbenchers' – not taking the whip from any of the main parties.

Not only is membership of political parties predominant in the House of Commons, but parties also organize the work of the Commons. The majority of time available for debate is allocated along party lines with most time set aside for government legislation and opposition supply days (see page 92). The few days that remain are available for private members' bills (see page 89). In addition, places on Commons committees are allocated according to party strength in Parliament. Finally, and most importantly, most votes are taken along party lines, with the overwhelming majority of MPs voting according to their **party whip**.

MPs have strong incentives to 'toe the party line' because parties have such a firm grip of the electoral process and on the allocation of offices. Therefore, MPs are aware that their present jobs, as MPs, are dependent on continued party support and any future promotion depends on their own ability to impress the leaders of their party.

The result of such strong **party discipline** is that the business of the Commons is highly organized. Only occasional backbench revolts disturb the predictability of the procedures of the House of Commons. In the modern British system of government, political parties are the oils that lubricate the constitutional system, providing candidates, policies and organization.

Comparison

The weak electoral role of politics in the USA, combined with a weak party line, mean that party discipline in Congress is relatively weak. Members know that they owe their election to their constituents, and so they keep their interests at the forefront of their political actions.

The party system

When examining the roles that political parties perform in the British system of government, we tend to concentrate on the Labour and Conservative parties. This is because Britain has what is commonly referred to as a two-party system. However, in practice Britain has far more than two political parties. So, what exactly does 'two-party system' mean, and is it an accurate description of the state of affairs in the UK?

A two-party system

A party system is a way of describing not only the number of political parties in a country but also the relative power of the parties and the issues around which they are formed. Britain is referred to as having a two-party system because the House of Commons is currently *dominated* by two parties – Labour and Conservative. After the 1997 election these two major parties held 88 per cent of constituencies (a percentage which was one of the lowest since 1945). During the 1950s and 1960s it was more typical for the two major parties to hold 98 per cent of the seats in the Commons. As a result, every postwar government has been formed by one of these parties alone, with its rival forming the official Opposition.

A multi-party system

The two-party system looks less convincing when looking at election campaigns and voting. It is very easy to assume that the look of the House of Commons reflects the nature of party political activity across the country. It does not.

The two-party division in Britain has its roots in the class system. Even though in the 1960s and 1970s the relationship between class and voting behaviour weakened (see page 34), the Conservative party is still perceived as the party of the middle class and the Labour party as that of the working class. However, such a view of the party system is Anglocentric. The English party system may be dominated by class divisions, but those of Scotland, Wales and Northern Ireland are not.

Parties and class

According to Lipset and Rokkan ((eds) *Party Systems and Voter Alignments: Cross-national Perspectives*, Collier–Macmillan, 1967), political parties form around four main divisions in society, known as 'cleavages' – they are class, centre–periphery (nationalism), religion, and urban–rural (agricultural interests). In Britain only the first three of these cleavages are present.

In Scotland and Wales, competition between Conservative and Labour is complicated by the nationalist parties. The Scottish Nationalist party and Plaid Cymru in Wales have arisen from the desire of many people in these countries to have greater independence from central, London-based, government.

Scotland and Wales

Northern Irish politics offers a completely different party picture. The dominant cleavage in the province is religion, with party affiliations being drawn around the division between Catholic and Protestant. Here the Conservative and Labour parties, as they are known in England, play no role at all, although the Conservative party is allied to the Unionist parties.

Northern Ireland

In fact, a simple contest between the Labour and Conservative parties is not even the case in England. Support for each of the two main parties has a geographical aspect. In the rural areas of the south, with the exception of London, the Conservative party is dominant, while the Labour party is dominant in the north of England. In each of

North and south

51

these areas the main challenger has been the centre party, in the form of the Liberals, the Liberal–Social Democratic Alliance and, most recently, the Liberal Democrats. Therefore, it might be said that a multi-party system exists since straight contests between Labour and Conservative are rare.

Votes · The strength of the Liberal Democrat vote across the country confirms that Britain does not in practice have a two-party system. The renaissance of the Liberal party began in the election of February 1974, under the leadership of Jeremy Thorpe, when its share of the vote rose to 19.3 per cent from 7.5 per cent in 1970. The centre party's fortunes reached a high point in 1983 when the Alliance polled 7.8 million votes (25.4 per cent), only 0.7 million votes behind the Labour party. Since then Liberal Democrat support has fallen to 6.1 million (18.4 per cent), but this remains sufficient to warrant talk of a 'three-party system', at least in the minds of many voters. In 1997 the Liberal Democrats increased their representation in the Commons by 26 seats to 46 – their highest since 1945. However, they did so on the basis of only 16.8 per cent of the votes cast. This was their lowest vote since 1970, but the distribution of support and the targeting of 'winable' seats proved successful.

The 1997 general election seemed to confirm the multi-party nature of British politics. In terms of candidates there was a plethora of parties putting up multiple candidates. They included the British National party (57 candidates; 35,833 votes), the Natural Law party (178 candidates; 28,073 votes), the Green party (94 candidates; 63,452 votes) and the Pro-Life Alliance (53 candiates; 18,545 votes). However, the largest 'small' party was the Referendum party, led by millionaire financier Sir James Goldsmith. It won 811,827 votes but failed to win any seats. Furthermore, the nationalist parties of Scotland and Wales increased their representation by four seats.

Preservation of the two-party system

Despite pressure from the Liberal Democrats and the nationalist parties, the two-party system in the House of Commons has remained in place. The main reason for its survival can be found in the anomalies of the British electoral system.

First-past-the-post · The first-past-the-post system (see page 23) rewards winners only. A candidate wins a constituency by accumulating more votes than their nearest rival. Traditionally with their support concentrated in geographical areas, the Labour and Conservative parties are able to win seats in the north, for the former, and the south, for the latter. This leaves the Liberal Democrats to accumulate a considerable number of votes, but to be placed second in many constituencies. Therefore, the centre party is unable to convert its widespread support into seats in the Commons.

Duverger · Another interpretation of the survival of the two-party system has been offered by Maurice Duverger. The French political scientist has argued that the Labour and Conservative parties can be placed at each end of a political spectrum with the Conservatives on the right and Labour on the left, reflecting their political ideologies. At times, both parties slide along the spectrum as their policies become more moderate or more extreme.

Consensus · For much of the postwar period, the two main parties were not seriously divided on key policy issues. Both were agreed on a Keynesian approach to economic management,

---

Comparison

The USA has a two-party system. American politics has been dominated by the Democratic and Republican parties since 1860. Whilst other parties do exist they have never succeeded in taking on the two main parties on equal terms. The first-past-the-post electoral system, the lack of funds, the tendency of these parties to be parties of protest or vehicles to further the ambitions of individuals, and therefore make these parties shortlived.

---

the importance of the National Health Service, the desirability of full employment, and the need for a British nuclear deterrent. The period of British politics from 1945 to 1970 has often been called the postwar **political consensus** or Butskellism, after Rab Butler (Conservative) and Hugh Gaitskell (Labour) whose economic policies were virtually indistinguishable. This can be represented on Duverger's spectrum as the two main parties sitting near the centre (see Figure 3.1)

Figure 3.1 Duverger's spectrum: political consensus

Economic policy

Keynesian economic theory was based on the idea that a government could exert some control over the twin economic evils of inflation and unemployment by influencing the demand for goods and services in the economy. If unemployment rose, the government could try to increase demand through its control over state spending, taxes and interest rates. More demand for their products would encourage firms to produce more and to take on more workers. The higher the level of demand, the more people would be employed.

If demand continued to rise, however, it would eventually outstrip the capacity of industry to supply it. Then competition for the insufficient supply of goods and services would cause persistent price rises – inflation. The government would then try to cut inflation by spending less, increasing taxes and raising interest rates. Demand would fall, and unemployment rise as firms laid off the workers they no longer needed.

While Keynesian economics tolerated a trade-off between inflation and unemployment – producing a cycle of economic booms and recessions – monetarism is based upon the theory that inflation should not be tolerated as part of an economic cycle, but attacked head on. Given the right incentives and economic conditions, monetarists argue, firms will become more competitive on the world market and will then take on more workers.

As the two main parties were so close together there was little room for the Liberal party to make an impact on electoral politics, and they polled fewer than three million votes in every general election except 1964.

In the 1970s the Conservative and Labour parties began to move further apart. First the Conservative party under Edward Heath confronted the trade unions, then the Labour party embarked on a series of nationalizations that lacked cross-party support. The adversarial nature of party competition was intensified when Margaret Thatcher became leader of the Conservative party in 1975 and when Michael Foot was elected leader of the Labour party in 1980. Margaret Thatcher moved the Conservatives to the right with radical policies such as privatization, the sale of council houses, trade union reform and monetarist economic policies (see page 69). Michael Foot committed the Labour party to renationalization, unilateral nuclear disarmament, full employment and higher public spending.

Adversarial politics   As the postwar political consensus crumbled, the two main parties moved to **adversarial politics** and towards more polarized positions on the left–right spectrum. This left the middle ground free for the centre party to capture (see Figure 3.2). The Liberal party was revitalized under the leadership of first Jeremy Thorpe and subsequently David Steel. It formed the Alliance with a group of moderate Labour MPs who had broken away to form the Social Democratic party.

Figure 3.2 Duverger's spectrum: the centre party captures the middle ground

Under these circumstances, Duverger argues, the two main parties will adjust their policies in order to recapture the middle ground, crushing the centre party as they do so. To support this argument, we can point to the election of John Major as the Tory leader with a more moderate image and approach than his predecessor, and the Labour party's gradual move towards the centre, or even the right, of the spectrum under the leadership of Neil Kinnock, John Smith and Tony Blair.

According to Duverger, the two-party system is maintained as the two main parties take back the centre ground, leaving the Liberal Democrats to be a party of protest unable to break the mould of traditional two-party politics.

A one-party system

Conservative
dominance   The idea of a two-party system implies that the two main parties alternate in power on a fairly regular basis. For much of the twentieth century this has not been the case. Since 1918 the Conservative party has participated in government for 54 of 78 years, and by the time of the 1997 general election had been in power continuously for 18 years.

However, one should again bear in mind that Conservative dominance was in the House of Commons alone. With regard to voting patterns, the Conservative party in the last four general elections prior to 1997 had never polled more than 44 per cent of the vote, so its 'dominance' in terms of votes has never taken it beyond 50 per cent of the popular vote. Its dominance of the Commons has been based on the tendency of the British electoral system to exaggerate the popular support of the Conservative party by over-representing it in the House.

Of course, the over-representation of large parties in the Commons also contributes to the possible one-party system because the victorious party usually has an overall majority. Therefore, the party in government is virtually in an unassailable position and can govern almost without reference to the opposition parties.

Although the 1997 general election has seen the collapse of Conservative dominance of almost the last two decades, the structure of the British system of government combined with the effects of the first-past-the-post electoral system means that, at least for five years, the dominance has been handed to the Labour party. The biggest postwar parliamentary majority (179 seats) should, barring mismanagement, allow Tony Blair's government to dominate and control Parliament almost unchallenged.

Party organization and structure

Most people are aware of political parties only when they fulfil the roles of government or opposition. However, parties are organizations in their own right outside the governmental structures of Parliament and Cabinet and have their own constitutions, bureaucracies and members. All British parties consist of:
- the parliamentary party
- the extra-parliamentary party
- the party's bureaucracy.

The Conservative party

The Conservative party originated as a loose grouping of Tory MPs in the House of Commons in the nineteenth century. As the electoral franchise was extended, they set up a system of constituency associations which were intended to give MPs the support they needed to be re-elected in a more democratic environment. The extra-parliamentary party was set up in support of the parliamentary party. The distribution of power within the party reflects these origins.

Origins

The parliamentary Conservative party

The parliamentary party is the focus of power inside the party with all other branches being subordinate to it. Although party discipline is as strong in the Conservative party as in any other party – perhaps stronger given the Conservatives' respect for authority – the experiences of the Major government (1992–97) clearly illustrates that it is by no means absolute, and it would be a mistake to imagine that the party would always follow its leader no matter what the issue.

Since 1945, two wings of the modern Conservative party can be identified. The first is commonly associated with the **one-nation Toryism** of Disraeli. The second is the **neo-liberal** wing of the party associated with Margaret Thatcher.

One-nation Tory

The one-nation Tories dominated the party until the 1970s. Neville Chamberlain, Winston Churchill and Harold Macmillan all believed that their main aim was to unite the country behind policies that would allow prosperity, while also taking care of the needs of the poor. Traditionally, the MPs supporting this view were from the landed gentry who saw it as their duty to govern in the best interests of all classes. As their wealth was usually inherited, their comfortable position was due to luck, and – in their eyes – poverty was often the result of bad luck. Both were, therefore, two sides of the same coin and so the poor should be supported, not judged. Hence the state should be used to provide benefits, the National Health Service, employment and security for everyone in society. This is sometimes referred to as the paternalist wing of the party.

Recently, members of this wing have become known as **Wets**. This is a derogatory term applied to them by the Thatcherite or neo-liberal wing.

Thatcherites
: The Thatcherites believed in the free market, in which the forces of supply and demand allocate resources, individual effort determines success or failure, and state intervention is doomed to failure because it interferes with the delicate balance of capitalism (see page 69).

Tendencies
: Traditionally, the Conservative party is a party of loosely organized groupings, 'tendencies', rather than the more formal groupings, 'factions', associated with the Labour party. However, as conflicts over ideological issues intensified in the 1970s and 1980s, so have the conflicts between the groupings within the party.

Monday Club
: The right of the party has a number of groupings which promote their views. The **Monday Club** was formed in 1961 in response to fears of some MPs that Harold Macmillan's government was moving too far to the left, particularly on issues

Election of the Conservative leader

Traditionally, the Conservative leader 'emerged' as the natural leader. It was not until 1965 that the leader, Edward Heath, was elected.

A sitting Conservative leader can be challenged only within a period three months before and fourteen days after the opening of Parliament. The support of 10 per cent of MPs is required for the **1922 Committee** to grant a ballot (see page 96).

To win on the first ballot a candidate needs an overall majority and a lead of 15 per cent over his or her nearest rival. If a candidate does not achieve this, a second ballot is required. In 1990 Margaret Thatcher was four votes short of the required majority.

At the second ballot stage candidates can enter or leave the contest. To win, a candidate needs an overall majority. In 1990 Margaret Thatcher withdrew after the first ballot. Michael Heseltine was left to compete against John Major and Douglas Hurd in the second ballot. John Major gained 49.7 per cent of the vote and the other candidates conceded defeat.

If no candidate gains the majority, a third ballot is needed, but only the two leading candidates go forward. A fourth ballot is only required in the event of a tie.

concerning the empire and immigration. In recent years this group has gained considerable notoriety as a rather extreme right-wing group, possibly infiltrated by far-right groups from outside the party, such as the National Front, which were attracted by its strong line on immigration.

The Selsdon Group was formed in 1973 to keep alive the ideas that Edward Heath had adopted in the late 1960s but seemed to have abandoned in a dramatic U-turn in 1972. Similar groups have been formed more recently in order to keep alive the legacy of Thatcherism. The No Turning Back Group (1985) and the Conservative Way Forward (1991) are pledged to promote Thatcherite ideals in economic and social policy, while the Bruges Group (1988) concentrates its energies on an anti-federalist approach to Europe.

Right-wing groups

The Conservative leadership election in 1997

Almost immediately after the devastating general election defeat of the Conservative party in 1997, John Major resigned his leadership to return to the backbenches.

Two long-standing favourites for the contest were unavailable – Michael Portillo, owing to the loss of his parliamentary seat, and Michael Heseltine, owing to poor health. This left the way open for Kenneth Clarke, former Chancellor of the Exchequer and candidate of the Europhile left of the party, and a host of right-wing candidates – Michael Howard (former Home Secretary), Peter Lilley (former Social Security Secretary), William Hague (former Welsh Secretary) and John Redwood (a lone challenger to John Major's leadership in the summer of 1995).

In the first ballot Kenneth Clarke secured 49 votes as compared with 41 for William Hague. John Redwood came third, with Peter Lilley and Michael Howard bringing up the rear. Whilst this victory for Clarke was an achievement it masked his real difficulty – how to defeat the combined forces of the right wing of the party.

Lilley and Howard now withdrew from the contest and threw their support behind William Hague. John Redwood remained in the contest. The second ballot was inconclusive and the party moved into a seventh week of campaigning before the third ballot.

This period saw the forging of an extraordinary pact between Ken Clarke and John Redwood. Each from an opposite wing of the party – Clarke, a moderate, one-nation, pro-Europe Tory and Redwood, a Thatcherite disciple and avid euro-sceptic – they agreed to work together, with Redwood putting his support behind Clarke in exchange for the promise of the chancellor's portfolio in the shadow cabinet.

Such a marriage of opposites drew much condemnation. It was criticized by Margaret Thatcher, *The Times* and the *Daily Telegraph* ('a marriage made in the Tory party's hell'). Most importantly, many of Redwood's former supporters voted with their feet – straight into the Hague camp. In the final ballot William Hague beat Kenneth Clarke by 92 votes to 70.

Party left | The left of the party, or the 'Wets', includes the Tory Reform Group (1975) and the One Nation Group. They provide a counterbalance to the right-wing groups and allow the left to discuss ideas.

Within Parliament, the Conservative party has a series of committees that examine specific policy areas. However, the most important one is the 1922 Committee which is made up of all of the party's backbench MPs. The executive committee of 'the 1922' is a powerful force within the party and both wings compete for control of it.

Conservative Central Office

Party chairman | Central Office is the bureaucracy of the party and is staffed by full-time party officials. It is responsible for fundraising, research, assisting in selecting candidates and organizing election campaigns. It is headed by the party chairman and vice chairman, both of whom are appointed by the party leader. The appointments are of vital importance to ensure that the central bureaucracy will be loyal to the leader and also to ensure that the wheels of the party machine will be well oiled in the run up to a general election.

Tory reform

William Hague became leader of the Conservative party in July 1997 promising to reform and revitalize the party in the wake of its worst electoral defeat of the century. Like the Labour party of the last 18 years, and in keeping with the cyclical flows of politics and history, the Conservatives now seem set for a period of soul-searching before emerging, some time in the future, as a stronger, more modern party once again ready for government.

William Hague's recipes for renewal were put before the annual party conference in October 1997 – albeit in embryonic form. His first proposal is to bring all the elements of the party together within one organization. At the moment the MPs, Central Office and the National Union (see next page) are all separate entities, but Hague hopes to bring greater unity and more efficient organization by creating a single 'Conservative party'.

This party would also have members. At the moment individuals join their local constituency association and so there is no list of national party members. Hague intends to create one and to build that membership up to one million members by the year 2000. This is particularly important because membership has been on the wane and the majority of those who remain are over 60 years of age.

Having been elected by Conservative MPs, the smallest number since 1832, William Hague put himself forward for ratification by the annual conference. In future, leadership elections are unlikely to be the preserve of MPs alone. Hague proposes an electoral college made up of constituency members, MPs, peers and possibly MEPs (members of the European Parliament).

Candidates for election will continue to be chosen by constituencies from a list approved by Central Office, but Hague's aim will be to have women making up at least 25 per cent of potential candidates.

The National Union of Conservative Associations

The National Union was set up by Disraeli following the 1867 Reform Act. It is made up of all of the constituency associations and headed by an executive committee. As an extra-parliamentary body its role is to support the leadership, by offering advice and organization, rather than to regulate the leaders in any way.

The executive council is also responsible for organizing the party's annual conference. This has long been criticized as a party rally designed solely as a promotional exercise for the party, and more specifically, the leader. It is true that the Conservative party conference is highly stage-managed, and open warfare – so associated with the Labour party – rarely breaks out there. However, the conference can provide a forum for serious debate and offers members an opportunity to influence policy, although it does not have the power to make policy. Also the conference raises the morale of the party and sends party activists out into the country to campaign with a new vigour and enthusiasm.

Conservative party conference

The Labour party

The Labour party originated outside Parliament with the broader Labour movement. Trade unions, co-operative societies and Fabian organizations (see below) decided to set up the Labour Representation Committee in 1900 in order gain a voice for the workers in the House of Commons. Its first success came in 1906 when 29 Labour MPs were elected. It was at that time that the committee became the Labour party.

Origins

The fact that the party originated outside Parliament means that the parliamentary party was created as an extension of the extra-parliamentary party, not the other way round – as was the case with the Conservative party. As a result, the extra-parliamentary sections of the party have considerable power, and constitutional authority flows upwards from the grassroots to the leadership. The party is described as a **bottom-up** party, in contrast to the Conservative party which is **top-down**.

'Bottom-up'

The parliamentary Labour party

The Labour party was created from a number of diverse groups, so it is perhaps natural that these divisions should be evident in the parliamentary party. In fact, one of the best-known groups, the **Fabians**, was established in 1884 and was involved in the creation of the Labour party. Its influence on party policy was probably at its greatest in the 1920s when the Fabian Society was headed by Beatrice and Sydney Webb. Today the Fabians provide a forum for debate about new policy ideas and constitutional reform for the party.

Fabians

Other groups within the party tend to be clustered around the division between those seeking rapid and radical reform as opposed to those promoting a more gradual approach. This division between left and right has often been personified by conflict between senior figures in the party, perhaps most famously between Hugh Gaitskell and Aneurin Bevan; Harold Wilson and Michael Foot; and James Callaghan and Tony Benn.

Left and right

On the left are the **Tribune Group** and the Campaign Group. Tribune was set up in 1966 in an effort to push the policies of Harold Wilson's government further to the left

Left-wing groups

59

Election of the Labour leader

Prior to the rule changes in 1981, the Labour leader was elected by a ballot of Labour MPs. Since then it has been opened up to the whole party.

The leader or deputy can be challenged only with the support of 20 per cent of Labour MPs. Candidates must win the support of 12.5 per cent of MPs.

The subsequent ballot is via an electoral college which weights the votes of the three components of the party: the MPs and MEPs, the trade unions and the constituency parties. Since 1993 each component has had 33⅓ per cent of the votes.

In July 1994, Tony Blair was elected Labour leader after the death of John Smith. He gained 57 per cent of the vote, winning the votes of 61 per cent of the MPs and MEPs, 58 per cent of constituency members, and 52 per cent of trade unionists.

on issues such as unilateral nuclear disarmament and nationalization. Michael Foot, a leading member of Tribune, became leader of the party in 1980 and Tribune's line on policy began to soften as Michael Foot moderated his policies. This trend was continued when he was replaced as leader by another member of Tribune, Neil Kinnock, in 1983.

In view of the softening of Tribune's line, the 'hard left' set up an alternative group known as Campaign. This has proved a rallying point the left-wingers, promoting greater links with the trade union movement, fundamental reform of the constitution, including abolition of the monarchy and reform of the House of Lords.

Groups of the hard left have been retreating in recent years as first Neil Kinnock, then John Smith and Tony Blair, moved the party further to the right. A high point of the conflict between the moderates and the hard left occurred in 1986 when Neil Kinnock confronted members of Militant Tendency at the Labour party's annual conference. Militant, a Trotskyist group, had infiltrated many constituency associations and had taken control of Liverpool City Council. The moderates objected to such a revolutionary group within their ranks and many members of Militant were expelled from the party in 1987.

More recently, in 1996 the **Labour Reform Group** was established. Ironically this is not a vehicle for Tony Blair's modernizing ideas. In fact, it is quite the opposite and is seen as a force to counterbalance Blair's tendency to centralize control of the party.

Right-wing groups   The main groups on the right of the party are the **Manifesto Group** and Solidarity. The former was formed in 1974 in order to fend off the advance of the left. This was also the motive behind the creation of Solidarity in 1981 by Roy Hattersley and Peter Shore.

During recent years in opposition the Labour party worked hard to give the impression of a responsible, united party prepared to take office. In fact, as the political scientist Gillian Peele points out: '… that image was in many ways deceptive, for during this time Labour's parliamentary party managers operated a regime in which many votes were one-line whips or free votes … Such a practice would be impossible in government.' ('Political parties', in *Developments in British Politics* Volume 5,

Macmillan Press, 1997). She goes on to point out that during the course of the last Parliament from 1992 to 1996, no fewer than 184 Labour MPs (70 per cent) voted against the leadership on a variety of issues.

The Labour party remains divided on a range of issues, from the economy to Europe. Many left-wing MPs are opposed to the leadership's view on government spending and taxation, and the party is fundamentally divided on the issue of European integration – just as it was in 1975 when Harold Wilson called the referendum on membership of the then European Community.

These divisions are unlikely to disappear during the course of Labour's five years in government office. In fact, Blair's large majority of 179 MPs is likely to make management of the party more difficult – although defeats are likely to be rare. The very fact that the majority is so large might encourage backbenchers to revolt, safe in the knowledge that the government is unlikely to be defeated and seriously embarrassed.

The extra-parliamentary party

The Labour constitution of 1918 and the reforms of the early 1980s have given considerable power to party groups outside Parliament. This is most clearly illustrated in the annual conference and the National Executive Committee (NEC). Constitutionally, the annual conference is the policy-making body in the Labour party.

This body is dominated by the trade union movement whose members account for 50 per cent of the votes cast at conference (down from 70 per cent), with constituency parties holding the remaining 50 per cent (up from 30 per cent). The role of the unions was strengthened by the block vote. This was a type of winner-take-all system which enabled a trade union leader to cast all of a union's votes in one direction, either for or against a proposal, regardless of how close the division of opinion might be inside the union. This system gave the five biggest trade unions an enormous amount of power as they commanded the vast majority of votes at the conference. The system was abolished in 1993 when John Smith persuaded the conference to adopt the one-member-one-vote proposal, which means that the union block is now divided between the 'yes' and 'no' groups on a proportional basis.

Trade union role

Labour democracy

As the Labour party was created by extra-parliamentary bodies, the power constitutionally lies with the institutions of the whole party rather than with the parliamentary party – it is a 'bottom-up' party.

However, the broader party has often criticized the leadership for ignoring NEC and annual conference decisions. Therefore, in 1981 there was a move to make the party more democratic through changes to the election of the leader, the selection of parliamentary candidates, and the formulation of the manifesto (the latter was unsuccessful). This move was largely initiated by the left of the party.

Since then the right has responded by pushing internal democracy further by adopting the OMOV proposal which removes the power of the block vote.

There has been concern from the left of the Labour party that it is Tony Blair's intention to further distance the party from the trade union movement. In fact the issue caused some controversy at the annual conference in 1996.

NEC As the conference is in session only once a year, the day-to-day running of the party is the responsibility of the National Executive Committee (NEC), which is elected by conference. Here, too, the trade unions have a great deal of power. Twelve members of the 30-strong NEC are elected by the trade unions alone, but they also have a substantial voice in the election of the party treasurer and the five women members of the NEC who are elected by the conference as a whole. The remaining members of the NEC are elected by the constituency parties (seven), the Young Socialists (one), the socialist societies (one), with the exception of the leader, deputy leader and party secretary who are automatically members by virtue of their office (*ex-officio* members).

Despite the constitutional fact that the conference, and in its absence the NEC, has policy-making power, its impact on party leaders has been variable. Harold Wilson, James Callaghan and Neil Kinnock all ignored conference decisions at times, helped by the distinction between the party programme and the party manifesto. Although any proposal carried by a two-thirds majority at conference automatically becomes part of the party programme, that is not the same as the party manifesto. The latter is officially the responsibility of the Cabinet and the NEC, when in government, or the Parliamentary Labour Party Committee and the NEC, when in opposition. However, the party leader wields the main influence on the manifesto. Tony Blair employed his technique of appealing to the mass membership over the heads of the NEC on this issue. In 1996 the first draft of the manifesto was presented to the mass membership for approval in readiness for the general election in the following year.

Reform In view of the tendency of the leadership to ignore the wishes of the conference, the party initiated a number of notable rule changes in the early 1980s. First, the election of the Labour leader was thrown open to the whole party, rather than simply the parliamentary Labour party. Second, MPs were required to face mandatory reselection before every general election. However, the left, which was pushing for these reforms, was unable to achieve its aim of giving control of the manifesto to the NEC.

OMOV The constituency Labour parties, as we have seen, have a role in the work of conference and the NEC, although they tend to be overshadowed by the trade unions. The 1993 conference went some way to rectifying this situation with regard to the selection of parliamentary candidates. Traditionally, candidates had been chosen by an electoral college in which the trade unions controlled 40 per cent of the vote. This system has now been replaced by the OMOV principle which allows constituency members only the right to vote. Trade union members are required to pay an additional levy if they wish to participate.

Sponsorship Many of the candidates chosen to fight elections are sponsored by various sections of the party. In 1992 the trade unions sponsored 173 candidates, while the Co-operative Society sponsored another 26. Sponsorship money, which is about £2000–£3000, is used as a contribution to election expenses.

Central headquarters

The Labour party bureaucracy is based at John Smith House, Walworth Road in south-east London and is headed by the party's General Secretary. Under Neil Kinnock and John Smith, 'Walworth Road' became responsible for coordinating the various policy reviews, launched to 'update' socialism and make the party more electable.

Walworth Road

Like Conservative Central Office, Walworth Road is responsible for party finance and the organization of election campaigns, but it has often been considerably weaker than its Conservative counterpart because of the Labour party's relative shortage of funds. However, since the 1992 election, roles have been reversed and the Conservative party has experienced cash-flow difficulties.

The Liberal Democrats

At the end of the nineteenth century the Liberal party was the main rival to the Conservatives. However, it consistently lost support after World War I and was eventually surpassed by the new Labour party. Its fortunes did not improve after 1945 as the Conservative and Labour parties occupied the centre ground of British politics and squeezed out the Liberals.

Third party

The renaissance of the party occurred in the 1970s under the leadership of Jeremy Thorpe and subsequently David Steel. As the two main parties took up more extreme positions the centre ground was left vacant for the Liberals, and as a result their level of electoral support increased.

1970s revival

In 1981 the Liberal party joined with the Social Democratic party (SDP), formed by a group of breakaway MPs from the Labour party, to create the Alliance. The SDP was headed by the 'Gang of Four' (David Owen, Roy Jenkins, Shirley Williams and Bill Rodgers). It put forward many of the policies associated with the right of the Labour party and aimed to displace Labour as the main party of opposition in Parliament.

The Alliance

In 1983 the centre parties polled their highest proportion of votes (25.4 per cent) of the postwar period. However, the first-past-the-post electoral system prevented them converting these votes into seats in the House of Commons. After a similar election result in 1987 the Liberals and SDP merged to form the Social and Liberal Democratic party, which changed its name to the Liberal Democrats in 1989.

The Liberal Democrats, like the Liberals before them, are committed to greater devolution of power in the UK. This aim is reflected in the structure of their party. Local constituency parties are run by three 'state' organizations in England, Wales and Scotland. Each state body is responsible for local organization, including the selection of local candidates and finance. Above the 'state' level are three federal bodies, the Federal Executive, the Federal Policy Committee (FPC) and the Federal Conference.

Devolution

The FPC is made up of the leader, the president, four MPs, one peer, three local government councillors, two Scottish and two Welsh representatives, plus thirteen members elected by the conference. It is responsible for drawing up the party's manifesto and circulating proposals for changes to party policy. The FPC can also call a ballot of party members on any issue that threatens to question fundamental party values.

Policy-making

The Federal Executive manages the party at national level. It is made up of the president and three vice presidents; the leader, two MPs, one peer, two councillors and fourteen members elected by the annual conference.

The Green party

Origins The Green party was formed in 1985 from the Ecology party. Its policies are concerned with the preservation of the planet and the need to switch our focus from continuous economic growth in favour of greater spiritual fulfilment. As such, it is breaking the traditional pattern of UK politics and its own internal organization reflects this new approach. It is committed to decentralized decision-making and emphasizes the local parties as the main units of organization, responsible for policy ideas and overall leadership.

Speakers The party conference elects a national council which is responsible for day-to-day administration and six 'speakers' who speak on behalf of the party on particular issue areas. However, these officials are not considered 'leaders'.

Euro-election success In 1987 the party gained only 90,000 votes in the general election and seemed doomed to be a peripheral force in UK politics. However, in the 1989 elections to the European Parliament the party won 15 per cent of the vote and appeared set to take advantage of the growing concern for 'green issues'.

After the 1989 success the party was unable to capitalize on this breakthrough. The main parties put forward their own environmental policies and so squeezed the Greens out of mainstream politics. In the popular imagination they moved still further from the mainstream when a well-known Green spokesman claimed to be the Son of God. Perhaps the worst setback for the Greens came as a result of the advent of the economic recession in Britain in 1990. As the electorate became more concerned about jobs, prosperity and security, environmental issues slipped down the political agenda.

In the 1992 general election the party's 253 candidates polled a total of 171,000 votes, compared with 2 million in 1989. In 1997 the party fielded only 94 candidates, who polled a total of 63,452 votes.

Exercises

Short questions

1 **a** How do the Conservative and Labour parties replace their leaders?
   b Which of the two procedures is the more effective?
   (ULEAC, January 1993)

2 **a** Explain how the Labour party selects parliamentary candidates.
   b How democratic is this selection process compared with those used by other parties?
   (ULEAC, June 1994)

3 What is the role of parties in a democracy?
   (ULEAC, January 1994)

4 a   Describe two factions in the Conservative party.
   b   Explain their origins.
   (ULEAC, June 1991)

5 What is meant by: (a) one-nation Toryism, and (b) neo-liberal Conservatism?
   (ULEAC, January 1994)

6 To what extent have the constitutional changes in the Labour party since 1987
   made it more democratic?
   (ULEAC, January 1991)

7 What influence can rank and file party members exert?
   (EdExcel, June 1996)

Essay questions

1 To what extent has Britain a two-party system?
   (ULEAC, June 1992)

2 To what extent does party competition contribute towards democracy?
   (ULEAC, January 1992)

3 To what extent is there consensus politics in Britain today?
   (ULEAC, January 1993)

4 What are the main functions performed by parties in the British political system?
   (Cambridge, June 1993)

5 What problems might arise from having a permanent party of government in Britain?
   (EdExcel, January 1995)

6 Does Britain now have a permanent party of government?
   (EdExcel, June 1994)

Data response question

The following is adapted from John Benyon, 'The fall of a Prime Minister', *Social
Studies Review*, Vol. 6, No. 3, January 1991.

Changing the prime minister

'27–28 October 1990
*Margaret Thatcher, the British Prime Minister, is isolated at the Rome European
Council meeting. Opinion polls show Labour 16 per cent ahead.*

30 October
*In the Commons, the Prime Minister accuses the European Commission of "striving to
extinguish democracy".*

1 November
*Sir Geoffrey Howe resigns as Deputy Prime Minister and Leader of the House on the
grounds that he can no longer support the Prime Minister's approach to Britain's role
in Europe.*

13 November

In his resignation speech Sir Geoffrey Howe concludes by saying: "The time has come for others to consider their response to the tragic conflict of loyalty with which I have myself wrestled for perhaps too long."

14 November

Heseltine announces: "I intend to let my name go forward."

16 November

Opinion poll claims that a Labour lead of 6 per cent would become a Conservative lead of 10 per cent under Heseltine.

20 November

Result of first ballot announced: Margaret Thatcher 204 votes, Michael Heseltine 152. The Prime Minister, just four votes short of the necessary majority, announces she will fight on.

22 November

Margaret Thatcher decides to step down. Douglas Hurd and John Major enter the fray before nominations for the second ballot close.

24–25 November

The candidates are interviewed on television and present "manifestos", all of which include a review of the poll tax as a high priority; opinion polls suggest that John Major would win more votes than Michael Heseltine.

27 November

The result of the second ballot is announced: John Major 185 votes; Michael Heseltine 131; Douglas Hurd 56. Although John Major is two votes short of the winning figure, Cranley Onslow, Chairman of the 1922 Committee, declares him elected when both other candidates state they will vote for him on a third ballot.'

1   Why did the Conservative party decide to change its leader?

2   Describe the formal process for removing a Conservative party leader.

3   How acceptable is this process as a means of changing the Prime Minister?

(ULEAC, June 1992)

4 Political ideologies

Questions to be answered in this chapter

- What is ideology?
- What are the main beliefs behind liberalism, conservatism and socialism?

Terms to know

- Clause 4
- Consent
- Conservatism
- Equality
- Evolutionary change
- Freedom
- Ideology
- Individualism
- Liberalism
- Liberty
- Limited government
- Meritocratic
- Order
- Rational
- Revolution
- Rule of law
- Socialism
- Toleration

Introduction

British politics, and European politics in general, is often considered to be quite ideological. The division between left-wing and right-wing political parties dominates politics in most European countries. Parties from both wings of the political spectrum adhere, at least in name, to the ideologies of **socialism** or **conservatism**. However, there is often a wide gulf between the theories behind these ideologies and the practice of everyday politics.

What is ideology?

Traditionally, the terms '**ideology**' and 'ideological' have been used in a derogatory way, most commonly by politicians against their opponents. As a result, the accuser believes they know the true way while the opponent merely follows an 'ideology'. For example, the view from London is that British courts are non-political and trials are 'fair'; while courts in the People's Republic of China are ideological, political and unfair. In Beijing the opposite view is held.

A more open-minded definition of ideology is that it is a system of ideas and beliefs that offer a means of understanding the world. The ideas allow the believer to interpret the past as well as providing a programme for shaping the future. Thus, to politicians

System of ideas

ideology provides a framework within which to analyse issues and to prescribe future action.

Liberalism

Importance **Liberalism** has probably contributed more to the development of the British political system than any other ideology. John Locke, Jeremy Bentham, John Stuart Mill and Adam Smith can all be considered the founding fathers of liberal thought and their ideas lie at the centre of British politics. Indeed, a great deal of Western constitutional thinking is based on liberalism, and the demise of communism has left it with no real ideological rival.

When examining liberalism we are looking at an ideology that was developed in the eighteenth century and which has a life of its own, independent of the British Liberal party, now known as the Liberal Democrats. In fact, many liberal ideas are to be found in conservatism and, indeed, many commentators have viewed Margaret Thatcher as a nineteenth-century liberal rather than a Conservative. Therefore, even though the Liberal Democrats are faring poorly in British electoral politics, liberal ideology is flourishing.

Human nature John Locke (1632–1704) believed that human beings, being **rational**, made decisions according to analysis rather than emotion. Therefore, people sought proof and evidence to support theories while retaining a healthy scepticism.

Toleration The scepticism of liberal thinkers encouraged political **toleration**. Liberals do not claim to have sole access to the truth and so encourage open debate. They strongly defend freedom of speech for all, including minority groups. They tend to be opposed to censorship of any sort. For the early liberal thinkers toleration was particularly important given the background of conflict between Catholic and Protestant and between the monarch and Parliament.

John Stuart Mill and liberalism

'... *the sole end for which mankind are warranted, individually or collectively, in interfering with the liberty of action of any of their number, is self-protection. That the only purpose for which power can be rightfully exercised over any member of a civilized community, against his will, is to prevent harm to others. His own good, either physical or moral, is not a sufficient warrant. He cannot rightfully be compelled to do or forbear because it will be better for him to do so, because it will make him happier, because in the opinions of others, to do so would be wise, or even right. These are good reasons for remonstrating with him, or persuading him, or entreating him, but not for compelling him, or visiting him with any evil in case he do otherwise. To justify that, the conduct from which it is desired to deter him, must be calculated to produce evil to someone else. The only part of the conduct of anyone, for which he is amenable to society, is that which concerns others. In the part which merely concerns himself, his independence is, of right, absolute. Over himself, over his own body and mind, the individual is sovereign.*'

Source: J S Mill, *On Liberty*, 1859

Individualism is at the heart of liberalism. John Locke believed that in their natural state people were independent individuals capable of making their own decisions. If they decided to come together in society, they would do so as equal individuals. Therefore, individuals would **consent** to government. In return the government's duty is to preserve the rights and liberties of individuals.

Individualism

Thatcherism

In name, Margaret Thatcher was a Conservative; in practice she was a liberal. If one looks at the words used to describe her personal philosophy, three come to mind: individualism, competition and choice – all cornerstones of liberalism.

Unlike many politicians, and particularly unlike the pragmatist tradition of the Conservative party, Margaret Thatcher attempted to implement her beliefs through policy.

Privatization: The Thatcher governments embarked on a radical programme of privatization, either by selling public sector assets to the private sector or by bringing private sector principles into the public sector. British Aerospace (1981 and 1985), Jaguar (1984), British Telecom (1984), British Gas (1986), British Airways (1987), British Steel (1988), and the twelve electricity companies (1990) were all returned to private ownership in the belief that private industry would manage these businesses more efficiently and profitably than the government.

Local authorities were forced to make many of their services open to tender from private companies, rather than provide every service by their own employees. Private companies have the right to compete to provide these services and the local authority merely becomes an 'enabler' rather than a 'provider'. Once again, competition would encourage greater efficiency and better services to customers.

Health: The National Health Service, long the jewel in the crown of the 1945 Labour government, also came under scrutiny. General practitioners (GPs) were allowed to manage their own funds ('fund-holding GPs') in purchasing care for their patients. In turn that care would be purchased from 'hospital trusts', self-governing hospitals, rather than local health authorities. This was intended to encourage hospitals to pay more attention to the needs of patients than to the needs of their own staff.

Education: Schools were permitted to opt-out of local government control, receiving funds directly from central government ('grant maintained schools'); examination results were published and transformed, by the media, into league tables, and parents were allowed to choose their maintained school rather than have one allocated by the local authority. These policies were intended to improve school performance through competition, and to give parents choice.

Housing: Council houses were sold to their tenants and some council estates were transferred into the hands of housing trusts. The government believed that if people owned their own houses they would be encouraged to value their property.

69

The individual's rights are political, economic and legal. Politically, individuals have the right to participate in the political system through voting, forming political parties and pressure groups. Economically, individuals have the right to private property and to pursue their own happiness. This liberal view of individualism is perhaps best expressed by the American Declaration of Independence, written by Thomas Jefferson:

'*We hold these truths to be self-evident, that all men are created equal, that they are endowed by their Creator with certain unalienable Rights, that among these are Life, **Liberty** and the pursuit of Happiness. That to secure these rights, Governments are instituted among Men, deriving their powers from the consent of the governed ...*'

Rule of law

Legally, all people should be treated equally before the law and the judiciary should be free from political interference; in other words, liberals support the **rule of law** (see page 172). John Locke stated: 'Where there is no law there is no freedom. For liberty is to be free of restraint and violence by others, which cannot be where there is no law.' This view is in line with the liberal view of the role of the state. Government should be **limited** and subject to checks and balances to prevent power being concentrated in the hands of one individual or institution. This was a means of preventing government infringing on the freedom of the individual.

Freedom

Liberals have traditionally conceived **freedom** in a negative way. This means that the individual is best placed to determine their own interests. Therefore, they should be free from government interference in order to pursue those interests. This is clearly seen in the economic philosophy of Adam Smith (1723–90). Smith believed in the free market and that if individuals pursued their own best interests, society as a whole would benefit.

Equality

In line with this thinking, liberals define economic **equality** not in terms of equality of outcome but equality of opportunity. They believe that everyone should have the same opportunities in life and should have the freedom to make whatever they will from those opportunities. Therefore, they believe in a **meritocratic** society, rather than a class society based on privilege.

Conservatism

Origins

Conservative thought has its roots in the eighteenth century as philosophers, such as Edmund Burke, responded to the French Revolution at the end of the century. Conservatives are conservative by nature and are opposed to **revolution**, preferring incremental, **evolutionary change**. Radical change, according to the conservative view, is rather like jumping from the frying pan into the fire – the revolution is usually painful without any guarantee that the end result will be any better than before. They believe that politicians who pursue radical change to create a grand scheme are arrogant and foolish and that their designs will flounder on their own inadequacies. As a result, the people will be worse off. Therefore, the Conservative party has generally seen itself as the party of pragmatism – making policy to suit the circumstances – rather than coming to office with a programme designed to take the country to a clearly defined target.

Margaret Thatcher was, however, an exception to this. Her approach to politics was

Edmund Burke and conservatism

'It is a presumption in favour of any settled scheme of government against any untried project, that a nation has long existed and flourished under it. It is a better presumption even of the choice of a nation, far better than any sudden and temporary arrangement by actual election. Because a nation is not an idea only of local extent, and individual momentary aggregation; but it is an idea of continuity, which extends in time as well as in numbers and in space. And this is a choice not of one day, or one set of people, not a tumultuary and giddy choice; it is a deliberate election of the ages and of generations; it is a constitution made by what is ten thousand times better than choice, it is made by the peculiar circumstances, occasions, tempers, dispositions, and moral, civil, and social habitudes of the people, which disclose themselves only in a long space of time ... The individual is foolish; the multitude, for the moment, is foolish, when they act without deliberation; but the species is wise, and, when time is given to it, as a species it always acts right.'

Source: Edmund Burke, *Reform of Representation in the House of Commons,* 1792

based on conviction, was radical and there was a distinct aim in mind – a free market system in which individual enterprise could flourish. Margaret Thatcher's divergence from traditional conservative thought on this point accounts for some of the criticism she received from within her own party during her leadership.

Evolution

Conservatives believe that the economy, the political system and social structure change gradually over time in order to adjust to changing circumstances. This, they believe, is the reason behind the success of the British constitution which has evolved, in its unwritten form, as the nature of British society has changed (see page 11). Therefore, conventions are an important part of the British constitutional arrangement. They are a major source of the constitution's flexibility, and to remove them in favour of a codified document would be to create system that would be more likely to break than bend as society changes.

The idea of evolutionary change is linked to the conservatives' view that society is a living organism, not a constructed machine. It has grown through numerous transformations to reach its present state. Therefore, all parts of the organism are important and play a function. This is as true of the older as well as the more modern institutions. Traditional institutions, such as the monarchy and the House of Lords, contain wisdom because they have developed over such a long period of time. Therefore, they should be preserved.

Nationalism

Institutions also bind society together. They are part of the common heritage and experience of the nation and, therefore, help to build the identity of the nation. Nationhood, patriotism and unity are major principles of conservative thought. This can be clearly seen in the unwillingness of the Conservative party to devolve power to Scottish and Welsh parliaments. The nation is also important on the world stage. Conservatives tend to see the nation as the basic unit of currency of international

71

> ### Conservatism, 1951–55
>
> Traditional, pragmatic conservatism is probably best illustrated by one of the Conservative governments of the 1950s. Winston Churchill returned to government following six years of radical Labour reforms and adopted a pragmatic approach rather than radical revisionism.
>
> *'To the left and moderate sections of the Conservative party ... the Churchill government remains a definite success ... The government ... decided to avoid dismantling many of the social reforms instituted (if not initiated) by Labour during 1945–51, and denationalization was kept to a bare minimum. Social conflict was avoided, and the trade unions were brought closer to a Conservative government than for many years. In economic policy, a middle-of-the-road course was pursued by R A Butler at the Exchequer, and unemployment was kept to a minimum. Abroad, the transition from Empire to Commonwealth was given a moderate boost in certain areas. Defence expenditure was meanwhile reduced, and expensive commitments, such as the Suez base, were abandoned ... With that type of middle-of-the-road record, Labour cannot find much with which to quarrel.'*
>
> Source: Anthony Seldon, 'The Churchill administration, 1951–1955' in Hennessy and Seldon (eds) *Ruling Performance*, Blackwell, 1987

politics and one of the roles of government is to be guided by the national interest at all times.

Institutions   It is not only political institutions that are important in society. Marriage, the family, the church and the educational system are all important means of maintaining social control. For conservatives, social control is particularly important because their view of human nature is generally pessimistic – they believe that people are basically greedy, selfish and imperfect. Given the state of human nature, it is important to control that nature rather than to try to reform it. The conservative's emphasis on law and order also reflects their belief in the wicked nature of humankind.

Order   Within society, conservatives believe in a natural **order** that is hierarchical. Everyone has their place in society, performs a useful function and it is damaging to upset this structure. Included in this natural order is rule by an elite or a ruling class. Only a few are blessed with the qualities required of a leader and so the mass of people will be prepared to follow such an individual or group. Such authority could be derived from natural charisma or from tradition. Often leaders of the Conservative party have been drawn from the aristocracy where there is a tradition of public service. Furthermore, leaders should have been trained in the correct methods of leadership, and so conservatives turn to the traditional institutions of public schools and the ancient universities (particularly Oxford and Cambridge) for that preparation.

Liberty   In public life conservatives believe that the power of leaders should be limited. If power is concentrated in the hands of a few people, there is a danger that the liberty of the people will be infringed. The conservatives' view of liberty tends to be negative, in that they tend to emphasize freedom from government interference. Therefore, conservatives believe in balanced government with the power of one institution checked by the power of another.

Another method of diffusing power within a society is to encourage property ownership. This is a fundamental principle of conservatism. However, property ownership is also a means to educate people in the benefits of stability. Individuals can keep their possessions only in a stable society in which public order is maintained. This is linked to the conservatives' view that the rule of law is the basis of all freedom – everyone must be subject to the law and the law must be applied equally.

Socialism

Socialists differ from both liberals and conservatives in their view of human nature. To a socialist, individuals are inherently good but can be made wicked by the society in which they live. Capitalism brings out the worst characteristics of human beings. It encourages them to be selfish, competitive and greedy, and in order to survive in the system those characteristics are necessary. However, if people can be made wicked by a

Human nature

The Labour government, 1945–51

Clement Attlee brought a Labour government to power with an overall majority for the first time in 1945. What followed was arguably one of the most radical periods of reform in British history.

The government nationalized key industries: the Bank of England (1946), the railways (1948), electricity companies (1948); iron and steel production (1951). The National Health Service (NHS) was created (1948). Taxes became more progressive – the better off paid more. Public housing increased. Trade unions were brought into the policy-making process.

Whether this government actually represents 'socialism' is a matter of great dispute. The government did attempt to control some of the heights of British industry. It did launch the greatest act of wealth redistribution ever seen in Britain – the NHS. It did put public money into replenishing the housing stock: 'In terms of achievement, the Attlee governments set the standard against which all subsequent administrations have been marked. As Anthony King expressed it, "The fit between what the Labour party said it would do in 1945 and what the Labour government actually achieved between 1945 and 1951 is astonishingly close." ' (Peter Hennessy, 'The Attlee governments, 1945–51', in *Ruling Performance*, Blackwell, 1987)

An alternative point of view suggests that the Labour government was not really socialist at all. It simply continued with the planning process begun during World War II, a strategy made necessary by the devastation caused by the war. It was not truly socialist because capitalism remained at the heart of the British economy and society, and the main effect of capitalism is to make profits for the proprietors by exploiting the working class.

system, then logically, the reverse must be true. Therefore, socialism seeks to build a society in which individuals can cooperate with other human beings.

Society and individuals

While liberals and conservatives believe that people shape the environment, socialists believe that individuals are influenced by the environment in which they live. This can be clearly illustrated by a socialist's views on crime which often identify poor social conditions as a cause of crime. Poor housing, unemployment, alienation from the political system all contribute to the frustration that a large section of the society feel and so they turn to crime as a means of escape and as a method of drawing attention to their plight. Again, if society could be improved the individual within that society would be so much better.

Cooperation

Methods to change that society range from reform to revolution. Socialists believe that capitalism divides people, while their natural inclination is to come together in a cooperative and fraternal manner. Therefore, society must be transformed into one in which everyone is free to work together, where each is rewarded according to their effort and their function, rather than by the forces of supply and demand.

Equality

A fundamental requirement for a future society is greater equality. While conservatives and liberals stress political equality, socialists emphasize economic equality. Without greater economic equality, they argue, true political equality cannot be achieved. The wealthy will always have more political power and better access to the protection of the rule of law. Therefore, they advocate redistribution of income via a progressive tax system, in which the wealthy pay a greater proportion of their income in tax. The tax revenue can then be used by the government to create a network of services such as social security, universal health care and public education, so that everyone may benefit from the country's wealth.

Some socialists also argue that considerable public ownership of the means of production is also necessary to ensure that production is properly planned for the good of the whole society and that industrial life is not dominated solely by the demands of the marketplace. Under its 1918 constitution, the British Labour party is committed to the nationalization of the 'means of production, distribution and exchange'. This is

New Labour: 1997

Tony Blair's version of socialism, many would argue, is very far removed from that of Clement Attlee in 1945, let alone from a theory of socialism.

Left-wing critics would argue that the government that came to power in 1997 pledged not to nationalize any of the industries privatized by the Conservative governments, not to raise income taxes and not to depart from the spending plans of its predecessors. It has courted the middle classes, the City and industry, and has almost disowned the trade union movement.

On the other hand, one could argue that the Labour party has effectively learned to operate within a capitalist structure. By doing so it has achieved an electoral victory and, while in power, can aim to help the less well off, reduce unemployment and put more money into education and health.

known as **Clause 4**. The Labour party leader, Tony Blair, sparked some controversy within the party in the autumn of 1994 when he recommended that Clause 4 be replaced by a more modern version of what many saw as a sacred commitment of the party.

It is clear, then, that socialists place much emphasis on the well-being of the group rather than the individual. In socialist ideology the needs of the individual are combined with the needs of society as a whole in an effort to create more freedom for everyone, rather than just for those who can afford it.

Exercises

Short questions

1   How do the Conservative and Labour parties differ in their understanding of (a) authority, and (b) equality?
    (ULEAC, June 1992)

2   How do the Conservative and Labour parties differ in their understanding of (a) freedom, and (b) justice?
    (ULEAC, June 1994)

Essay questions

1   How accurately, and in what ways, may the Labour party be regarded as 'socialist' and the Conservative party as 'individualist'?
    (AEB, June 1991)

2   How radical has Thatcherism been?
    (ULEAC, June 1990)

3   Is the Labour party a socialist party?
    (ULEAC, January 1991)

Data response question

The following is taken from Paddy Ashdown, *Citizens' Britain: A Radical Agenda for the 1990s*, Fourth Estate, 1989

'*Under the Conservative administration of the 1980s, the emphasis has been on unrestrained individualism, consumption and private property. Public life has deteriorated, standards of behaviour have declined and our shared environment has become at best down at heel and at worst downright dangerous. People are encouraged to prize chiefly what can be owned exclusively, hoarded or displayed in their homes. Status depends on money and possessions. Private greed has been elevated to the status of a public virtue ...*

There is a paradox at the heart of the Conservative government's vision of society. They proclaim the enterprise culture yet their policies trap people in dependency. They promote adaption to change, yet they have created real fear of change among the most vulnerable. Instead of "rolling back the frontiers of the state", the Conservatives have rolled over the safeguards which protect the citizen. That is why they have to spend so much more ... on crime, on police, on punishment, on officialdom, on surveillance.'

1   How accurately does the extract describe the contemporary political values of Conservatives?

2   To what extent and in what ways is it possible for a government to influence or change the long-term, underlying political values of society?

(AEB, 1992)

5 Parliament

Questions to be answered in this chapter

- What are the functions of Parliament?
- How effectively is Parliament performing its functions?
- How could Parliament be reformed to improve its performance?

Terms to know

- Backbench revolts
- Backwoodsmen
- Crossbenchers
- Guillotine motion
- Hereditary peers
- Judicial review
- Legislation
- Legitimization
- Life peers
- Opposition
- Parliamentary sovereignty
- Question time
- Referendum
- Representative democracy
- Representatives
- Royal assent
- Select Committees
- Separation of powers
- Standing Committees
- Vote of no confidence
- Working peers

Introduction

The 1990s have seen Parliament under fire from the media and declining in stature in the eyes of the general public. The main focus for these changes has been the allegations of 'sleaze' surrounding MPs. Against **representatives** of the people these are obviously important charges. In the long term, perhaps more significant are fears that Parliament has failed to keep up with advances in governmental power and responsibilities. As a result commentators have expressed concern about modern government's ability to dominate Parliament. However, the last two decades have seen Parliament take significant steps to rectify the imbalance and to gain a firmer grip on the government's activities.

The composition of Parliament

The Queen-in-Parliament

Parliament was formed in medieval times as a forum of 'great men' to be summoned by the king to discuss the state of the kingdom. It was divided into two 'houses' or parts,   Origins the Lords and the Commons. The former consisted of the aristocracy and senior figures from the Church. The latter was made up mostly of gentry.

The third branch of Parliament was the monarch, referred to as the King-(or Queen)-in-Parliament. This reflected the fact that Parliament was originally formed by the king and remained at his disposal. It could be summoned by him, existed to consider royal business, looked to him for the solutions to problems, and could be wound up (dissolved) by him.

Civil War

However, the balance of power between the monarch and Parliament began to change when it became generally accepted that the king needed the consent of Parliament to raise new taxes and to pass new laws. Gradually, the power and stature of Parliament began to grow until it attempted to usurp the power of the monarch – Charles I. The result of this conflict was the Civil War of 1642–45, which ended in defeat for the royalists, the beheading of Charles, and the subsequent abolition of the monarchy by Oliver Cromwell.

Glorious Revolution

The monarchy was reinstated in 1660, but with greatly diminished power. This was particularly so after the 'Glorious Revolution' in 1688 – the Bill of Rights was accepted in 1689 which limited the power of the monarchy and laid the foundations of the 'constitutional monarchy' we know today.

Constitutional monarchy

Queen Elizabeth II has a largely ceremonial role in Parliament, with most of her powers, or prerogatives, having passed to the government of the day – often to the Prime Minister. The opening of Parliament, signing a bill into law and the dissolution of Parliament are largely ceremonial functions for the monarch. (For a full discussion of the monarch's powers, see Chapter 8.)

Therefore, when we discuss the role of Parliament it will be confined to an examination of the workings of the House of Lords and the House of Commons.

The House of Lords

Composition

Traditionally, the House of Lords has been made up principally of **hereditary peers**, archbishops and bishops, and the law lords.

There are currently about 1200 peers in total. Those who have inherited their titles account for 769 peers, the clergy 26, and the law lords 20. The remainder are all **life peers** (377). Life peers are appointed by the Prime Minister and have become the main means of entry to the House since the Life Peerages Act of 1958. It is currently still *possible* to appoint hereditary peers; however, only four have been created since 1964 – they include Lord Whitelaw and Lord Tonypandy (the ex-Speaker of the House of Commons, George Thomas, who died in 1997 without leaving a male heir).

The unrepresentative House of Lords

Backgrounds

The Life Peerages Act of 1958 allowed the government to appoint people to be peers only for their lifetime; i.e. the peerage cannot be passed on to a son or daughter. The aim of the Act was to broaden the composition of the House of Lords, both in terms of its social background and its political attitudes. Traditionally, the House of Lords was composed of male aristocrats whose political views were largely conservative (hereditary titles cannot normally be passed to female heirs, although some Scottish titles are exceptions to this rule and 17 hereditary peers are women). The vast majority of the hereditary peers were educated at public schools, which leads to the common criticism that the House of Lords was unrepresentative of the nation as a whole, both socially and politically.

However, the range of peers includes ex-politicians, actors, trade union leaders and businesspeople. Perhaps, more significantly, the representation of the Labour party has increased since 1958. During the Labour governments of 1964–70 and 1974–79, 160 Labour life peers were created, compared with 28 from the Conservative party.

Labour

The creation of so many Labour peers has gone some way to correcting the balance between the Conservative and Labour party representatives in the House of Lords. It has also contributed to the distinction between **working peers** and **backwoodsmen**. Of about 1200 members of the House of Lords, only some 400 attend more than one-third of its sittings. In fact, less than two-thirds of the eligible peers have ever attended the Lords. Those who attend on a regular basis are known as working peers because it is they who conduct most of the business. Life peers account for 56 per cent of the working peers.

Working peers

Backwoodsmen

Despite the creation of a number of Labour life peers, the Labour party – with only 120 peers – is outnumbered among the Lords as a whole and even among the life peers. The Conservative party can often rely on a majority among working peers, but when backwoodsmen attend a majority is almost guaranteed. The number of peers with a declared allegiance to the Conservative party in 1996 was 476.

Some 287 peers choose not to take the whip (see page 94) of either party, and these are known as **crossbenchers**. Theoretically, crossbenchers are considered independent, but the majority have tended to vote in sypathy with the Conservative party's stance on most issues. Their attendance has been poor.

Crossbenchers

The undemocratic House of Lords

A second criticism of the House of Lords is that it is undemocratic. Until the nineteenth

Unelected

The Lords in 1867

'*When we come to look at the House in which I have now the honour to address your Lordships, I ask how it will be affected by this great democratic change? So long as the other House of Parliament was elected upon a restricted principle, I can understand that it would submit to a check from a House such as this. But in the presence of this great democratic power and the advance of this great democratic wave ... it passes my comprehension to understand how an hereditary House like this can hold its own. It might be possible for this House, in one instance, to withstand a measure if it were violent, unjust and coercive; but I do not believe that the repetition of such an offence would be permitted. It would be said: "The People must govern, and not a set of hereditary peers never chosen by the people."*'

Source: Lord Shaftesbury during the debate on the 1867 Reform Act century the fact that the Lords was not elected had not aroused disquiet. In fact, it had long been acknowledged that the voice of the elected Commons would hold sway over the Lords. However, constitutionally, the House of Lords held a **veto** over all **legislation** and the Conservative majority there was keen to quell the tide of liberalism from the House of Commons.

Electoral reform

As the electoral franchise was widened in 1832 and 1867, the power of the unelected house seemed increasingly untenable. The constitutional crisis came to a head under the Liberal government that was elected with an overwhelming majority in 1906. In 1909 the Lords rejected Lloyd George's 'Peoples' Budget' and a bill to reduce the powers of the Lords quickly followed. The Lords opposed the bill, but after two further election victories for the Liberals in 1910 and a threat to create enough Liberal

Suggested reform of the Lords

Attitudes to the Lords are often summarized as 'retain, reform, replace or remove'. To retain the Lords in its present form is favoured by Conservatives who wish to avoid radical reform. Currently, it is a mild check on the Commons, it can help save the Commons' time, it has time for debate, and it is not hamstrung by strong party discipline.

Reform of the Lords has been undertaken throughout the twentieth century but has never attacked the very basis of the Lords. In 1969 the Labour party proposed the gradual phasing out of hereditary peers, but this was defeated by Labour left-wingers who believed it did not go far enough and right-wing Conservatives who thought it went too far. Alternative ideas might be to allow only life peers or only working peers to vote.

Replacing the Lords with a democratically elected senate is a more radical proposal, suggested by the Liberal–SDP Alliance in 1987. Problems, though not insurmountable, would include the constituencies to be drawn in order to prevent a replica of the Commons and the electoral system to be used. Adopting a system of proportional representation would make the senate more democratic than the Commons, in many people's eyes. The creation of a senate would also remove the need for the limits on the powers of the second chamber. Therefore, the veto could be restored, possibly leading to deadlock between the senate and the house.

Removing the Lords in favour of a unicameral chamber, the most radical solution of all, was proposed by the Labour party in 1983. This would remove the second chamber as a check on the Commons, which might be considered foolhardy given the workload that the Commons faces and the extent to which the executive dominates the work of the Commons. However, the logic behind this view is that if the Commons is the voice of the people, why should it be checked at all?

Project

Draw up your own plans to reform the House of Lords, indicating the powers that the reformed house would have and the advantages and disadvantages of such a scheme.

peers to end Conservative control of the house, permanently, the Lords backed down and accepted reform.

The 1911 Parliament Act removed the Lords' veto power over public legislation and replaced it with the power to delay a bill for two parliamentary sessions. The Act also removed the Lords' power to amend, veto or even delay any 'money bills' – those bills relating to national finance. The power of the Lords was further restricted by the 1949 Parliament Act which reduced the delaying power to one session of Parliament.

Reform

The House of Commons

The lower house of Parliament is elected. The right to vote in parliamentary elections was gradually extended throughout the nineteenth century. The 1867 Reform Act was one of the most significant extensions of the franchise as the male, urban, working class was allowed to vote for the first time. In 1884 the franchise was widened further, and in 1918 women were allowed to vote for the first time. In 1969 the voting age was reduced from 21 to 18.

Currently there are 659 Members of Parliament (MPs), each representing a constituency of approximately 65,000 voters. Since the 1911 Parliament Act the lifetime of a Parliament has been limited to five years, so the Prime Minister must ask the monarch to dissolve Parliament – i.e. call a general election – before the five-year limit is reached.

The Speaker

The office of Speaker developed in the Middle Ages as an agent of the monarch. This link was not broken until 1642 when Speaker Lenthall told Charles I: 'I have neither eyes to see, nor tongue to speak in this place but as the House is pleased to direct me, whose servant I am here.'

Since the mid-nineteenth century the Speaker has been seen as a neutral figure. Elected by MPs, the Speaker resigns from their party on taking office. Although traditionally chosen from the governing party, in 1992 Betty Boothroyd was elected, with considerable cross-party support, from the Opposition.

The Speaker has four main functions:
- chair of the house
- referee of proceedings
- administration of the Commons
- ceremonial duties.

By convention, members of the government are drawn from either the House of Lords or the Commons. It is the composition of the latter that dictates the colour of the government in that a government depends on the support of the Commons only. Hence, under normal circumstances, the largest party forms the government, often with an overall majority of seats resulting from the first-past-the-post electoral system (see page 23). As the House of Commons is set up on adversarial lines, the second largest party forms the official **Opposition**.

> **The impact of political party organization on the Commons**
>
> *'During this period [1832–67], Parliament and primarily the Commons came to form what was effectively part of the decision-making process. It did not itself govern – it has never done so – but it did exercise an effective negative (checking) and sometimes positive (initiating) power in the decision-making process … Members could and did replace one government with another without suffering a dissolution (as, for example, in 1852, 1855, 1858 and 1866), and could and did remove individual Ministers who had erred (as, for instance, Lord John Russell in 1855 and Lord Ellenborough in 1858). Members collaborated in the shaping of various government measures as well as in amending or rejecting legislation on the floor of the House … ministerial policy on various occasions was overruled; the Ministry was sometimes forced to divulge information (for example, about negotiations with foreign powers); and debate really counted for something … The golden age was to be short-lived. It came to an end essentially in consequence of the effects of the Reform Act of 1867.*
>
> *The Act [1867] itself put into practice the principle recognized by the 1832 Act, that of the extension of the franchise, and increased the electorate by 88 per cent … For the political parties, such an enormous and sudden growth of the electorate meant that "a system of centralization became inevitable".' Political leaders realized that they would have to make efforts to cater for the political aspirations of middle-class and some working men, and to attract their support, through constituency-based organizations and through legislation in Parliament. This could be achieved only by the development of large-scale party organizations … with Members united in the House of Commons to ensure the passage of promised measures.*
>
> *… The result of a large electoral role, the growth of party competition, and the development of large, centralized party organizations all modified the position of Members of Parliament. The parliamentary action of an individual Member was no longer his own concern or that of a limited few – it was now that of his constituents and party, electors no longer identified with Members as individuals but increasingly with a party, and it was on the strength of their party labels that Members were elected. The dominant force of British political life became the political parties, a development which was gradual but sure. As mass parties assumed positions of dominance, the effect on Parliament and parliamentary life was profound.'*
>
> Source: Philip Norton, *The Commons in Perspective*, Basil Blackwell, 1985

Parliamentary sovereignty

Dicey The main principle of the British constitution is **parliamentary sovereignty**. This means that Parliament holds the supreme authority in the UK. According to A V Dicey, this meant Parliament 'has under the English constitution, the right to make or unmake any law whatever; and further, that no person or body is recognized by the law of England as having a right to override or set aside the legislation of Parliament.'

Since 1885, when A V Dicey wrote those words, the nature of parliamentary sovereignty has changed. Inside Parliament, as we have already seen, the power of the House of Lords has been reduced through the Parliament Acts of 1911 and 1949. As a result, the balance of power has shifted towards the House of Commons, and to some extent practical sovereignty now lies here rather than with Parliament as a whole.

The impetus for reform of the House of Lords came from electoral reform. However, the Reform Acts also had an impact on the organization of the House of Commons. With more people eligible to take part in elections and the introduction of the secret ballot in 1872, MPs could no longer rely on corruption or contacts to ensure their re-election and so they developed political parties. Since the turn of the century, political parties have dominated elections and the organization of the House of Commons. MPs are organized into tightly disciplined parliamentary groups that make the business of the House of Commons relatively predictable. Some would argue that parliamentary sovereignty has moved towards the political parties and away from a house of MPs with independent voices.

Party control

Comparison

The political system in the USA is such that no single institution holds sovereign power. The President needs the support of Congress and vice versa; both fall under the scrutiny of the Supreme Court (the constitutional court of the USA) and the ability of the central government to interfere in all affairs is limited by the powers of the state governments.

The USA has a system of government based on the separation of powers and a network of checks and balances which prevents any single institution being omnipotent.

Executive sovereignty?

The strength of political parties, combined with an overall majority of seats in the Commons, has augmented the power of the executive branch of government. The British government is determined by the composition of the House of Commons and so, given the workings of the first-past-the-post electoral system, it usually has an overall majority. The strong party discipline makes that majority reliable and almost guarantees the government victory in Commons votes. When the fact that the executive is backed by the civil service is taken into account, it is easy to see why sovereignty might actually be considered to lie with the executive, not with Parliament.

Executive dominance

Popular sovereignty?

At least once every five years the House of Commons is elected and so, in political terms, at those times, sovereignty could be said to lie with the people. However, once the general election has taken place, sovereignty passes to Parliament with the people having no power to change governments, although they are occasionally given the opportunity to voice opinions in a **referendum**.

The referendum

A referendum involves the electorate being asked for their opinions regarding a specific issue. This is usually done by the government posing a question and asking the voters to cast a 'yes' or 'no' answer.

Until 1997, only three referendums had been held in Britain. The first, in 1975, was initiated by Harold Wilson's government over Britain's membership of the European Community (EC; now the European Union). The second and third were held in 1979, under James Callaghan's administration, over the devolution of power to Scottish and Welsh parliaments.

All these referendums were justified by the seriousness of the constitutional decision facing the government, making some element of popular participation desirable. However, constitutionally, they are more difficult to justify because MPs are elected to make decisions on behalf of their constituents, not to refer them back to the electorate.

Often a referendum is organized in order to help the government out of a difficult political situation. The 1975 referendum was held because the Labour Cabinet was split over membership of the EC. The 1979 referendums were held because James Callaghan's government hoped to be kept in power by offering devolution proposals in return for continued Liberal support of the Lib–Lab Pact.

Problems of referendums include the over-simplification of issues into 'yes'/'no' responses, the cost and the fact that the electorate may be ill-equipped to make an informed choice. Advantages include popular participation, the education of the electorate on an issue and the resolution of a difficult problem.

1997 saw referendums touted as the solution to a number of difficult problems by both the Labour and Conservative parties: devolution of power to Scottish and Welsh parliaments; the reform of the electoral system; and the single European currency. To date the Labour government elected in 1997 has used referendums in Scotland and Wales.

European sovereignty?

Perhaps the most fundamental change to the concept of parliamentary sovereignty occurred in 1973 when Britain joined the European Community (EC), now known as the European Union (EU). By joining this supranational organization, Britain accepted that decisions regarding British society could be made by European institutions, on which Britain would be represented.

European law

By becoming a signatory of the Treaty of Rome, which set up what became the EC, Britain accepted that European law has superior status to British law. Now, British law must be in line with the provisions of European law, and British courts have the power of **judicial review** over Acts of Parliament. This means courts can scrutinize Acts of Parliament, refer them to the European Court of Justice, and even suspend those Acts (see page 182).

R. v Secretary of State for Transport ex parte Factortame Ltd (No 2) (1991), the so-called Factortame case, was the first example of a British court reviewing an Act of Parliament. In this case, the Merchant Shipping Act (1988) was suspended by the British courts and referred to the European Court of Justice, where it was found to contravene European law.

Judicial review

Although membership of the EU has affected Parliamentary sovereignty on a day-to-day basis, it has not brought it to an end. Parliament is free to withdraw Britain from the EU at any time, although the Treaty of Rome does not explain how it could be done. (For a fuller discussion of the EU, see Chapter 11.)

The functions of Parliament

Although Parliament is sovereign, it is important to realize that it is *not* its function to govern the country. Paliament does not govern and it does not make policy. As political scientist John Norton has suggested, the British Parliament is a 'policy-influencing' legislature rather than a policy-making legislature. It is able to reject and amend legislation, but it cannot propose its own alternatives. In the UK there is an opportunity for backbenchers to put forward their own bills, but these opportunities are limited and likely to fail if the government does not cooperate with a bill's passage.

Comparison

Policy-making legislatures are relatively few and far between. An exception is the US Congress. The clear separation of powers in the United States has enabled Congress to maintain its independence from the executive. While it does spend much of its time responding to proposals from the President's team, it does have the power – often used – to put forward its own policies. For example, the President's budget is put forward in January of each year but both houses of Congress – the Senate and the House of Representatives – will suggest their own alternatives.

A third type of legislature is one with little or no policy power. It has little influence over policy and is there simply to 'rubber-stamp' proposals placed before it by the executive. To a large extent it exists solely to give credibility to the decisions of the executive. Such assemblies were typical of those found in the Communist countries of Eastern Europe.

The British Parliament has four main functions:
- representation
- legislation
- control of the executive
- financial control.

Most are performed by both the Lords and the Commons. However, the lower house is undoubtedly the senior partner.

> **Comparison**
>
> The American Congress is also bicameral and is made up of the House of Representatives and the Senate. Each house is elected but each represents a different constituency.
>
> Members of the Senate represent US states – two senators from each state regardless of the size of the state. Members of the House represent districts within the states – each district being approximately the same size, around 450,000 people.

Representation

Britain is a **representative democracy**. Since 55 million people cannot participate in political decision-making on a day-to-day basis, the voters elect a small group of others to make decisions on their behalf.

Burke Since members of the House of Lords are not elected, they have no role to play with regard to the representative function. This falls entirely on MPs in the Commons. To what extent members of the Commons actually represent their constituents depends on the type of representation being sought. The Commons is representative in that the whole country is divided into constituencies of approximately equal size (65,000 people) with one member elected for each one, and the MPs should act on behalf of all of their constituents, not merely those who voted for them. MPs speak on behalf of their constituents, but they are not mouthpieces for their views: they are representatives, not delegates, and do not have to vote or speak as instructed by their constituents (for Edmund Burke's distinction between representatives and delegates, see page 23).

MPs and constituents In this role MPs promote the interests of their constituency, trying to foster commerce in the area, taking care of the environment and the infrastructure. They will also help individual constituents with problems relating to government. Common areas of difficulty include the bureaucracies of the National Health Service and the social security system. MPs can put forward oral and written questions on behalf of constituents (see page 93) and can refer problems to the parliamentary Ombudsman.

Electoral reform However, critics of the electoral system argue that constituents are not adequately represented in that the system distorts election results by exaggerating the popularity of the Labour and Conservative parties and understates that of the Liberal Democrats. This is demonstrated clearly by Table 5.1.

The members of the House of Commons are also unrepresentative of the public in terms of social background. The majority of Labour and Conservative MPs are from professional or business backgrounds. In 1997, three-quarters of newly elected Labour MPs had a university education; the equivalent statistics in the Conservative and Liberal Democrat parties were respectively 90 per cent and 74 per cent. Ethnic minorities, who make up 5 per cent of the UK's population, are seriously under-represented – there were just nine MPs in 1997 (less than 1½ per cent of the Commons).

Table 5.1 The 1997 election result

Party	Votes	Seats
Labour	13.5m	418
Conservative	9.6m	165
Liberal Democrats	5.2m	46
Others	4m	30

Perhaps the most striking anomaly in the Commons has been the low number of women MPs – there were only 60 after the 1992 general election. The Labour party's policy of placing female candidates in vacant safe seats was an attempt to address this issue. This policy was struck down in 1996 as being based on sex discrimination, but those candidates already adopted were not affected. As a result the total number of women elected in 1997 reached an all-time high of 119. One hundred and one of those were on the Labour benches, with only twelve coming from the Conservative party.

As well as their constituents, MPs also represent their party. As a result, they are expected to follow the party line by voting with the party whip on key issues. MPs' responsibilities to their party have now grown to such an extent that some observers have labelled MPs 'lobby fodder' – meaning that they are merely party-voting robots needed to feed the voting lobbies.

Party delegates

Over recent years considerable attention has focused on the conflict between MPs' responsibility to represent their constituents and their willingness to act on behalf of pressure groups and businesses. This came to a head in 1994 when two Conservative MPs, Tim Smith and Neil Hamilton, were accused of failing to declare in the Register of Members' Interests that they took money in return for asking questions on behalf of Mohammed Al-Fayed, the Egyptian-born owner of Harrods. However, concern over divided loyalties in the Commons encompasses MPs who are company directors outside Parliament, those who are sponsored by pressure groups, as well as those who accept payments from professional lobbyists.

Outside interests

Currently, the Register of Members' Interests is supervised by the Committee on Members' Interests, but this lacks the power to investigate allegations of corruption. Therefore, the Prime Minister set up the Nolan Committee to look into standards of behaviour in public life. The report, published in May 1995, proposed that MPs undertake no paid parliamentary services for lobbyists; that former Cabinet ministers, for two years after leaving office, be subject to vetting before taking jobs in industry; and the creation of an independent Parliamentary Commissioner for Standards to monitor the arrangements.

Nolan Committee

Since 1995 all of these recommendations have been implemented. There is a new Select Committee on Standards and Privileges, and a Parliamentary Commissioner for Standards. There is a ban on paid advocacy on behalf of a particular cause or group, and MPs now declare any income received in connection with their position as an MP. However, this does not include any income received from second jobs.

Legislation

Parliament is the legislative branch of government and, as its name suggests, one of its key functions is to make law. The House of Lords also has a law-making function, but the main responsibility lies with the Commons. The legislative function also incorporates a secondary function of Parliament, i.e. a forum for debate.

The majority of bills are sponsored by the government and the most important are announced in the Queen's Speech at the opening of the parliamentary session. Most

The passage of a bill

Most bills originate from the government and are first introduced in the House of Commons. This is known as the 'first reading' and involves no debate. The 'second reading' takes place on the floor of the house and involves debate about the principles lying behind the bill. This is followed by the committee stage at which point the bill is considered, clause by clause, by a **Standing Committee**. Amendments can be suggested at this point and are then considered on the floor of the house at the report stage. There follows the 'third reading' on the floor of the house and MPs vote on the final stage of the bill.

Figure 5.1 Passage of a bill through the Commons

Bills follow much the same path through the House of Lords. If the Lords suggest amendments, these must be reconciled with the Commons' version of the bill. Once a final version is agreed, the bill becomes law with the **Royal Assent**.

bills take a few months to be passed and controversial legislation can take even longer. However, no bill may be carried over from one session to the next – allowing about a maximum of eleven months for consideration.

MPs who do not hold ministerial office can introduce 'private members' bills'. However, their opportunities to do so are limited because the schedule is so packed with government bills. Private members' bills are rarely successful without government support at least in terms of time. The government often chooses to support private members' bills in order to legislate on controversial issues of social morality. Such a strategy allows bills to be debated and voted on without bringing them into the centre of party political conflict. Votes on these bills are usually free votes, so MPs may vote as they choose, without having to follow the party whip (see page 94). Well-known private members' bills have dealt with abortion, homosexuality, and the abolition of the death penalty.

Private members' bills

Control of the executive

In the British parliamentary system the executive is drawn from Parliament and is responsible to it. The structure of British government creates another set of major and minor functions for Parliament. Both houses are responsible for training and cultivating recruits for ministerial ranks and for checking government and individual ministers once in office.

The scrutinizing function has become particularly important in the twentieth century as the role of the executive has grown. Government is expected to take responsibility for all of society's troubles. The 'Peoples' Budget' of 1909 pushed government responsibilities into unemployment benefit and pensions. The end of World War II saw the government adopting the ideas of Keynesian economics (see page 53), which identified the need for government intervention to solve the problems of inflation and unemployment, and in 1948 launching the National Health Service.

Growth of the executive

Increased government intervention requires greater government initiation of policy programmes and their implementation. Therefore, it is important that Parliament be able to scrutinize the government's policies and the effectiveness of their implementation.

The government is also the centre of foreign policy activity. Summit meetings, the technology of war and the advanced telecommunications that have made the world a global village have also reinforced the government's command of foreign policy. The role of Parliament in this regard is limited to scrutinizing the work of the government.

Foreign policy

The world outside Parliament also focuses on the government. The majority of the public understand the British system of government only through the personalities of the government. Therefore, the Prime Minister, in particular, takes the credit and criticism for government policy. Of course, this is reinforced by the media which tend to concentrate on personalities as much as issues. The fact that the government is the focus of political attention adds to the need for parliamentary scrutiny.

Public perception

Both houses of Parliament are responsible for the investigation and scrutiny of the government. This takes place through debate, oral and written questions to ministers, and the **Select Committee** systems in both houses (see page 100).

Financial control

Control of the purse strings has been a function of Parliament since the assembly was convened in order to approve the monarch's plans to raise revenue. Today the government presents Parliament with its budgetary proposals and seeks the approval of the House of Commons only. In fact, the Commons only considers requests for funds from the government – it does not initiate spending plans itself. For example, in November 1994 the Commons defeated the government's plan to increase value added tax (VAT) on domestic fuel to 15 per cent, but did not suggest alternative methods of raising the revenue. The House of Lords' involvement in financial matters has been restricted since the 1911 Parliament Act.

Budget Until 1994 the government traditionally presented its spending plans and revenue expectations in two separate procedures. Its estimates of public spending were given in November and its approach to the raising of the necessary revenue in the budget in March. Since 1994 both elements have been combined into a single budget presented in November.

Committee of the whole house Once requests for funds have been made, they are incorporated into a finance bill which is debated by the house. The committee stage of the bill is undertaken by the committee of the whole house. This means that the finance bill is examined clause by clause on the floor of the house, rather than through the usual Standing Committee.

In addition to debate, the Commons scrutinizes the ways in which the money is spent through the Public Accounts Committee and the departmental Select Committees. The Public Accounts Committee is probably the hardest working Select Committee in the Commons. It is usually headed by a member of the Opposition and is served by the National Audit Office which provides financial information.

It should be clear that the Commons' financial role is one of scrutiny, rather than full responsibility. The government is responsible for finance and it alone can initiate financial proposals. The Commons does *not* have the power to usurp the function of the government by putting forward its own budget.

The interaction of Parliament's main functions

A question frequently asked is: 'Which of Parliament's main functions is the most important?' Representation is a popular choice, because in Britain's representative democracy parliamentary elections are the chief form of political participation for the public and so the House of Commons becomes the voice of the people. However, if the voice of the people has no power the system is not truly democratic. Therefore, the legislative, investigative and financial powers are also of vital importance.

Some commentators argue that in the twentieth century the government has become more dominant and so the investigative and financial functions are the most significant because they might enable Parliament to check the power of government. However, this power is closely linked to the legislative function because debate of government policy is a means of checking the executive.

Therefore, all of Parliament's key functions are *interlinked*. They are dependent upon each other and they reinforce each other. Without any one of its functions Parliament would be a significantly weaker assembly.

Perhaps the best way to draw all of Parliament's main functions together is under the heading **legitimization**. As the House of Commons is composed of the elected representatives of the people, the government must put financial and legislative proposals before MPs for their approval and MPs are able to criticize the government. In doing so, they are indirectly putting the people's seal of approval, or veto, on government actions. As a result, the people are expected to obey laws and so public order is maintained.

Legitimization

Factors affecting Parliament's performance

Given the importance of the executive branch of government in the twentieth century, the chief determinant of the effectiveness of Parliament is the degree to which it is dominated by government.

The structure of government

British government is characterized as *parliamentary*. This means that the government is drawn from Parliament and depends upon the support of the House of Commons for its survival.

Parliamentary government

Comparison

In the *presidential* system of the USA, the President – who heads the executive branch – is elected separately from the election of Congress members, who make up the legislature.

The distinction between these two styles of government illustrates an important factor influencing the effectiveness of the British Parliament. The American President is not drawn from Congress and therefore is not sustained by a congressional majority. The British government depends on a majority of support in the Commons, without which it may be brought down.

Presidential government

The first-past-the-post electoral system has created an overall majority of seats for all but one government since 1945 (the Labour government of February 1974 was a minority government). Therefore, all but one government, since 1945, has begun its term of office with the benefit of its own supporters controlling the House of Commons. The bigger the majority, the more likely the government is to dominate Parliament. This contrasts sharply with the experiences of postwar American Presidents. Only three – John Kennedy, Lyndon Johnson and Jimmy Carter – have faced a Congress controlled by their own party throughout their term of office.

Control of the assembly

As well as having an almost guaranteed majority in the lower house, the parliamentary system also allows the executive considerable scope to interfere in the affairs of the legislature. In a parliamentary system, members of the government are drawn from the assembly so the members of the executive are also members of the legislature. Strictly speaking, this is an infringement of Montesquieu's **separation of powers** (see page 7) and it allows government ministers to introduce their own bills, to take part in the debates, and even to manipulate the time available for consideration of legislation.

Guillotine

A **guillotine motion** is a mechanism available to the Commons to curtail debate of a bill. It is usually proposed by the minister concerned with the bill, and the whole house is required to vote on the guillotine motion. The guillotine motion has been defeated only once since 1945.

Comparison

Since the US President is elected seperately from the Congress, he or she cannot rely on having a majority in either house. Furthermore, neither the President nor any of his or her staff are allowed to be members of Congress, they have no control over Congress' timetable, they cannot introduce their own legislation, or take part in congressional debates.

Despite the opportunities available to a government to dominate Parliament, the parliamentary structure does create openings for the Commons to check government. The ultimate censure for a government that loses the support of the house is a **vote of no confidence**.

Vote of no confidence

A no-confidence motion can be tabled by the Opposition. Typical phrasing of such a motion would be: 'This house has no confidence in Her Majesty's government.' A government losing a vote of confidence should resign or call a general election. Since 1945 only one government has lost such a vote – the Labour government of James Callaghan in March 1979. The Labour party lost the subsequent general election.

Question time

The parliamentary system also allows **question time** to take place. This most famous of Commons occasions takes place every afternoon from Monday to Thursday and

---

The Opposition

Normally, the second largest party in the Commons forms Her Majesty's Opposition. The leader of the Opposition, the chief whip and two deputies are paid a salary by the state.

The Leader of the Opposition expects to be consulted on issues that are a matter of the national interest and which might require bipartisan support.

Twenty Opposition days are set aside for use by the second largest party (17 days) and the third party (3 days). On these days the opposition parties can chose the subject for debate.

If the government has a majority and party discipline is strong, the Opposition is in a very weak position. Therefore, it tends to concentrate on appearing as a government in waiting, criticizing the government and airing important issues.

involves ministers, on a strict rota, answering questions regarding departmental business. Prime Minister's questions, traditionally held on Tuesdays and Thursdays but now moved to Wednesday, attract the most attention.

Questions

Question time is the aspect of parliamentary procedure that has most caught the public imagination since the house was first televised in 1989. The first 45 minutes of the sitting from Monday to Thursday are occupied with oral questions to ministers. Oral questions to the Prime Minister are allocated 30 minutes on Wednesday.

MPs must table their question ten days in advance if they are to have a chance of being called. The initial question tends to be bland in order to disguise the topic of the *supplementary question* that follows, for which no notice is required and which usually contains the main point.

MPs can also ask *written questions*. Ministers' replies are published in *Hansard*, the official record of Parliamentary business.

Even though the time available is short, question time gives backbenchers the opportunity to ask ministers difficult and searching questions. Prime Ministers and departmental ministers are judged critically on their performance on these occasions, and Prime Ministers, in particular, are very conscious of the need for good performances. Former Prime Minister Harold Macmillan believed:

'*You have to know who is your questioner ... like a prep school, there are boys who are popular, whom you must never slap down, even if they are asking a silly question ... then there are the unpopular, the tiresome, and the House rather enjoys their being slapped down ... You must remember that, like a school, on the whole it dislikes the front bench (the masters) ... often you can turn an enemy into a friend, by some slight recognition. Always keep your temper ... and always have a good control of questions and supplementaries ... in many ways it is the most anxious work; I would never have lunched out on question day.*' (Quoted in Andrew Adonis, *Parliament Today*, Manchester University Press, 1993)

Comparison

In the USA, Cabinet members can be asked to answer questions before congressional comittees, but the President is never questioned by members of Congress and is required to appear in Congress only once a year to deliver the State of the Union Address. So the separation of powers is much stronger than in Britain and, while it does release the President from some duties, on balance, this tends to strengthen Congress and prevent it being dominated by the executive. In Britain the parliamentary structure gives Parliament a great deal of potential power, but few opportunities to use that power.

Possible reforms

- Electoral reform to reduce the size of a government's majority and possibly create a hung parliament and a coalition government.

- Abolition of the guillotine to prevent the curtailment of debate.

- Removal of the notice period for oral questions.

Party discipline

A majority in the House of Commons is not sufficient to allow government to dominate the house. The majority must be *cohesive* and the government must be relatively confident that its supporters will stick together.

The whips

Virtually all MPs are also members of a political party. As such, they are subject to the 'party whip'. When an important vote is due to be taken, MPs receive a voting instruction. This comes in the form of a 'three-line whip' if the issue is of crucial importance, a 'two-line whip' if it is very important, and a 'one-line whip' if it is fairly important. A vote without an instruction is known as a 'free vote'.

MPs who ignore a three-line whip are in danger of retribution from their party. In November 1994, nine Conservative MPs had the whip withdrawn after abstaining in a confidence vote over Britain's financial contributions to the EU.

When the whip is withdrawn, MPs are effectively ostracized from the party. They are not allowed to vote in party elections, nor to represent the party on parliamentary committees.

We have already seen that since the late nineteenth century political parties have been a powerful force in British politics. As a result of this development, parties have forged two clear roles in the political system: an electoral role and a governing role.

Strength of parties
    At election time, parties control the nomination of candidates, the organization of the campaign, the finance of the campaign, the provision of policy – and they command voter loyalty. Therefore, MPs are aware that their electoral success is largely due to their party, rather than their own candidature. As a result, when pressed to vote for the

Comparison

The weak electoral and governing roles of American political parties mean that party discipline in Congress is relatively weak. Unlike the House of Commons, Congress does not always divide along party lines. This makes it much harder to push legislation through Congress but also makes it much harder for the executive to dominate Congress.

party line, MPs often do so, aware that the withdrawal of their party's whip could mean the threat of deselection as a candidate before the next election.

The parties' governing roles include the provision of policy for government, the staffing of government offices, and the organization of the assembly. Therefore, MPs know that if they have ambitions to gain promotion into the ranks of government ministers they must meet the approval of the party leader and the party whips. They are unlikely to gain this promotion if they persistently vote against the party line.

So, MPs depend on the party for their present job and for any future job. These are strong weapons in the hands of the party whips who are employed to keep the MPs in line with party policy.

Promotion

The strength of the party whips means that party discipline in the British Parliament is almost certain and governments can usually rely on their supporters to vote with them. In 1969 the political writer Samuel Beer described party discipline as 'so close to 100 per cent that there was no longer any point in measuring it'. Beer expressed amazement at the level of party loyalty:

Discipline

'In the House of Commons were two bodies of freedom-loving Britons, chosen in more than six hundred constituencies and subject to influences that ran back to an electorate that was numbered in the millions and divided by the complex interests and aspirations of an advanced modern society. Yet day after day with a Prussian discipline they trooped into the division lobbies at the signals of their whips and in the service of the authoritative decisions of their parliamentary parties. We are so familiar with this fact that we are in danger of losing our sense of wonder.' (Samuel Beer, Modern British Politics, Faber, 1969)

Between 1945 and 1970, this high level of party loyalty can be clearly seen. For example, between 1950 and 1959, 97 per cent of all votes in the Commons showed absolute party cohesion. So confident were parties of their supporters' constancy, that a government defeated on a major issue – not necessarily a vote of confidence – would resign.

Backbench dissent

However, since 1970 the level of party loyalty has begun to slip, as backbenchers have found their voice. Between 1970 and 1979 only around 75 per cent of votes witnessed absolute party loyalty. Edward Heath's Conservative government (1970 to February 1974) was defeated six times, and the Labour government of October 1974 to 1979 was defeated 23 times as a result of backbench dissent (quoted in Philip Norton, 'The pattern of backbench dissent', Parliament in the 1980s, Basil Blackwell, 1985). These defeats contrast sharply with the record of no defeats at all for previous postwar governments.

Conservative governments since 1979 have also experienced backbench defections. The 1979–83 government saw at least ten Conservative backbenchers voting against it, or abstaining, on 16 occasions, while at least 40 did so on four occasions. The 1983–87 government also experienced backbench dissent. In 1986, despite a majority of 144, the government was defeated in the Commons on proposals to legalize Sunday trading.

Rebellions

In 1990, 32 Conservative backbenchers voted against the government's poll tax proposals.

Maastricht

John Major's Conservative government weathered a series of **backbench revolts** over the Maastricht Treaty in 1992 and 1993, and the treaty was finally passed only when the Prime Minister made the vote an issue of confidence – a defeat would have led to the resignation of the government.

An alternative course of action is to make a vote against the party a punishable offence. John Major used this tactic against nine 'Euro-rebels' in the Conservative party in December 1994. When they voted against the government on the issue of contributions to the budget of the European Union, the party whip was withdrawn from them. For the MPs this meant that they became independent members of Parliament, unable to participate in party activity. Unfortunately for the Prime Minister it meant that his parliamentary majority was, at least theoretically, wiped out.

Communication and the whips

Of course, government defeats at the hands of its backbenchers gain considerable publicity, but to be effective a backbench revolt does not need to result in a government defeat. Party whips are not merely party enforcers. A good whip will be the eyes and ears of the party leadership, reporting on the mood of backbenchers and counting likely party support. An astute government will take account of backbench feeling and move to head off a rebellion before the voting stage is reached.

The Conservative governments between 1979 and 1992 made a number of tactical retreats, including dropping the sale of the car manufacturer British Leyland to an American company, and dropping the Police and Criminal Evidence Bill. In the autumn of 1994, John Major's government withdrew a proposal in the Queen's Speech to privatize the Post Office. This resulted from objections from about a dozen MPs. The Conservative party's majority at that time was so small that even the dissent of just a few Conservative backbenchers could have meant defeat in the Commons.

The Labour party is by no means immune from backbench dissent. The 1992-97 parliament saw 143 occasions (20.5 per cent of total votes in the Commons) in which Labour MPs dissented from the party line. These disagreements within the party are not likely to disappear now that they are in government. In addition, the very fact that the Labour party currently has an exceptionally large majority in the House of Commons could make the party more difficult to control, because backbench MPs will be aware that their dissent is unlikely to bring down the government and so should be more permissible.

Party committees

In addition to the party whips, the leaders can also gauge backbench opinion via party committees. The major parties form specialist committees that are made up of backbenchers only, when the party is in government, and backbenchers and shadow cabinet spokespersons when in opposition. Party committees provide a voice for backbenchers on specific issues and can provide a counterweight to leadership policies.

1922 Committee

Political parties also form larger committees consisting soley of their own their MPs. Perhaps the most famous is the Conservative party's 1922 Committee, which consists of all backbench Conservative MPs. The executive committee of the 1922 is an extremely powerful force within the party, particularly at times of crisis.

Parties in the Lords

Party discipline in the House of Lords is not as strict as in the lower house. This is because its members are not elected and so owe less to their party. Some are crossbenchers, others adopt no affiliation whatsoever. Relative independence, combined with a higher degree of regular attendance (owing to the advent of working peers – see page 79) has made the behaviour of the Lords much more unpredictable over the last twenty years. Conservative governments have been as susceptible to House of Lords defeat as have Labour governments. In fact, during the Conservative government of 1983–87, the House of Commons majority was so great (144) that many considered the Lords the only practical opposition to government policies.

However, it is easy to exaggerate the importance of the Lords' independence. The Conservative party has a majority of both working and voting peers, including a majority of crossbenchers.

The House of Lords has suggested numerous amendments to government legislation, but once an amendment has been defeated in the Commons, the Lords have not taken up the fight. On only one occasion since 1979 have they voted against a bill outright; the War Crimes Bill (1990) was finally passed without the approval of the Lords in 1991.

Possible reforms

- More free votes in the House of Commons.

- Fixed-term elections, with candidates being chosen by the voters through primaries, rather than by the parties. As a result MPs would owe their election to their constituents rather than the party.

- Reduction of the whips' control over committee appointments to remove the need for party loyalty in order to gain a committee place.

Time

Since 1945 the workload of Parliament has grown tremendously. This has resulted from the government taking responsibility for society's problems, technological advances, greater pressure-group activity, membership of the EU, and more letters from constituents. Also, in the 1990s approximately 2000 pages of laws have been passed *each year*, three times the quantity passed in the 1950s. While the amount of work that an MP is expected to do has risen, the time available for debate and investigation has barely increased at all.

Workload

Parliament's timetable has often been criticized as inefficient, with sessions starting in the afternoon and often continuing late into the night. The original intention of this schedule was to allow MPs to hold other jobs in the morning, particularly barristers who could attend court before coming to the Commons after lunch. It still serves that

Outside interests

purpose today, although there is growing controversy about whether MPs should be allowed part-time jobs. The argument is that, with a salary of over £40,000, there is no need for a second job and MPs should devote all of their time to their parliamentary and constituency business. On the other hand, defenders of the practice argue that it broadens their perspective and better equips them for their parliamentary duties.

Women   The unsociable hours of parliamentary business are also believed to discriminate against female members of the house and are likely to discourage more women from coming forward as parliamentary candidates. All-night and late-night sittings, in particular, may be difficult for women MPs who often shoulder the responsibilities of family life alongside their parliamentary duties.

Parliamentary reform in 1980 introduced a 9 a.m. start for Friday sittings to allow MPs more time to travel home to their constituencies for weekend business ('surgeries'). In fact, ten Fridays are set aside as non-sitting days to allow the MPs longer weekends in their constituencies.

> **Pressure on MPs**
>
> *'The pressure on Members of Parliament has increased dramatically in recent years, and it continues to increase. There is legislation to scrutinize, Select and Standing Committees to take part in and a flood of European Community directives to take note of and to follow through. At the last count, about two years ago, I found that I had dealt with about 6000 individual constituency cases in a year. I hold five surgeries a month, each lasting for five or six hours. The flow of correspondence from constituents gets greater and greater every year.'*
>
> Source: Chris Smith in a House of Commons debate on allowances, 1992

Opposition days   A series of reforms were passed in the 1980s aimed at preventing government business completely dominating parliamentary time. In 1983 it was agreed that three days would be set aside as estimates days to allow discussion of specific items of expenditure. Furthermore, 20 Opposition days have been set aside since 1985 to allow the leader of the Opposition and leader of the third largest party to choose the topics for debate.

Jopling Report   In 1992, the Jopling Report on parliamentary procedure recommended that more time

> **Possible reforms**
>
> - Reduction of the workload of the Commons by devolving more power to Scottish, Welsh and Northern Irish parliaments.
>
> - Greater use of morning sittings and a fixed time of adjournment to prevent anti-social hours.
>
> - MPs could be prevented from taking other employment, thus creating full-time, career politicians.

should be set aside to debate private members' bills. As a result, in January 1995 the House of Commons' procedure was changed to allow Wednesday mornings to be set aside for private members' bills.

A traditional strength of the House of Lords has been the amount of time it has at its disposal compared with the Commons. This perhaps results in a relatively high level of debate, particularly when the quality and experience of many of the peers is considered, and allows the Lords to introduce a great deal of uncontroversial legislation, so saving the Commons time.

Information and facilities

Any deliberative body is only as good as the information available to it and there is concern in Britain that Parliament is starved of information.

The government itself has the backing of over 500,000 civil servants who draft bills, brief ministers and prepare them for parliamentary scrutiny. Parliament, on the other hand, has very limited facilities. In 1988, MPs employed 1344 members of staff – equivalent to 2.1 each – and many engaged unpaid researchers. Since 1991 and the opening of new offices, most MPs have an office of their own. In addition, MPs make use of the Commons library as a research facility.

Staff

Comparison

The US Congress is much better served by facilities than its UK counterpart. Senators have, on average, around 30 staff, and Congress in general is staffed to ensure efficient running. Of course this is partly due to the fact that their constituencies are much larger than those in the UK.

The lack of facilities available to British MPs also contrasts greatly with those available to members of the US House of Representatives, each of whom represents approximately 450,000 constituents. On average, a member of the House of Representatives has 25 staff, access to the Library of Congress and to the Congressional Budget Office which prepares information on financial matters.

Possible reforms

- Civil service back-up for the Opposition.

- A Freedom of Information Act to improve the availability of information to MPs, the media and the public.

- More staff for MPs.

Committees

In order to save time and to improve the flow of information, assemblies throughout the world set up committee systems. Parliament has two main types:

- Standing Committees
- Select Committees.

The role played by the former in the legislative process has been outlined above.

Select Committees The House of Commons has had a Select Committee system for some time, including the Public Accounts Committee. The committees are made up of personnel selected from the house and their main purpose is to scrutinize the work of government.

In 1978, the system of Select Committees was reviewed and the need for a new system was made clear by the Procedure Committee's report:

'The House should no longer rest content with an incomplete and unsystematic scrutiny of the activities of the Executive merely as a result of historical accident or sporadic pressures, and it is equally desirable for the different branches of the public service to be subject to an even and regular incidence of select committee investigation into their activities and to have a clear understanding of the division of responsibilities between the committees which conduct it.'

Select Committees

'A quiet revolution has transformed Parliament. Its real work is no longer done on the floor of the House of Commons, where debate, save for set-piece occasions such as the budget, is confined to ritual partisan abuse. The action has moved upstairs, to the all-party select committees, where MPs now focus their efforts to hold the executive to account ...

... the new generation of select committees, introduced in 1979 by Norman St John Stevas, then leader of the Commons, took time to make an impact. Allowing television into the committees' hearings has helped. An MP can make his name by skilfully quizzing a minister before the cameras. This explains why committees have a 70 per cent attendance rate, though attendance in the Commons chamber often drops below a miserable 5 per cent ... According to a MORI poll of MPs, 88 per cent rate the committees effective. Only 45 per cent think that questioning ministers in the Commons itself works.

In 1992–93, the departmental select committees published 74 reports. One, from the Trade and Industry Committee, forced the government to modify its pit-closure programme. Another, from the Treasury Committee, exposed the Bank of England's mishandling of BCCI. And yet another, from the National Heritage Committee, lambasted the high price of compact discs.

The committees could do still better ... The committees need more resources. Their outside advisers – crucial to their authority – work for peanuts, and they commission little original research. Their reports should be regularly debated on the floor of the Commons. Then ministers who lost their arguments in front of select committees would be forced to justify publicly their all-too-frequent decisions to take their revenge by turning down the committees' recommendations.'

Source: The Economist, 12–18 March 1994

In 1979, Margaret Thatcher's government set up a new Select Committee system. Each committee is responsible for scrutinizing the work of a government department, but has the remit to stray beyond departmental boundaries in pursuit of an issue. Each committee is made up of eleven backbenchers, with the balance between the parties reflecting the distribution of seats in the Commons. In 1992 the Conservatives had a majority of one on each committee.

The role of chairing the committees is divided between the two parties, depending on their relative strengths. Traditionally, the Public Accounts Committee is chaired by a member of the Opposition.

Members of the committees are chosen by the Committee of Selection. Traditionally, the selections are made without any intervention from the party whips. However, in 1992 there was controversy over the omission of Nicholas Winterton from the chair of the Health Committee; he had held positions on the Social Services and Health Committees since 1979 and there was some suspicion that he had not been reappointed because of his failure to toe the party line.

Composition

Many members of the government feared that select committees would swing the balance of power from the government to the Commons. With this in mind, their powers were curtailed: they are unable to force ministers to come before them; there is

---

... And as for Parliament, parties and government ...

'The whips, the party policemen who press members to vote for the government, have a long history and MPs exchange horror stories of rough treatment by former chief whips. They hold the keys to promotion and favours, ranging from free trips to knighthoods or jobs in the government. And as fewer members have independent means or jobs, still fewer can resist the lures of office. The Tory whips became much dreaded and effective under Thatcher; they could compel MPs with their three-line whips to stay up at night, to prevent the opposition laying an ambush to deprive the government of a majority.

When Major took over, Members of Parliament hoped for a freer regime, but the whips are even tougher under their chief, Richard Ryder, Major's close ally; and when they lost patience with the rebel MP, Nicholas Winterton, they sacked him from his chairmanship of the Select Committee on Health – a new degree of vengeance. The whips faced a greater challenge from the 63 new Tory MPs elected in 1992 who were cockier and less respectful than earlier intakes; many of them were "Thatcher's children" with a strong dislike of Europe.

But they were also even more ambitious to join the government; and the whips' real secret is that their side of Parliament, after thirteen continuous years, has become an annexe or waiting room to the government and once in office Parliament looks much less important. "It wasn't until I joined the government," said one just-retired minister, "that I realized just how irrelevant Parliament was."'

Source: Adapted from Anthony Sampson, *The Essential Anatomy of Britain*, Coronet, 1993 no obligation to find the time to debate committee reports on the floor of the house; and there is no time limit within which departments must respond to reports.

Suggested reforms

- Select Committees could be given the power to force ministers to attend.

- An end to government majorities on Select Committees.

- Time could be set aside to debate Select Committee reports on the floor of the house.

- The functions of Select and Standing Committees could be combined and carried out by permanent committees on each issue area. This would increase the expertise of committee members.

Comparison

The American Congress has a more specialized comittee system than the UK Parliament. In America Standing Committees are permanent and are responsible for legislation and scrutiny for their particular area of responsibility, for example agriculture. This allows greater specialization and improved flow of information, but it also makes committees incredibly powerful and, in effect, mini legislatures in their own right.

Exercises

Short questions

1 Distinguish between the role of an MP and a member of the House of Lords.
   (ULEAC, January 1993)

2 a What is the role of Her Majesty's Opposition?
   b How effectively is it carried out?
   (ULEAC, January 1991)

3 Distinguish between the power and authority of (a) the House of Commons, and (b) the House of Lords.
   (ULEAC, June 1991)

4 Why do Members of Parliament devote so much time to constituency work?
   (EdExcel, June 1996)

5 a Why is the British system of government described as 'parliamentary'?
   b Outline a case against such a description.
   (EdExcel, June 1994)

Essay questions

1 Read the extract on page 101, '… And as for Parliament, parties and government …'. To what extent do parties make unreasonable demands on their MPs? How far and in what ways can the claim that Parliament is 'irrelevant' be justified? (AEB, June 1994)

2 In what ways could government be made more accountable to Parliament? (ULEAC, June 1991)

3 Is there any realistic sense in which Parliament controls the government? (ULEAC, January 1993)

4 How much power and influence do backbenchers have in Parliament? (Cambridge, June 1994)

5 'Reform of the House of Commons is not urgent; reform of the House of Lords is.' Discuss. (Oxford & Cambridge, June 1992)

6 Evaluate the importance of the whips in the Parliamentary process. (Cambridge, June 1993)

7 'The government controls Parliament but cannot always rely on getting its way, though it is virtually impossible in normal circumstances to bring the government down and, in practice, very difficult to engineer any defeat in the House of Commons.' (Adapted from Coxall and Robins, *Contemporary British Politics*, Macmillan.)

To what extent and in what circumstances may the wishes of the government be thwarted by Parliament? How far could the claim be justified that MPs of all parties have become more assertive and less disciplined in recent years? (AEB, June 1992)

8 Recent political debate has revealed considerable support for proportional representation, referendums and the replacement of the House of Lords by an elected second chamber. Consider the likely impact of such changes on the House of Commons. If Parliament were no longer dominated by a party majority, what roles might it usefully fulfil? (AEB, June 1993)

9 Discuss the implications of an elected second chamber. (EdExcel, June 1996)

10 Discuss the role which Parliament plays in British democracy. (EdExcel, January 1996)

Data response question

The following is taken from M Rush, 'Recent parliamentary developments', *Developments in Politics*, Vol. 2, 1991.

'The evidence for arguing that by the mid-twentieth century Parliament has become

little more than a rubber stamp for whichever of the two major parties was in power is compelling ... In some respects this paints too stark a picture ... Nevertheless, backbench MPs were not particularly well equipped to keep a check on the government.

There can be no doubt that significant changes have taken place in the role of the House of Commons. That role has changed dramatically – the British parliamentary system remains executive-dominated, but it has changed nonetheless. Parliament in general and the Commons in particular is more assertive, more critical, more demanding and significantly less subservient.'

1 What is the case for and the case against the view that 'by the mid-twentieth century Parliament had become little more than a rubber stamp'?

2 According to the author, how has the role of Parliament changed?

3 To what extent are MPs now 'well equipped to keep a check on the government'?

(ULEAC, January 1994)

6 The Prime Minister and the Cabinet

Questions to be answered in this chapter

- What is the traditional and constitutional role of the Cabinet?
- Where do concepts such as collective and individual ministerial responsibility fit into the system?
- To what extent is a Prime Minister able to dominate the Cabinet?
- To what extent are such factors under the Prime Minister's control?

Terms to know

- Agreement to differ
- Bilateral meetings
- 'Bottom-up'
- Cabinet committees
- Cabinet government
- Coalition government
- Collective ministerial responsibility
- Efficiency Unit
- 'Kitchen Cabinet'
- Minority government
- Patronage
- Policy Unit
- Politicization
- Presidential government
- Press Office
- Prime ministerial government
- *Primus inter pares*
- Reshuffle
- Thatcherite
- 'Top-down'
- Unwritten constitution
- 'Wets'

Introduction

Theoretically, the Cabinet lies at the head of the British system of government and in turn it is headed by the Prime Minister. This description might sound a little vague and open to interpretation. Does Britain really have a system of **Cabinet government**? If the Cabinet is headed by the Prime Minister, is it not possible that the Cabinet could be *dominated* by that one politician – perhaps even to such an extent that it is the Prime Minister who lies at the head of government rather than the Cabinet as a whole?

Such questions have dominated this area of British politics for some years. The balance of power between Prime Minister and Cabinet has been high on the political scientists' agenda since 1979 when Margaret Thatcher arrived at 10 Downing Street, but it is by no means a recent development. All Prime Ministers have different characters and styles, as do their ministers, and they are all face different political realities.

Cabinet government

Composition

The Cabinet is the committee that heads the executive branch of British government. It has around 18 to 26 members, drawn from either house of the legislature. The size of the Cabinet must balance two requirements. It must be small enough to allow its members to discuss issues and make political decisions, but at the same time it should be large enough to allow all the departments of state to be represented.

Prime Ministers have often favoured smaller Cabinets to enhance decision-making. The war cabinets of Lloyd George (1914–18) and Winston Churchill (1939–45) all contained fewer than ten members, but Harold Wilson's (1964–66) contained 24. Margaret Thatcher and John Major both favoured 22 members. The size of Tony Blair's Cabinet is 24.

In cases where the governing party has an overall majority in the House of Commons, the members of the Cabinet are all likely to come from the majority party. In the case of a **coalition government**, members would be drawn from two or more parties – this is currently the case in Italy and Germany.

Most Cabinet ministers head a department of state – for example, the Department of Trade and Industry or the Department for Education and Employment. Traditionally, the senior ministers in the Cabinet, other than the Prime Minister, are the Chancellor of the Exchequer, the Foreign Secretary and the Home Secretary. Beneath them, most Cabinet ministers have a number of junior ministers who have specific responsibilities within the department, but do not have Cabinet rank. The exception is the First Secretary to the Treasury who usually has a seat in Cabinet.

The Cabinet provides the collective leadership of the executive branch of government. As such it oversees the work of government, planning legislative proposals for Parliament, coordinating the work of government departments, and confirming government policy. These functions are important not only for the government but also for the governing party. As it is made up of the senior members of the governing party it should also give leadership to the party in the country.

Collective decisions

Decision-making within Cabinet should be collective, rather like the board of a company. This means that all members of the Cabinet have a right to be present when decisions are made and have the right to make their views known at that time, but the view of the majority on the committee prevails.

Collective ministerial responsibility

The concept of collective decision-making is supported by the idea of collective Cabinet responsibility or **collective ministerial responsibility**. According to the convention of collective ministerial responsibility, decisions should be made collectively and once a decision has been made, all ministers must publicly support the decision. If they cannot back the decision, they should resign. The doctrine is intended to ensure that the

---

Comparison

The Cabinet in the USA consists of the heads of each of the civil service departments – as in the UK. However, members of the Cabinet cannot hold seats in the legislature at the same time as a Cabinet position. This is due to the strong separation of powers between the institutions of central government in the USA.

The executive branch of government in the USA is headed by the President who is elected by the people. He is not a member of the legislature and may face a legislature controlled by a party different from his own.

While most European countries have a cabinet system with members, including a 'prime minister', drawn from the legislature, France has a little of both. Since the beginning of the Fifth Republic in 1958, France has had a President who is directly elected by the people *and* a Prime Minister who is drawn from the elected legislature.

This system was created principally for General de Gaulle, France's heroic leader from World War II. He ruled much like a powerful monarch – he appointed the Prime Minister, and the French parliament had relatively little power. This was made easy while the same party controlled the Parliament and the presidency, but this has not always been the case. François Mitterand and Jaques Chirac have served as President under a system known as *cohabitation*.

Forty years after the formation of the republic it is still not clear what the powers of the French President are, nor to whom the Prime Minister is responsible – the President or the Parliament.

Cabinet stands or falls together. All members are responsible for government policy and so they should all unite behind it.

However, collective ministerial responsibility is a constitutional convention and how vigorously it is applied depends on the attitudes of the Prime Minister and Cabinet colleagues. In 1975, Harold Wilson found his Labour Cabinet divided over membership of the European Community (EC; now European Union). Afraid that he would not be able to enforce collective Cabinet responsibility without mass resignations, Wilson decided to allow the people to decide via a referendum. He then permitted his Cabinet to adopt an **agreement to differ** which allowed ministers to speak either for or against EC membership during the referendum campaign.

Agreement to differ

More recently, John Major's Conservative government was divided, also over Europe. Government policy stated that Britain might decide to return to the European Monetary System (EMS) with a single European currency if the circumstances were right. In a speech in 1994, Michael Portillo as Secretary to the Treasury interpreted this policy to mean that Britain would never return to the EMS and would never subscribe to a single European currency. In fact, throughout John Major's entire period as premier he presided over a divided Cabinet. The European issue – the extent of British integration into Europe, the single European currency, etc. – divided Major's government from the very beginning, with senior members such as Michael Portillo

John Major

(Defence), Michael Howard (Home Office), Michael Forsyth (Scottish Office), Peter Lilley (Social Security) and John Redwood (Welsh Office until 1995) all taking a profoundly anti-European stance. An equally important figure in the government, Kenneth Clarke (Chancellor of the Exchequer) took a strongly pro-European line and, allegedly, threatened to resign on a number of occasions if the government adopted a robustly anti-European stance. As a result observers looked to John Major to reinforce Cabinet responsibility.

Time   The doctrine of collective responsibility has also come under some pressure as the nature of Cabinet's work has begun to change. As the workload of government has grown, it has become impossible for every decision to be discussed in full Cabinet. Traditionally, Cabinet met twice a week, on Tuesdays and Thursdays, for approximately three hours. A committee of around 25 ministers could not cover all of the work on every issue in such a short time. The pressure on Cabinet became even greater during Margaret Thatcher's term of office, as Cabinet meetings were reduced to only once a week. Cabinet meetings have continued at this level of frequency since Margaret Thatcher's departure. However, at times of crisis the frequency of meetings has been increased; for example, under John Major three Cabinet meetings were held on the final day of the passage of the Maastricht Treaty through Parliament in July 1993.

The broader Cabinet system

If one confines an explanation of Cabinet government simply to the Cabinet itself, one seriously underestimates the breadth and sophistication of the system. The system of Cabinet government stretches far beyond the Cabinet room into formal and informal aspects of executive government.

We have already seen that Cabinet meetings have been reduced to one per week while Parliament is in session, but beneath the level of senior Cabinet there are a number of committees, meetings and conversations that together constitute a multi-layered Cabinet system.

The workload facing the modern Cabinet has made it impossible for a committee of 22 to effectively take decisions regarding the whole of government policy. Indeed, many of the factors, such as technology, which have led to the increased workload also lead to a greater complexity of decisions being made by government. Cabinet ministers do not always have the expertise and competence required to make these decisions. As a result much of the preparation, discussion and decision-making takes place elsewhere.

The 'elsewhere' can be as formal as a **Cabinet committee** meeting attended by senior ministers and civil servants with an agenda, documentation and minutes in the hands of the civil service, or something as informal as a chat in the corridor between two ministers after a meeting of the full Cabinet. Both are means by which the political executive in Britain is evolving to cope with the pressures placed upon it.

As Britain has an uncodified constitution, both the formal and informal aspects of the Cabinet system are gradually brought within the constitutional framework as they become normal and accepted patterns of behaviour. In other words they become *conventional*.

Cabinet committees

As a result of this workload, an elaborate system of Cabinet committees has developed. These committees examine particular issues in depth, allow discussion between the ministers most closely concerned, and then make the final decisions. Cabinet committee decisions carry the weight of full Cabinet decisions and need only be referred to the full Cabinet if there is disagreement on the committee. Therefore to all intents and purposes a decision taken in Cabinet committee is the equivalent of one made in full Cabinet, so Cabinet committees are obviously and clearly a part of the formal structure of the Cabinet system.

The exact nature of the Cabinet committee system has been a closely guarded secret for much of the postwar period. This was an attempt to preserve collective Cabinet responsibility across the Cabinet system by giving the impression that decisions were being made by the government as a whole. After 1992, John Major pledged to make more details of the committee system open to public scrutiny. As a result we now know that in June 1997 there were 19 ministerial Standing Committees of the new Labour government (see Table 6.1, page 110). These committees favoured by Tony Blair represent a fall from the 26 Standing Committees used by John Major in 1992.

Cabinet committees fall into three categories:

- **Standing Committees** are permanent during the Prime Minister's term of office. They have specific terms of reference. Key committees include Northern Ireland, Economic and Domestic Policy, and Intelligence Services.

- **Ad hoc committees** are set up when needed by the Prime Minister, who has the power to shape their terms of reference. Perhaps the best-known is the 'Star Chamber' or MISC62, which determines the allocation of funds to spending departments.

- **Ministerial committees** are made up of civil servants only. They help to coordinate the work of government departments.

The Prime Minister

The head of the Cabinet is the Prime Minister. He or she chairs meetings, sums up discussions and often acts as the chief government representative. However, the Prime Minister is only one member of the committee and so can be outvoted by colleagues. This position has been variously described. For example, the constitutional lawyer Sir Ivor Jennings (1903–65) termed the Prime Minister as 'the sun around which the planets revolve', but perhaps best known is Walter Bagehot's phrase ***primus inter pares*** or 'first among equals'. To this day, his description probably sums up the Prime Minister's special position most accurately.

Primus inter pares

Leadership for the government

As head of the Cabinet, the Prime Minister has become *de facto* head of the executive branch of government. Ultimately he or she will be held responsible for the government's policies and so must be a dominant force in the implementation of policy

Table 6.1 Cabinet committees after the 1997 election

Chair	Title	Members
Prime Minister	Defence and Overseas Policy	6
Prime Minister	Constitutional Reform Policy	13
Prime Minister	Intelligence Services	6
Prime Minister	Northern Ireland	6
Deputy Prime Minister and Secretary of State for Environment, Transport and the Regions	Home and Social Affairs	20
Deputy Prime Minister and Secretary of State for Environment, Transport and the Regions	Environment	18
Deputy Prime Minister and Secretary of State for Environment, Transport and the Regions	Local Government	19
Deputy Prime Minister and Secretary of State for Environment, Transport and the Regions	Sub-Committee on London	12
Chancellor of the Exchequer	Economic Affairs	18
Chancellor of the Exchequer	Public Expenditure	9
Chancellor of the Exchequer	Sub-Committee on Welfare to Work	13
Lord Chancellor	Queen's Speeches and Future Legislation	11
Lord Chancellor	Devolution to Scotland and Wales and the English Regions	19
Lord Chancellor	Sub-Committee on Incorporation of the European Convention on Human Rights	17
President of the Council and Leader of the House	Legislation	14
President of the Council and Leader of the House	Sub-Committee on Drug Misuse	12
President of the Council and Leader of the House	Sub-Committee on Health Strategy	15
Secretary of State for Foreign and Commonwealth Affairs	Sub-Committee on European Issues	19
Secretary of State for Social Security	Sub-Committee on Women's Issues	14

as well as its initiation. Under Margaret Thatcher many government policies originated from the Prime Minister – hence the title Thatcherism. Even if most policies do not originate from the leader, that person will undoubtedly have a hand in the determination of key policies.

Giving leadership to the government also involves appointing, reshuffling and dismissing members of that government and a host of other official figures. Like so many of the premier's other powers, this power of patronage has been inherited from the monarch. Cabinet secretaries, junior ministers, senior civil servants, bishops and judges are all appointed by the Prime Minister, either in their own name or on behalf of the monarch. As we shall see later in the context of the relationship with the rest of government, this is a crucial power.

Ultimate leadership of the government involves the decision to put the future of the government on the line by asking for a dissolution of parliament – calling a general election. As Britain does not have fixed-term parliaments (the 1911 Parliament Act lays down only that the *maximum* term should be five years) it is at the discretion of the Prime Minister to choose the exact timing of the next general election.

Obviously the timing of such a request can be a key factor in determining the success of the leader's party in the election, and it is interesting to note that relatively few British governments since 1945 have seen through a full five-year term. Most Prime Ministers have decided to 'go to the country' at a time of their own choosing rather than at the very last minute – assuming they have not been forced to go through a vote of no confidence.

Leadership in foreign policy

Although the head of state in Britain is the monarch, the *de facto* representative abroad is the Prime Minister. Every year the media cover major foreign policy visits, meetings and summits, most of which are – from a British point of view – dominated by the Prime Minister. Official engagements such as European Union summits and G7 meetings are supported by many informal, **bilateral meetings** of premiers and presidents.

Leadership of the party

The Prime Minister is not expected to be a neutral figure at the head of an impartial government. Having been selected as the leader of a political party, in government he or she speaks for that party, in Parliament and in the country.

Other layers

As the workload of government has increased since 1945 there has not been an equivalent increase in the number of Cabinet committees. In fact they have decreased. Clement Attlee created 148 Standing Committees and 313 *ad hoc* committees between 1945 and 1951, but in the first two years of his premiership John Major used only 26 and 24 respectively.

This trend would suggest that either Cabinet committees are becoming phenomenally

The Deputy Prime Minister

Consitutionally there is no place for a Deputy Prime Minister in the British political system. The Prime Minister is not directly elected to that position – he or she occupies 10 Downing Street simply through being the leader of the majority party in the House of Commons. Therefore if the current leader resigns or is ousted, a new leadership election occurs and the victor becomes Prime Minister. A Deputy Prime Minister might step into the breach on a temporary basis but does not have the right to assume office.

In contrast, the US Vice-President automatically assumes office if the President is incapacitated, resigns, is impeached or dies.

Nevertheless, Margaret Thatcher appointed William Whitelaw (1983–88) and subsequently Geoffrey Howe (1989–90) as her deputy. John Major did without a deputy until 1995, when Micheal Heseltine was appointed Deputy Prime Minister and 'First Secretary of State'.

The role of a deputy premier can vary according to the wishes of the Prime Minister and the circumstances. William Whitelaw was a trusted advisor of Margaret Thatcher and was given some authority to coordinate the work of government. In contrast, Geoffrey Howe was a political rival and so was given with only limited powers.

Michael Heseltine was given a particularly important role as deputy – coordination of government policy and the chairmanship of some key Cabinet committees. Heseltine's appointment came in the wake of John Major's re-election as Conservative party leader in 1995. He was not challenged by Michael Heseltine in this leadership contest and the arrangement smacked of political expediency.

The Labour Party elects a deputy leader in the same manner as the leader is chosen. In 1994, John Prescott was elected to the position and upon Labour's 1997 election victory he became Deputy Prime Minister. Unlike Heseltine, John Prescott has taken on responsibility for a Ministry – transport – and so does not have such a 'wandering brief' as his predecessor. Peter Mandelson does have such a brief, as Minister Without Portfolio, and the summer of 1997 reportedly saw some conflict between the two men.

successful, or that decisions are being taken elsewhere. The latter seems more likely, and increasingly decisions are being taken in bilateral meetings made up of the Prime Minister and the relevant Cabinet minister and both sets of their respective advisors, through correspondence – letters and memos – and a selection of committees, varying in their degree of formality, chaired by the Prime Minister.

All these layers of decision-making are examined in greater depth in the following section as we look at the decline of Cabinet decision-making in the context of the balance of power between Prime Ministers and their colleagues.

Summing up the role of Cabinet

Simply by scratching the surface of the broader Cabinet system, and even without beginning to assess its relationship with the Prime Minister, it should be clear that the traditional constitutional view of Cabinet government is outdated. The committee of 22 senior ministers that heads the executive branch of government is not the main day-to-day decision-making body of government. By borrowing from Martin Burch ('Prime Minister and Cabinet: an executive in transition', in Pyper and Robbins (eds) *Governing the UK in the 1990s*, St Martin's Press, 1995) we can begin to delineate its real role more clearly. Burch suggests that Cabinet has four main functions:

1 *As an information clearing house.* The fact that every Cabinet meeting begins with a briefing about foreign affairs and the state of parliamentary business allows all ministers to be brought up to date on those specific areas and in discussion on government activities in general.

2 *Dealing with issues not settled at a lower level.* The aim of the government and its administration is to settle as many issues as possible on the lower tiers of the Cabinet system. Only if they cannot be agreed will they be brought before full Cabinet.

3 *Clinching major policy decisions.* Some decisions may be considered so important that they must be taken by full Cabinet. This might not involve extensive discussion but Cabinet ratification of the policy may be sought.

4 *Airing politically sensitive issues.* A meeting of full Cabinet may be the opportunity to make everyone aware of a political decision that has the potential to jump up and bite any member of the government at any time. Ministers may be briefed on the issue and how to deal with it, as well as consulted as to the timing of the decision. As much as anything this is a means to bring collective responsibility into play to ensure that all members of the government are 'on board'.

Prime ministerial government

The views of Walter Bagehot and Richard Crossman

Walter Bagehot's interpretation of the British political system, *The English Constitution*, was written in 1867. Since then, it has become a classic text and indeed has become part of Britain's **unwritten constitution**. In it, Bagehot distinguished between efficient and dignified parts of the constitution – that is, those parts that are working elements of the constitution and those that play a largely ceremonial role in British politics. At the time, the Cabinet was considered to be an efficient part of the constitution; since then some might argue that it has been relegated to dignified status.

Efficient and dignified

In 1964, the then Labour Minister of Housing, Richard Crossman was asked to write a new introduction to *The English Constitution*. He used the opportunity to argue that

113

Presidential government

While there is perhaps some merit in describing the British government as prime ministerial government, we must be much more careful about using terms like 'presidential' because they bring with them a whole new set of specific constitutional rules and relationships.

The President

A presidential system of government usually involves a chief executive being elected separately from the legislature, directly by the people. This is the case in the USA where the President is elected every four years, the House of Representatives every two years and the Senate every six years (one-third of members every two years). The President is not allowed to be a member of the legislature while holding a position in the executive. He is not allowed to introduce bills into Congress, he cannot take part in Congressional debate, and he cannot be removed by Congress, unless impeached – for which he or she must be formally charged.

British government is not presidential; it is parliamentary. The British Prime Minister does not have the constitutional independence of an American President. This was clearly illustrated by the fall of Margaret Thatcher in 1990. Few postwar Prime Ministers have been so closely associated with the 'prime ministerial/presidential thesis' of British government. Many commentators saw her as the 'Iron Lady' subjecting the Cabinet to her will. However, it was this same Cabinet that finally convinced her that she should resign. Without the support of the Cabinet, her party and, therefore, of the House of Commons, Margaret Thatcher had little choice but to go.

Perception

However, the idea of presidential government in Britain should not be dismissed completely – Prime Ministers have sometimes given the impression of being presidential. The media focus on the premier and now, for their part, Prime Ministers employ image-makers and advertising agents to ensure that the public gaze remains on them. But it is more than merely image. Some Prime Ministers have gathered about them a great deal of political power. In many cases such a concentration of power would be the envy of an American President.

Bagehot's analysis had been superseded by events almost immediately after its publication. In the spirit of Bagehot's original analysis, Richard Crossman offered a new analysis of British government.

Crossman wrote that British government had moved away from **Cabinet government** towards **prime ministerial government** – or even **presidential government**. By this he meant that decision-making at the top of the executive branch of government was becoming increasingly dominated by one person – the Prime Minister.

His analysis of the growth of the power of the Prime Minister rests on three points:
- the power of political parties
- the development of a unified civil service
- the growth of the Prime Minister's private office and the Cabinet secretariat.

Richard Crossman was describing prime ministerial government at the time of Harold

Wilson's first Labour government (1964–66), and the idea gained a new lease of life during Margaret Thatcher's eleven years of office. However, the concept of dominant Prime Ministers was not a new one, even in the 1960s. David Lloyd George, Neville Chamberlain and Winston Churchill were all considered dominant Prime Ministers.

Nevertheless, Richard Crossman's ideas still offer a comprehensive framework in which to assess the power of a Prime Minister.

The power of political parties

Until the second half of the nineteenth century, British political parties were little more than clubs for MPs. Bagehot stated: 'At present the member is free because the constituency is not in earnest; no constituency has an acute, accurate doctrinal creed in politics.' As we have seen in Chapter 5, this began to change as the electoral franchise was widened and organized political parties developed.

This trend moved a stage further with the development of the Labour party. This new party of the working class was intended to break the middle-class stranglehold on the House of Commons. It did so by being well-funded and highly disciplined.

Today political parties have two broad roles in the political process: an electoral role and a governing role. In elections parties nominate candidates, organize their campaigns, finance their campaigns, provide manifestos, and command voter loyalty. As a result, MPs know that their position in the Commons is dependent on the continued support of the party because without party backing few potential MPs secure a seat.

Comparison

In the USA, the President and legislature are elected seperately. Therefore the President is not guaranteed a majority in Congress. Furthermore, even the President's own party does not dominate both houses of Congress, so he or she cannot rely on it for support. The electoral and governing roles of American political parties are relatively weak, and so members of Congress tend to show greater loyaly to their constituents than they do to their party.

The parties' governing role includes provision of policy, the organization of the assembly and the allocation of government offices. In Britain, provision of policy is largely the function of the party, via the election manifesto, and there are few opportunities for MPs to depart from the party line. The strong electoral role of British parties is a further incentive to party cohesion in Parliament because MPs rely on party backing to retain their seat. Furthermore, if they harbour ambitions to be promoted into government or to the Opposition front bench, MPs do well to vote as instructed by the party.

This combination of strong electoral and governing roles for British political parties has strengthened the position of the Prime Minister. As the head of the party, the disciplinary machinery of whips is at prime ministerial command and, therefore, a Prime Minister with a majority in the Commons is unlikely to lose a vote.

Party strength

Patronage

Appointments

The Prime Minister has an additional means of control over the party in the form of **patronage**. Traditionally, the monarch held the power of patronage (i.e. the power of making appointments), but this has now passed to the Prime Minister. Therefore, an MP's future in government depends on the Prime Minister. It is the Prime Minister who has the power to appoint ministers and junior ministers. At the turn of the twentieth century, appointments would have involved around 20 ministers; today about 120 ministers are appointed. This accounts for almost one-third of government MPs and so is an extremely powerful weapon. It gives the Prime Minister a great deal of power not only over MPs but also over ministers.

To be appointed to government office is only part of the aim of many MPs. Once the status of junior minister has been achieved, an ambitious MP seeks promotion into the Cabinet. Once in Cabinet, a minister will be anxious to at least hold their position and possibly to advance in the Cabinet hierarchy, with the 'top jobs' of Home Secretary, Chancellor of the Exchequer or Foreign Secretary possibly their ultimate goal. Every minister knows that hiring and firing; promoting and demoting is the responsibility of the Prime Minister, so falling out of favour with your leader can mean the end of your career.

Comparison

In most European countries the chief executive or Prime Minister is given a free hand in the choice of the Cabinet. However, in some countries – such as the Netherlands and Finland – the head of state designates a 'formateur' to nominate members of the Cabinet.

In Britain and Ireland, ministers are always drawn from the legislature. In France, Norway and the Netherlands, members of Cabinet must resign from the legislature in order to hold office.

This power of patronage gives Prime Ministers, at least theoretically, the opportunity to shape the composition of the Cabinet to suit their own needs. In other words, the balance of Cabinet could be tilted towards their own supporters in an effort to bolster their own power.

Composition of the Cabinet

Margaret Thatcher used her power of patronage to move her Cabinet gradually away from the 'well-balanced' Cabinet of 1979 to the more right-wing versions of later years. Her first Cabinet included ministers who were from the left of the party, such as Norman St John Stevas, Lord Soames, Mark Carlisle, James Prior and Ian Gilmour. These ministers were soon to be labelled '**Wets**' – a derogatory term coined by Thatcher's supporters to describe lack of resolve in the face of difficult policy decisions. Within two years, all four ministers had been removed from the Cabinet. '**Thatcherite**' ministers, such as Cecil Parkinson, Leon Brittan and Nigel Lawson, were moved into the Cabinet.

However, the successful use of the power of patronage is not merely a question of numbers. It is not just the Prime Minister's desire to have more allies than critics. Distribution of the ministerial portfolios allocated to supporters is also of vital importance. In Margaret Thatcher's 1979 Cabinet, 'Wets' or moderates almost outnumbered Thatcherites. In addition to those already mentioned, they included William Whitelaw, Lord Carrington and Peter Walker. However, Margaret Thatcher ensured that the key economic ministries – the Treasury and Trade and Industry – were held by her supporters. The Chancellor of the Exchequer was Sir Geoffrey Howe, and the Trade and Industry Secretary was Sir Keith Joseph, who many considered to be the high priest of Thatcherism.

John Major used Cabinet **reshuffles** less successfully than his predecessor. Despite his alleged reference to the Euro-sceptics in his Cabinet as 'bastards', all except John Redwood remained within his Cabinet until the general election of 1997. The reason for this was Major's efforts to unite his party, which was fundamentally divided over Britain's role in the European Union. Major effectively had little choice other than to keep senior figures from all wings of the party within his government.

The development of a unified civil service

Although the British civil service has been permanent since the Northcote–Trevellyan Report of 1854, it has only been unified since 1919. Lloyd George circulated a paper in September 1919 that outlined the new powers of the Treasury. In it he stated that the Permanent Secretary to the Treasury would also be the head of the civil service, particularly with regard to appointments. This meant that from then on all appointments to the civil service would be made centrally rather than departmentally. In Richard Crossman's words:

'*Instead of a cluster of departments, each with its own traditions, characteristics, and standards of recruitment, there has emerged a new horizontal stratification, with the heads forming a single, like-minded group of super bureaucrats.*'

As a result of centralization, individual ministers have lost a great deal of control over the personnel of their department. When senior civil service appointments are due to be made in any department, the Prime Minister is given a shortlist prepared by the Senior Appointments Selection Committee. Hence, the Prime Minister has accumulated the power to influence the composition of staff in ministerial departments. In doing so, the Prime Minister can influence the advice and cooperation ministers receive.

Appointments

'Politicization'

Margaret Thatcher has often been accused of '**politicizing**' the higher civil service by seeking to appoint and promote civil servants who are, in her words, 'one of us'. She certainly had the opportunity to do so, because in the first six years of her premiership there was virtually a complete turnover of Permanent and Deputy Secretaries. However, observers have only been able to point an accusing finger at one instance of her interference leading to the promotion of one of her 'favourites'. This was Peter Middleton, who succeeded Douglas Wass as Permanent Secretary to the Treasury in 1983. Douglas Wass was thought to have been a believer in Keynesian economics, while Middleton was a devout monetarist (see page 53).

Recent reforms to the civil service to allow non-career civil servants to be drafted in from outside the executive, and the advent of executive agencies, have broadened the scope for Prime Ministerial intervention in the appointment of civil servants. However, it is too early to tell how much use Tony Blair might make of these opportunities.

The growth of the Cabinet Secretariat

Sections   In 1916, Lloyd George was responsible for another major reform of the British Cabinet system when he created the Cabinet Secretariat. Today the Cabinet Secretariat is divided into five sections: economic policy; home affairs and legislation; foreign and defence policy; European affairs; and national security and intelligence matters. A sixth section responsible for technology was transformed into the Office of Public Service and Science in 1992 and is headed by a Cabinet minister – the Chancellor of the Duchy of Lancaster. The 30–40 senior civil servants, usually on loan from other departments, are responsible for servicing the system of Cabinet government. Headed by the Cabinet Secretary – Sir Richard Wilson – they plan Cabinet business in advance, drawing up the agendas for full Cabinet meetings and for Cabinet committees, writing and circulating the minutes of these meetings, and coordinating and supervising the implementation of decisions made in Cabinet and its committees.

The Cabinet Secretary and key members of the secretariat work very closely with the Prime Minister. The key officials meet at the end of each week to plan business for the following week and at regular intervals to plan further head. All of these decisions are subject to the Prime Minister's approval.

The individual secretariats have become increasingly involved in the policy-making for their area of responsibility. Those concerned with Europe and the economy are particularly influential in their respective areas. The former has a broad-ranging function as the arm of the European Union stretches into many policy areas, and it is the secretariat's responsibility to make everyone aware of the implications of policy in the European context.

The secretariat, being there to serve the whole Cabinet, should not have real decision-making power. A number of ministers have drawn attention to the dangers of a close relationship between the Cabinet Secretary and senior members of the secretariat and the Prime Minister. The ability to control the agendas of meetings and to influence the writing of the minutes would give a Prime Minister considerable power over Cabinet decision-making. Richard Crossman and others suspected that Cabinet minutes were written in consultation with the Prime Minister, although the latter subsequently denied these accusations.

Margaret Thatcher was also subject to accusations of politicizing the Cabinet secretariat. In this case it was her relationship with the Cabinet Secretary that was a cause for concern, not only because of the control over agenda and minutes, but also because the Cabinet Secretary is, in addition, head of the home civil service – which might give the Prime Minister added leverage over civil service appointments.

Agenda   While there is no evidence of Margaret Thatcher, or any other Prime Minister, influencing the recording of Cabinet minutes, it is known that she fought hard to keep issues not to her liking off the political agenda. In the first two years of her premiership many ministers complained of the lack of Cabinet discussion regarding the state of the economy. During a period of severe economic recession, Margaret Thatcher successfully kept questions of economic strategy within the economic affairs committee rather than in the full Cabinet where her support was weaker.

The Cabinet Secretary for much of Margaret Thatcher's term of office was Sir Robert Armstrong, a career civil servant, devoted to the traditional civil service characteristics of permanence and neutrality. However, in 1987 David Owen, leader of the Social Democratic Party, described Armstrong as 'damaged goods' and the Liberal leader David Steel stated that 'his credibility is at a very low ebb … [he has] become a civil servant who's very much seen as a supporter of the government'. Both leaders were referring to a series of controversial incidents in which Armstrong had appeared not as an anonymous, faceless bureaucrat but as a very public agent of government policy. The incidents included the Ponting case (1985), Westland (1985) and GCHQ (1984) (for a fuller discussion of these, see Chapter 7).

Sir Robert Armstrong

The *Spycatcher* case (1986) in particular severely damaged Armstrong's standing in British politics. He was despatched to Australia to defend, in court, the government's decision not to allow former MI5 employee, Peter Wright, to publish his memoirs in Britain. Under cross-examination by an Australian lawyer, Armstrong seemed badly prepared and his credibility was severely undermined when, at one stage of the trial, he was forced to change earlier testimony, admitting that he had been 'economical with the truth'.

Spycatcher

The result of this was that Margaret Thatcher had appeared to hijack the Cabinet Office by politicizing the Cabinet Secretary. In fact, Armstrong was not a Thatcherite but did feel that he should work for his government to the best of his ability. As the historian Peter Hennessy wrote:

'*In so far as he ever let his own political views slip to his friends they were old-fashioned "one nation" Conservative … His friends were in no doubt that in Mrs Thatcher's terms, he was not "one of us".*' (*Whitehall*, Secker & Warburg, 1989)

Perhaps the choice of Armstrong's successor reaffirms that the appointment to the top job was not politicized. On Armstrong's retirement in 1987, Margaret Thatcher appointed Robin Butler, a traditional civil servant, as his replacement – and his appointment was widely welcomed without any fear of politicization. As Peter Hennessy said: 'Butler, like Armstrong, could have been picked as head of his profession at any time since 1870.'

Robin Butler

The historian Anthony Seldon has argued that John Major was reluctant to manipulate the Cabinet agenda and was happy for controversial issues to come before Cabinet in order to allow discussion. Seldon quoted a series of (unattributed) views of John Major's premiership from his colleagues: 'No one would stand up to Mrs Thatcher in Cabinet: now it is very different.' 'I can recall few, if any, times when John Major has been beaten in Cabinet: the reason for that is that he carries colleagues with him; when he sums up, he does so making people feel they have been consulted.'

At this stage it is difficult to assess Tony Blair's style as Prime Minister. Much of his style prior to the election, and during the campaign, seemed presidential. Like Neil Kinnnock and John Smith before him, he staked his personal authority on changing the Labour party. Since the general election he seems to have taken a similar position on the Labour party winning a second term of office. Given his determination it is possible that he will be tempted to adopt a fairly presidential style in government.

The growth of the Prime Minister's staff

A traditional weakness of the Prime Minister is the lack of civil service support. This remains the case in so far as the Prime Minister does not have a civil service department capable of implementing policy – for this he or she must rely on ministers. While Prime Ministers have gradually built up a staff based at 10 Downing Street, compared with their counterparts in Germany (450) and the USA (400) they remain under-staffed. John Major had a staff of 107.

The Prime Minister's staff is made up of a number of different units, including the Private Office, the **Press Office**, the Political Office, the **Policy Unit**, the **Efficiency Unit**, and Special Advisors. He or she also has a Parliamentary Private Secretary (PPS).

Comparison

Since 1939, the US President has been served by the Executive Office of the President (EXOP). This is made up of four core offices: the White House Office; the National Security Council, the Office of Management and Budget, and the Council of Economic Advisors.

The White House Office consists of the President's closest advisors – chief of staff, speech writers, press officer, etc. The National Security Council concerns itself with foreign policy. The Office of Management and Budget (OMB) and the Council of Economic Advisors both have economic roles; however, the OMB is a vital arm of the President's administration as it draws up the annual budget and hence has a key role in determining the legislative agenda.

The Private Office

The Private Office is the Prime Minister's main means of communication with the rest of the Cabinet, departments and the government machinery. The Office is staffed by a group of high-flying career civil servants who are on secondment from their departments and will return after two or three years to fill senior positions.

Under John Major there were five private secretaries. The group is headed by the Principal Private Secretary with the other five each taking responsibility for one of the main policy areas – parliamentary, home, economic and foreign affairs (2). The role of the secretaries is to brief the Prime Minister, make notes of meetings and converstations, organize his or her time, and control the flow of documentation.

The Principal Private Secretary is also responsible for running the Number 10 Office and is generally considered to be the third most powerful civil servant in the administration behind the Cabinet Secretary and the Permanent Secretary to the Treasury.

The Press Office

The Press Office was set up in 1931 to help the Prime Minister deal with the media. This remains its main brief and it has a staff of five press secretaries and a small support staff.

Throughout Margaret Thatcher's premiership, Press Secretary Bernard Ingham gained considerable notoriety through his briefings of the press lobby. The lobby system allows the Press Secretary to brief the lobby correspondents on a daily basis about government policy and the reaction from Downing Street to events. This is done in an 'off-the-record' format which results in media comments being prefaced with phrases such as 'A source close to the Prime Minister said …' or 'The view from Number 10 is …'.

Bernard Ingham was often accused of using the briefing sessions to undermine ministers within the Cabinet. News of the Prime Minister's displeasure with a particular minister would be leaked, either to prepare the media for the minister's dismissal or to encourage the minister to toe the line. In 1985, John Biffen's imminent departure from the Cabinet was touted in advance when Bernard Ingham referred to him as 'a semi-detached member of the government'.

John Major chose Gus O'Donnell, a career civil servant from the Treasury, to take over from Bernard Ingham. His approach was much less strident, but his influence was nonetheless significant. However, John Major did not use him to undermine Cabinet colleagues and, indeed, the bitter rivalries that characterized many of the Margaret Thatcher years were not apparent in Major's premiership. In 1994, Gus O'Donnell was replaced by Chris Meyer, a former diplomat (he was deputy ambassador in Washington), after some criticism of the administration's presentation skills.

The job of Press Secretary is nominally a civil service position, but a number have been drawn from outside the career civil service – including Tony Blair's choice, Alistair Campbell, who was a prominent figure in the Labour general election campaign in 1997.

The Political Office

Number 10 has a small political office which is responsible for the Prime Minister's relations with his or her party – in Parliament and in the country. The office will respond to letters, plan party political events, etc.

In 1994, John Major appointed Howell James as his political secretary. James was an ex-director of corporate and government affairs at Cable and Wireless plc and at the BBC. He was also head of press and publicity with TV-am, a position which earned him the label 'Roland Rat's press secretary'. Given his background in media and public relations, Howell was widely seen as John Major's 'spin doctor', responsible for manipulating media coverage in favour of the Prime Minister.

Lobby system

Bernard Ingham

John Major

The Policy Unit

In 1970, Edward Heath set up the Central Policy Review Staff, or 'Think Tank', which was designed to look at government policy in a wider context and to consider alternative options. It was eventually disbanded by Margaret Thatcher in 1983 and its role was absorbed by the Policy Unit – which had been set up by Harold Wilson in 1974. The unit is generally made up of staff from outside the civil service who have no pretensions to neutrality.

Sarah Hogg

Usually made up of six to eight people, the Policy Unit is much smaller than anything the White House has to offer, but nevertheless can be extremely influential. Previous heads of the unit have included John Redwood (1983–85), Professor Brian Griffiths (1985–90) and Sarah Hogg (1990–95), who was believed to be so influential that she was sometimes referred to as 'the real Deputy Prime Minister'. Under Sarah Hogg's leadership, the Policy Unit played an important role in a number of areas, including the strategies for non-inflationary growth; an approach to the Maastricht Treaty; an alternative source of local government revenue to replace the poll tax; and many of the ideas behind the 1992 election victory.

Sarah Hogg was succeeded in February 1995 by Norman Blackwell, a senior partner of the management consultants, McKinsey & Company. He was considered by some to be the 'policy fanatic' that John Major needed to sift the good ideas from the bad. It remains to be seen how Tony Blair will use the Policy Unit.

The Efficiency Unit

Margaret Thatcher established the Efficiency Unit in 1979 to monitor the use of resources in the civil service. Initially, it was headed by Sir Derek Raynor, managing director of Marks & Spencer. He was succeeded by Sir Robin Ibbs, an executive director of ICI. Derek Raynor made a number of suggestions to save money in the administration, but it was Robin Ibbs who made the most far-reaching suggestions for civil service reform. He proposed that a core of ministerial advisers remain in Whitehall while executive agencies be set up to administer many government functions (see page 154). These reforms continued under John Major's head of the Efficiency Unit, John Oughton.

Special advisers

Margaret Thatcher's special advisers also created some cause for concern in the 1980s. Prime Ministers appoint individuals, on a full- or part-time basis, to provide specialist advice on areas of policy such as foreign affairs and the economy. Margaret Thatcher's appointments included Anthony Parsons, a former British ambassador to the United Nations, who acted as her adviser on foreign policy, and Alan Walters, who was a part-time adviser on the economy until 1989.

Alan Walters

Conflict between Alan Walters and the Chancellor of the Exchequer, Nigel Lawson, led to the latter's resignation in 1989. The issue at the centre of the conflict was membership of the European Exchange Rate Mechanism (ERM). Nigel Lawson favoured membership while the economist Alan Walters was opposed. The Chancellor believed that Alan Walters' advice was causing a rift between the Prime Minister and himself and was also preventing the former from fully accepting government policy of membership of the European Monetary System.

Parliamentary Private Secretary (PPS)

Like all other ministers, the Prime Minister has a PPS whose job it is to keep them in touch with opinion in, specifically, the House of Commons – although John Major also had a PPS for the House of Lords.

A Prime Minister's Department?

Prime Ministers have thus succeeded in building up a great deal of power in their own hands, at the expense of Cabinet government. To many observers the development of the various units and staff at 10 Downing Street has appeared to mark the beginnings of a fledgling Prime Minister's Department.

Some, such as Sir Keith Berrill, an ex-head of the Central Policy Review Staff, have argued that such a department would be of great benefit to central government because it would give Prime Ministers the support they need to speak on behalf of the government on a wide range of issues. The alternative point of view is that it would be a major step towards full prime ministerial government. It would strengthen Prime Ministers to such an extent that they would become more detached from Cabinet and be encouraged to make policy in isolation from their colleagues.

At the most basic level it is certainly true that the developments outlined above have made it possible for the Prime Minister to stay in touch with the activities of the wider government. Thus if a Prime Minister wished to concentrate power in 10 Downing Street, he or she has a more efficient machine with which to do it than ever before. The extent to which they do so will depend at least partly upon their personality.

However, it is possible to identify other aspects of the changing role of the Cabinet that have also indirectly strengthened the position of the Prime Minister. These are considered next.

The decline of Cabinet decision-making

We have already seen that since World War II a considerable amount of Cabinet decision-making has been diverted towards the broader Cabinet system. This has been largely due to the increasing workload of the Cabinet. However, this is unavoidable and does not necessarily mean that decision-making lies solely in the hands of the Prime Minister.

It is important to grasp that a reduction in the power of the full Cabinet does not automatically result in an equivalent increase in the power of the Prime Minister. There are many players in central government, including the Prime Minister, the full Cabinet, individual Cabinet ministers, Cabinet committees and the elements of the Number 10 Office. Some or all can benefit from a reduction in the power of any one of the others.

The growth of Cabinet committees

The importance of Cabinet committees has already been noted. However, an astute use of this system can indirectly enhance the power of the Prime Minister. Prime Ministers set up the committee system, appoint the chair of each committee and, indeed, chair the most significant committees themselves. Margaret Thatcher, for example, headed the Standing Committees covering economic strategy, export policy, public sector strategy, foreign affairs and defence, and the Steering Committee on the intelligence services. In their turns John Major and Tony Blair have also headed the most important of the Standing Committees.

Composition

Since these committees are usually made up of the ministers most directly concerned with the issues, careful allocation of ministerial portfolios can strengthen the Prime Minister's control over government policy. We have already mentioned that Margaret Thatcher's Cabinet in 1979 contained a large number of critics of Thatcherite economic policies. However, Geoffrey Howe and Keith Joseph held the key economic ministries of the Treasury and Trade and Industry. As a result, Thatcherites dominated the Cabinet committee concerning economic strategy.

Numbers

In fact, Margaret Thatcher did not favour Cabinet committees as a method of decision-making and she created relatively few of them. Between 1979 and 1987 she set up fewer than 35 Standing Committees and 120 *ad hoc* committees. This compares with Clement Attlee's creation of 148 Standing Committees and 313 *ad hoc* committees in just over six years from 1945.

Prime Ministers can also manipulate *ad hoc* committees to their own advantage. While still part of the formal Cabinet system, *ad hoc* committees are, as their name suggests, temporary and so offer the Prime Minister an opportunity to manipulate their membership and terms of reference.

Another set of committees are even further removed from the institutionalized and formal world of Cabinet committees. They are officially not Cabinet committee meetings and are therefore not generally publicized. The Cabinet Committee on Coordination and Presentation of Government Policy set up under John Major was chaired by the Deputy Prime Minister, Michael Heseltine. Its all-embracing remit gave Heseltine the opportunity to take an interest, or interfere, in the whole range of policy issues and departmental affairs – particularly as he lacked departmental responsibilities himself.

Since 1997 in the new Labour administration, Peter Mandelson has occupied a similar position. The Minister Without Portfolio has the same freedom to 'take an interest' and has ackowledged that he chairs a daily meeting similar to that of Heseltine.

It is interesting to note that Mandelson was not given a Cabinet position. His position was to be within the Cabinet Office. Nevertheless, during the summer of 1997 he had accumulated sufficient power to engage in a very public battle for power with the Deputy Prime Minister, John Prescott, during Tony Blair's summer holiday. This is a clear illustration of the complexity of the power relationships within the machinery of central government.

Bilateral meetings

Margaret Thatcher's favoured method of doing business was by means of bilateral meetings with ministers. As issues arose and policy needed to be made, individual ministers, with their advisers, would be invited to 10 Downing Street to make a presentation to the Prime Minister. If policy ideas did not pass the Prime Minister's scrutiny, they could not be presented to Cabinet. The use of such bilateral meetings is another step further away from Cabinet government because they are *ad hoc* and, in constitutional terms, informal because they do not fall under the constitutional arrangements of full Cabinet meetings or Cabinet committees.

Margaret Thatcher's personal involvement in policy-making increased fears about prime ministerial government. These concerns remained undiminished given other elements of her style – for example, her reliance on the Policy Unit, rather than ministers, for initiatives, and her tendency to make policy without any consultation with ministers, perhaps on television or during party conference speeches.

'Kitchen Cabinets'

In addition, Margaret Thatcher came to rely on a **'kitchen Cabinet'** of advisers, including Charles Powell on foreign policy and Bernard Ingham, her Press Secretary. Prior to 1987 her range of advisers had been rather wider and included Robert Armstrong (Cabinet Secretary), William Whitelaw (Deputy Prime Minister), Robin Ibbs (Head of the Central Policy Review Staff) and Clive Whitemore (Principal Private Secretary). William Whitelaw, in particular, was instrumental in keeping the Prime Minister in touch with the feelings of Cabinet colleagues and the party as a whole. During the final years of her premiership, she appeared more isolated from colleagues.

John Major

John Major moved away from the use of bilateral meetings back to Cabinet committees. In 1993 Lord Wakeham, the Lord Privy Seal, gave his opinion: 'The move towards the use of *ad hoc* groups appears to have been halted ... my impression is that the balance has shifted back towards greater reliance on the Standing Committees'. (Quoted in *The Major Effect*, Macmillan, 1994)

In contrast to Margaret Thatcher, who liked to use bilateral meetings with ministers as these provided a better opportunity for her to dominate the discussion, John Major was anxious to maintain Cabinet unity on all key issues. He thus sought to avoid informal forums for decision-making – which could prompt objections and dissent from Cabinet ministers apparently excluded from the decision-making process.

John Major's leadership style was rather to attempt to build consensus than to defeat all the opposing views in the Cabinet. This reflects not only a different personality or leadership style, but also different political and economic circumstances. It has been reported that John Major relied on an inner Cabinet made up of his close colleagues. Kenneth Clarke (Chancellor of the Exchequer), Douglas Hurd (Foreign Secretary), Michael Heseltine (President of the Board of Trade), Michael Howard (Home Secretary), Malcolm Rifkind (Defence Secretary) and Tony Newton (Leader of the House of Commons) were all part of this grouping of senior colleagues.

Tony Blair

At the time this text is being written it is too early to give a full assessment of the premiership of Tony Blair. However, it appears that he is anxious to retain strong control of his government and colleagues. This tends to suggest that he will favour bilateral meetings to maximize his influence rather than large-scale collective decision-making.

For example, the *Sunday Times* reported on 19 October 1997 that the decision to declare British membership of the European single currency as 'highly unlikely' in the so-called 'first wave' of subscribers was made in a private meeting between the Prime Minister and the Chancellor of the Exchequer, Gordon Brown.

The Prime Minister's personality

Herbert Asquith said: 'The office of Prime Minister is what the holder chooses and is able to make it.' His remark, much quoted in examination questions, suggests that a great deal, if not all, of a Prime Minister's power depends on the office holder's personality. After comparing aspects of the premierships of Margaret Thatcher and John Major, and now of Tony Blair, it would be all too easy to agree.

Margaret Thatcher

It is well known that Margaret Thatcher was considered a 'conviction politician' who did not suffer fools gladly and opponents hardly at all. Margaret Thatcher's forcefulness also reflected the fact that she came to power with an agenda for change. Her 'conviction' was not based on power for its own sake, but rather she felt she had a mission to change Britain's economy, its industrial relations and its patterns of ownership, and she was unwilling to let others stand in her way. Francis Pym, a member of her Cabinet, once said:

'*The point about Mrs Thatcher is that she was against any suggestion of compromise; which meant that she had a very confrontational style, that was the automatic consequence of it and the idea that someone else might have a valid point of view, which might be a right point of view, wouldn't enter her mind at all.*' (Quoted in *The Major Effect*, Macmillan, 1994)

Margaret Thatcher was thought to enjoy argument, but Hugo Young quotes two senior Conservative politicians in his biography of her:

'*Arguing with her is an extremely unsatisfactory experience ... She doesn't have discussions, she states opinions ... These battles are totally exhausting. They can't be good for government. They're quite unnecessary expenditure of energy. They almost never result in any clarification, mainly because of her habit of going off at a wild tangent and worrying away for half an hour at a minor detail.*' (Hugo Young, *One of Us*, Macmillan, 1989)

John Major

John Major was often described as a consensus politician. Anthony Seldon quotes a senior Cabinet member: 'John Major's great ability is to get consensus, a position everyone is happy to accept' (in Kavanagh and Seldon (eds) *The Major Effect*, Macmillan, 1994). According to anecdotal evidence such as this, John Major's approach was more collective and far less dictatorial, but until Cabinet papers are released in about 30 years' time, this will be difficult to prove.

The atmosphere in Cabinet apparently changed following Margaret Thatcher's departure. Anthony Seldon once again quotes a Cabinet minister: 'The big difference before and after 1990 is that now if people feel they have something to say, they say it.' In Margaret Thatcher's time ministers were not always encouraged to speak and those who were overly tenacious often received withering rebukes. Former minister Jim Prior has recorded that in 1983 Michael Heseltine's continued opposition to the abolition of the Greater London Council 'led Margaret to deliver him one of the most violent rebukes I have witnessed in Cabinet' (James Prior, *A Balance of Power*, London, 1986).

However, it is not only a Prime Minister's temper and willingness to suffer opposition that is a determinant of their power. One of Margaret Thatcher's legendary attributes was her ability to work harder and to survive on less sleep than any of her ministers. When her phenomenal work rate was combined with her insatiable desire to interfere in all elements of policy, the mixture was potent. Having had only four hours of sleep, she would arrive regularly at meetings better prepared than the minister concerned.

Having briefly compared the personalities and leadership styles of Margaret Thatcher and John Major, it is tempting to conclude that Margaret Thatcher was the more powerful owing to her forceful personality. It is probably true that she made greater use of the tools of the Prime Minister's office in an effort to increase her power and to push through her policies. However, it is important not to confuse consensus politics with weakness. John Major certainly had a different leadership style from Margaret Thatcher, but it is open to debate whether he was a weaker Prime Minister because of it.

Margaret Thatcher was more dictatorial than John Major, but nevertheless she was defeated on some key issues. John Major may have employed a different leadership style and may have built a better record than his predecessor.

Finally, Tony Blair seems to relish control over his Cabinet, not only with a view to imposing his own agenda, but also – perhaps primarily – with a view to achieving his objective of a second full term for a Labour government – a feat never achieved by his Labour predecessors.

Tony Blair

Internal constraints on the Prime Minister

Whatever the Prime Minister's personality, there are a number of points about the relationship between the Prime Minister and the Cabinet that need to be considered.

The Cabinet agenda

We have seen that a Prime Minister can attempt to keep certain issues off the Cabinet agenda in order to avoid difficult discussions. In some cases, they can be very successful in doing so, particularly if it is not an ongoing issue; for example, Margaret Thatcher made decisions regarding the Americans' use of British air bases from which to attack Libya. But if the issue is likely to recur – for example, the economy – sooner or later it has to be discussed by the Cabinet.

How long an issue may be left off a Cabinet agenda depends partly on the personalities of Cabinet ministers. It is possible to argue that had the moderates been more forceful in their objections to Margaret Thatcher's handling of the economy, they would have been able to curb her power.

Primus inter pares

On occasions the Prime Minister will be defeated in Cabinet. As *primus inter pares* (see page 109) the Prime Minister – unlike the US President – is not able to overrule the Cabinet. In 1969 Harold Wilson was isolated in Cabinet over trade union reform, and in 1986 Margaret Thatcher was defeated in Cabinet over the proposed sale of the Landrover company to General Motors. Also, ultimately, it was Margaret Thatcher's Cabinet colleagues who persuaded her that to stand in the second ballot of the 1990 leadership contest would mean ignominious defeat, even given the fact that she had received most votes in the first ballot.

It has been reported ('Bye-bye Blues', Channel 4, 5 October 1997) that John Major was forced to accept the imposition of the second tranche of VAT on domestic energy supplies in Kenneth Clarke's budget of 1994, a measure that was ultimately defeated in the Commons in December of that year.

Civil service support

Despite the growth in the Number 10 Office, ultimately Prime Ministers are not self-sufficient. They cannot persistently make policy without the support of Cabinet colleagues, not least because they do not have the time to master and control every issue and, furthermore, cannot implement policy without the backing of ministerial departments.

External constraints on the Prime Minister

The relationship between the Prime Minister and the Cabinet does not take place in a vacuum. No matter what the relative merits of the Cabinet or the Number 10 Office are, neither is immune from outside influence. Events beyond the control of the Cabinet room will have as great an effect on the relationship as any of the internal factors (see Figure 6.1).

Parliamentary constraints

Majority   Between 1983 and 1987, Margaret Thatcher's government had a parliamentary majority of almost 150 seats. This left it almost immune from all but the most serious backbench revolts. John Major, on the other hand, came to power with a majority of only 21. This meant that just twelve government MPs needed to vote against their whip in order to engineer a government defeat. Naturally, John Major had to foster his majority most carefully. This situation partly accounts for his difficulties over the Maastricht Treaty in 1994. Eventually, a backbench rebellion was headed off only when he made the vote a test of confidence. A loss would have required a government resignation.

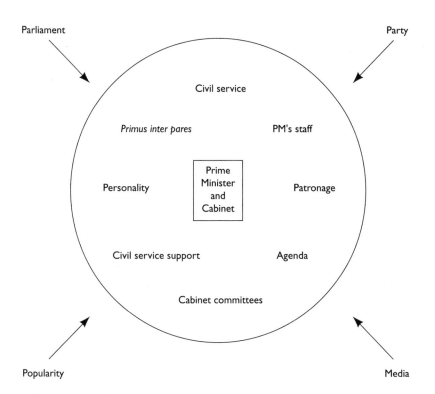

Figure 6.1 The context of prime ministerial power

Tony Blair leads a government with a majority of nearly 180 seats in the Commons – the largest of any postwar Prime Minister. Even though Margaret Thatcher's 1983–87 administration had a majority of 144 seats and lost a Commons vote on the Shops Bill in 1986, it would be surprising to see the present Blair administration losing a vote in the House of Commons. To do so would show carelessness on the part of the Labour Party's whips. The Labour administration might still face backbench revolts which could temporarily dent Tony Blair's standing, but they are unlikely to seriously undermine his position as Prime Minister. His party's majority certainly opens the way for a spell of prime ministerial government should he wish to take it.

Of course, the Prime Minister heading a coalition or **minority government** may be in the weakest position of all and would need to compromise either with other parties in

---

Comparison

Chief executives who lead coalition governments are not always weak. Helmut Kohl has led coalition governments in Germany since the early 1980s and has had a firm grip on German politics.

Margaret Thatcher in Britain and Felipe Gonzalez of Spain both held majorities in the legislatures but both ultimately were dismissed by their parties as electoral liabilities.

Cabinet or with parties on the floor of the house. Such circumstances make it much more difficult for a Prime Minister to take a strong line on any policy.

Perhaps an exception to this situation is the leader of a government of national unity. Winston Churchill led a coalition of national unity through World War II and gained considerable strength from the knowledge that the whole of Parliament was behind him.

Party political constraints

We have already seen the importance that Richard Crossman attached to the well-disciplined political party with regard to the development of Prime Ministerial power. However, political parties rarely follow their leader blindly and all Prime Ministers must nurture their party's support.

Patronage

Balance A Prime Minister's concern for party support is clear from the way they allocate ministerial office. It would not be prudent to offer Cabinet positions to their loyal supporters, hence fashioning a Cabinet in their own image. They must consider all wings of party opinion when making their selections.

James Callaghan's government of 1976–79 relied on the support of its leading left-wing member, Michael Foot, in order to gain continued co-operation from the trade union movement.

Similarly, Margaret Thatcher was advised to include in her Cabinet the supporters of her Conservative predecessor, Edward Heath. Hence Francis Pym, James Prior, Peter Walker and Lord Carrington all held office in her Cabinet in 1979. It was not until 1981 that moderates like Norman St John Stevas, Ian Gilmour and Mark Carlisle were removed from office and replaced by Thatcherites like Norman Tebbitt and Leon Brittan.

Careful placement of *opponents* inside the Cabinet can also protect a Prime Minister from criticism in the House of Commons. Harold Wilson included the left-wing MP Tony Benn in both his 1964–70 and 1974–76 Cabinets in order to bring him under the banner of collective Cabinet responsibility. In this way, Tony Benn was rather muzzled.

Dissent Margaret Thatcher was happy to retain a number of moderates in her Cabinet on the basis of the same tactics. She has said:

'*Far better to have them with you. even though they tried to slow you down, than to have them on the backbenches arguing against you, influencing other people against you instead of accepting the policies.*' (*Thatcher, The Downing Street Years*, BBC documentary, 1993)

It is not only all wings of the party that need to be represented in Cabinet. Some senior figures within the party expect to be given Cabinet positions. Some Cabinet positions require a certain degree of familiarity with the issues. For example, the Chancellor of the Exchequer must be knowledgeable about economics, and some – like the Scottish and Welsh Offices – require MPs from particular geographical localities. So the Prime Minister certainly does not have a totally free hand, and an astute one will try to keep the Cabinet balanced.

The need to keep the Cabinet balanced and to adjust its composition in the light of changing circumstances is clearly illustrated by the Cabinet reshuffle forced upon Margaret Thatcher in 1989. Nigel Lawson, the Chancellor of the Exchequer, resigned following conflicts with the Prime Minister over economic policy and the role of her economics special adviser Alan Walters. This was clearly a blow to the Prime Minister's standing, but she moved quickly to reinforce her position. John Major, a favourite, was moved from the Foreign Office, after only a few months, to the Treasury. His place at the Foreign Office was taken by Douglas Hurd, a senior Conservative and a 'safe pair of hands'. Douglas Hurd would probably not have been Margaret Thatcher's first choice, but given her position of weakness, his appointment settled the party's nerves and reinforced her position.

Party structure

A Prime Minister's ability to control his or her party does not depend only on the divisions within the party but also on the structure of the party. In the Labour party, power flows from the '**bottom-up**', while in the Conservative party power is distributed from the '**top-down**' (see page 59).

Labour party

Constitutionally, at least, policy-making power lies with the Labour party conference – that is, the grassroots. This makes it much harder for the leader to forge a particular path for the party. Labour leaders in opposition, including Hugh Gaitskell, Harold Wilson and Neil Kinnock, have all struggled to control their party. This has particularly been the case following the loss of an election. Gaitskell and Callaghan had to cope with a party in upheaval as a reaction to an election loss. However, during the 1980s and 1990s the Labour party had been out of power for so long it seemed to become increasingly compliant as successive leaders (Kinnock, Smith and Blair) attempted to reform the Party's organization and policies.

Power in the Conservative party currently lies at the top. The ministerial personnel, the manifesto and election strategies are all determined by the leadership. Although divisions undoubtedly exist within the party, as the European issue clearly illustrated, the party has tended to unite behind its leader and has largely been content to support their chosen path. A public display of disharmony is relatively rare in the Conservative party.

Conservative party

Popularity

Whilst the Conservative party may illustrate the strength a Prime Minister can gain from the backing of a united party, it also shows the weakness that can overtake the leader of the same party when it is divided. Nothing divides a political party like unpopularity and the fear of electoral losses.

Margaret Thatcher's three general election victories counted for nothing when her magic touch seemed to have deserted her in 1990. So long as the next election victory seemed assured, her colleagues were prepared to endure her dictatorial style of leadership. When she seemed doomed to lose, she was removed from office.

Similarly, John Major's power in the Cabinet suffered in 1993 and early 1994 as his standing in opinion polls slumped. If an election defeat seems likely, the Cabinet is much more difficult to hold together as colleagues begin to shape up for a possible leadership contest.

A leader's popularity is likely to depend on the state of the economy, the international prestige of the country or the general mood of the country, all of which are, to a greater or lesser extent, outside the control of the Prime Minister.

Tony Blair at the end of his first six months in office was experiencing a public approval rating of over 90 per cent – unprecedented in modern politics. His power within his Cabinet, party and Parliament will all benefit from his popularity in the country.

The media

The popularity of a Prime Minister depends, to some extent, on the media coverage he or she receives. Subject to more intense scrutiny than any other minister, they carry the whole of government policy in a way that other ministers do not. As a result, they gain the praise or the criticism that goes with those policies. A Prime Minister pilloried in the media is likely to be weakened in Cabinet.

Which party the Prime Minister represents can also affect media coverage. The press in Britain is biased in its coverage and editorials, with *The Daily Mirror*, *The Independent* and *The Guardian* being the only national daily newspapers not committed to some degree to the Conservative party. Newspapers, however, are fickle, and in the final years of the Major government many newspapers that had supported the Conservative party changed their minds. In particular *The Sun* decided to switch its support and promote the Labour party just before the 1997 general election, which undoubtedly helped to swing the election in favour of that party.

Conclusion

The debate surrounding the growth of prime ministerial power is by no means new. However, the premiership of Margaret Thatcher gave it new life. Throughout her terms of office she gave the impression of prime ministerial or even presidential government, but such an impression was misleading. Even a strong Prime Minister such as Margaret Thatcher is subject to constraints both inside and outside the Cabinet machine.

Inside the government machine we have seen that there are many players any one of whom can benefit from a slide in the standing of another. There is not a simple trade-off between the Prime Minister and the Cabinet. However, it is important to remember that it is the Prime Minister who maintains links with all elements of the government, and if any individual is well placed to dominate the proceedings it is definitely the Prime Minister.

Perhaps the most important of the constraints are those that act upon the Cabinet from outside Whitehall. Parliament, party, popularity and the media all set the context of the Prime Minister–Cabinet relationship, and all are, to some extent, beyond the control of the players. Furthermore, the context is in a continuous state of flux – it changes on a daily basis. As it changes, so the fortunes of the Prime Minister and the Cabinet also change. Sometimes the Prime Minister's star will rise at the expense of Cabinet; sometimes all of the players will benefit. So, as with so many constitutional issues, the reality is an ever-changing shade of grey.

A summary of external factors affecting the Prime Minister's power

- Parliament
- Party
- Popularity
- Media

Exercises

Short questions

1 a Define the convention of collective ministerial responsibility.
  b How effective is this convention in practice?
  (ULEAC, January 1995)

2 Outline the relationship of the Cabinet to the Prime Minister.
  (ULEAC, January 1994)

3 What is the role of the Cabinet?
  (ULEAC, June 1993)

4 Outline the factors that affect the powers of the Prime Minister.
  (EdExcel, June 1996)

Essay questions

1 Discuss the relationship between the office of Prime Minister and Parliament.
  (ULEAC, June 1994)

2 How could the power of the Prime Minister be reduced?
  (ULEAC, June 1993)

3 Does Britain have prime ministerial government?
  (ULEAC, January 1994)

4 Compare the relationship between the Prime Minister and Cabinet during the Thatcher and Major administrations.
  (Oxford, June 1994)

5 Does the fall of Mrs Thatcher indicate that prime ministerial power is not as great as some had argued?

6 Discuss the relationship between the office of Prime Minister and Parliament.
  (EdExcel, June 1994)

7   'The Cabinet has increasingly become a reporting and reviewing body, rather than a decision-taker.' Discuss.
(EdExcel, June 1996)

8   To what extent is British government becoming presidential?
(EdExcel, January 1996)

Data response question

The following is taken from Richard Crossman's 'Introduction' to Walter Bagehot's *The English Constitution*, Collins, 1963.

'The postwar epoch has seen the final transformation of Cabinet Government into Prime Ministerial Government ... Even in Bagehot's time it was probably a misnomer to describe the Premier as chairman and primus inter pares. *His right to select his own Cabinet and dismiss them at will; his power to decide the Cabinet's agenda and announce the decisions reached without taking a vote; his control, through the Chief Whip, over patronage – all this had already, before 1867, given him near Presidential powers. Since then his powers have been steadily increased, first by the centralization of the party machine under his personal rule and, secondly, by the growth of a centralized bureaucracy so vast that it could no longer be managed by a Cabinet behaving like the board of directors of an old-fashioned company.'*

1   What was meant by describing the Prime Minister as *primus inter pares* (first among equals)?

2   Describe recent examples of what 'had already, before 1867, given him near Presidential powers'.

3   Explain how the powers of the office 'have been steadily increased' since 1867.

4   State a case against the view that 'the postwar epoch has seen the final transformation of Cabinet Government into Prime Ministerial Government'.

(ULEAC, January 1993)

7 The civil service

Questions to be answered in this chapter

- What are the structure, role and characteristics of the civil service?
- What is the relationship between civil servants and ministers, and to what extent do civil servants have political power?
- If civil servants do have power, how do they use it?
- How have recent reforms affected the position of the civil service?

Terms to know

- Accountability
- Anonymity
- Bureaucracy
- Competitive tendering
- Continuity and stability
- Efficiency Unit

- Executive agencies
- Individual ministerial responsibility
- Interdepartmental committees
- Market testing

- Meritocratic
- Neutrality
- 'The Next Steps'
- Non-partisan
- Permanence
- Politicization

Introduction

The civil service, as perhaps the single aspect of British government most renowned for its stability and reluctance to change, has recently been the focus of some of the most profound changes of any British institution. For many years it had been the object of criticism from all parts of the political spectrum for its power without accountability, and for bias in the use of that power. Following the arrival of the first Thatcher government in 1979, it has been the object of reforms so long resisted in previous decades. The upheaval caused by the breaking up of civil service departments into executive agencies, the greater interest of politicians in the appointment of civil servants, and the drive for greater efficiency in the administrative branch of government, have left many of the conventions of British government struggling to keep up.

The executive branch of government

The executive branch of government can be divided into two parts: the political and the administrative. Ministers form the political part while their officials form the administrative arm.

In the public imagination, the term 'civil servant' means bowler hats, pinstripe suits and tightly rolled umbrellas. This image is associated with the higher civil servants of Whitehall, now immortalized in the television series 'Yes, Minister'. However, high-level civil servants account for less than one per cent of the total number; for most people, contact with civil servants is more likely to be in a local tax office or a Job-centre than in Whitehall.

Higher civil servants

This chapter looks at the 7000 higher civil servants, and in particular at the 600 higher civil servants who are in close contact with ministers at the centre of British government.

Functions of higher civil servants

Implementation of policy

The tentacles of the civil service reach deep into British society. This is understandable when we consider the main constitutional function of the civil service. As the administrative element of the executive branch of government, it is responsible for executing, or implementing, government policy. Civil servants ensure that statute law and government policy are put into practice.

Providing advice to ministers

At the highest level, civil servants have developed an additional function, that of

Providers of continuity

'Civil servants are servants of the Crown. In today's world, the executive responsibilities of the Crown are carried out by the elected government of the day. The civil service serves that government, irrespective of its political complexion ... It provides continuity through the changes of government ... On policy matters, the civil service is responsible for advising Ministers on policy options and ensuring the implementation of Minister's decisions. Ministers must decide on policy issues – and are accountable to Parliament and the public for them. But they expect civil servants to be expert in areas of administration and keep them under review; to analyse and evaluate the options for new approaches; and to provide them with thorough and objective advice on the implications, costs and benefits of alternative courses of action ... Outside the policy area, the Government relies upon the high standards of integrity, fairness and confidentiality of the civil service, upon civil servants' commitment to service for every citizen and economy and efficiency on behalf of the taxpayer, and upon the civil service's flexibility and sensitivity to changes in Government policy in handling some of the largest managerial and service delivery tasks in the economy.'

Source: 'The civil service: continuity and change', Government policy paper, 1994 advising ministers. As Charles Trevelyan, in many ways the founder of the modern civil service, wrote in 1854:

'... *the Government of the country could not be carried on without the aid of an efficient body of permanent officers, occupying a position duly subordinate to that of the Ministers who are directly responsible to the Crown and to Parliament, yet possessing sufficient independence, character, ability and experience to be able to advise, assist and to some extent influence those who are from time to time set over them.*'

According to the traditional, constitutional view of the advisory role of the civil service, the 'mandarins', as they are sometimes called, should be available to advise ministers on the decisions that need to be made, to brief ministers on the issues involved, and to present options to make the ministers' decision-making easier.

Functions and characteristics of the civil service

Functions
- Advise
- Implement

Characteristics
- Permanence
- Neutrality
- Anonymity

However, at no stage should civil servants be *responsible* for decision-making. Constitutionally, there is a clear dividing line between the decision-making role of the minister and the supporting role of the civil servant. As Margaret Thatcher said in 1989: 'Civil servants advise; ministers decide.'

> Advise, not decide

The division of responsibilities between ministers and officials is based on the fact that ministers are the representatives of the elected government of the country and, indeed, most ministers being MPs will have been elected themselves. Some ministers may be from the House of Lords, and therefore not elected. The government itself is not elected directly, but at least the government has some democratic credentials as it is drawn from the House of Commons. Civil servants have not been elected and for this reason should not hold political power.

> Unelected

The concept of **individual ministerial responsibility** underlies the division of responsibilities. According to this doctrine, ministers are responsible to Parliament for departmental policy, while civil servants are not. In the case of policy errors or mistakes in implementation, it is the minister who resigns rather than the civil servant. The implication of the doctrine is that civil servants should not be held responsible because they have no role in decision-making.

> Individual ministerial responsibility

This doctrine was clearly reiterated by the Home Secretary, Sir David Maxwell-Fyfe, in 1954 in the wake of the Critchell Down affair. In 1938 the Air Ministry bought a parcel of land under a compulsory purchase order to create a bombing range.

> Critchell Down

Eventually this land was handed over to the Ministry of Agriculture, where it was decided to lease the land back into agricultural use. The original owners of the land were not, however, first given the opportunity to buy back the land – as was required under the compulsory purchase order. It was believed – but this has since been questioned – that the Minister of Agriculture, Sir Thomas Dugdale, was not involved in this error. Nevertheless, Dugdale resigned.

Ministerial resignations

Whether ministers decide to resign or not depends not only on their sense of honour but also on the attitudes of those around them. Probably, the most influential opinions are those of the Prime Minister and the party's backbenchers. If the Prime Minister and other members of the party are prepared to give full backing to a minister, then the minister has a chance to survive criticism. However, if the backing of one or both of these bodies is lost the minister's fate is virtually sealed.

Ministerial
resignations

If a minister's department has made serious errors or if the minister has been guilty of misconduct, they should be prepared to resign. A number of ministers have resigned over misjudgments over policy. These have included: Lord Carrington, the Foreign Secretary, and his team of foreign office ministers who resigned in 1982 after failing to predict the Argentine invasion of the Falkland Islands; Leon Brittan, the Trade and Industry Secretary, who resigned in 1986 having been blamed for the unauthorized leak of a letter from the Solicitor-General to the Minister of Defence; and Michael Heseltine, the Defence Secretary, regarding the sale of the Westland helicopter company to a group of European companies.

In the case of Leon Brittan the leak was considered serious because all communications with government law officers are confidential. He later claimed that the release of the letter had been approved by a number of civil servants inside 10 Downing Street. Subsequently, civil servant anonymity was broken when a number of the civil servants

---

The drama of a ministerial resignation

Act I

On the 26 December 1993, *The News of the World* reveals that the Environment Minister, Tim Yeo, has fathered an illegitimate child through an extramarital affair – this against the backdrop of the 'Back to Basics' campaign announced by John Major at the Conservative Party Conference in October.

Through his solicitor Yeo issues a statement immediately confirming the story and explaining that his family already knew of the child. He confirmed that he had informed his government colleagues even though he felt that the matter was entirely private. By doing this he sought to defuse the situation but ran the risk of broadening interest.

The strategy appears to work – his ministerial colleagues are believed to be backing him and the national newspapers proclaim his survival. *The Sun*: 'Cheating Minister Told: Your Job's Safe'

Yeo and family leave for the Seychelles on holiday.

Act II

Conservative party chairman, Norman Fowler, is interviewed by the BBC and strongly supports Tim Yeo, claiming that the media and public should be sympathetic. More importantly, he pledges the Prime Minister's support for the minister. John Major had been strongly criticized for suppporting another minister a year earlier and had successfully kept out of the Yeo limelight until his party chairman dragged him into the full glare and gave new life to the story. He also invited retaliatory attacks from the media, having criticized their intrusive behaviour. *The Sun*: 'Carry on Bonking, Fowler Tells Tories'

Yeo returns from the Seychelles early in a blaze of publicity, including a photograph of the minister crouching down in the back of a car. *The Daily Mirror*: 'If You Don't Look – It Might All Go Away'

Act III

Yeo is attacked by a prominent constituent, Mrs Aldine Horrigan, Mayor of Haverhill and vice-chair of the Conservative constituency association. She writes to the Prime Minister asking him to reconsider his support. She is interviewed by the BBC and calls upon the PM to denounce Yeo's behaviour.

Fowler is attacked by Dr Adrian Rodgers, director of the Conservative Family Institute. He claims that the party chairman has misjudged the seriousness of the issue because 'immoral politicians' were 'potentially untrustworthy'.

Act IV

Interviewed for *The World this Weekend* (BBC Radio 4), John Major states that he will not be drawn into answering questions about the conduct of individual ministers. This is taken as a clear indication of a cooling of support for Yeo. Mrs Patricia Fitzpatrick, chair of the constituency association, announces a meeting to discuss the issue.

National newspapers print the full text of Mrs Horrigan's letter and confidently predict Yeo's resignation. Yeo insists that he will not be driven from office by media attacks.

Act V

Yeo attends the constituency meeting and expresses his deep regret for the embarrassment he has caused. At 10.00 the next morning Mrs Fitzpatrick reads a statement asking Yeo to reflect on the disappointment felt by constituency members. They back him as an MP but not as a minister. That evening Yeo resigns.

involved were named in Parliament, including Bernard Ingham, Margaret Thatcher's Press Secretary; Sir Charles Powell, one of her senior advisers; John Mogg, Leon Brittan's private secretary, and John Mitchell, an Undersecretary at the Department of Trade and Industry.

Staying on

While some ministers have been prepared to resign, in line with the doctrine of ministerial responsibility, many others have remained in office. For example, in 1991 the Home Secretary, Kenneth Baker, did not resign after two IRA prisoners escaped from Brixton Prison. In 1983 James Prior, Northern Ireland Secretary, retained his position after 38 IRA prisoners escaped from the Maze prison in Belfast, killing a prison officer.

In fact, demands for resignation appear to plague Home Secretaries, possibly owing to the tendency for their department to come into contact with British domestic law more than others. Michael Howard was a particularly controversial incumbent. He ran foul of the law a number of times in the 1990s as the courts found him to have been acting beyond his powers (*'ultra vires'*). A highly publicized example was his attempt to increase the minimum sentence given to the young murderers of two-year-old Jamie Bulger.

Personal misjudgements

Other ministers have resigned for a variety of reasons, all of which came under the heading of individual ministerial responsibility, but involved personal misjudgement rather than departmental errors (see Table 7.1). Cecil Parkinson (1983), David Mellor (1992) and Tim Yeo (1993) all resigned over scandals in their personal lives that raised doubts about their fitness to hold senior government office. In the case of Mellor, his downfall was a very public extramarital affair. In the other cases their extramarital affairs had resulted in illegitimate children.

Perhaps the most well known of these is the Profumo Affair (1963), dramatized in the film 'Scandal', in which John Profumo (Minister for War) was forced to resign following an ill-judged affair with Christine Keeler who was also having an affair with a member of the Russian embassy staff. More recently, two junior ministers have resigned as a result of alleged financial irregularities – the infamous 'cash-for-questions' saga. In 1996, businessman Mohammed Al-Fayed claimed to have given cash to nine MPs to ask questions in the Commons on his behalf during his fight with rival businessman 'Tiny' Rowlands for control of the Harrods department store.

Table 7.1 Ministerial resignations

	Edward Heath (1970–74)	Harold Wilson (1974–76)	Jim Callaghan (1976–79)	Margaret Thatcher (1979–90)	John Major (1990–97)
Sex scandal	2	0	0	1	4
Financial scandal	2	0	0	0	3
Failure	0	0	0	3	0
Political principle	2	5	4	7	4
Public criticism	0	0	0	3	1
Totals	6	5	4	14	11

Source: Jones et al., *Politics UK*, Prentice Hall, 1998

Characteristics of the civil service

In order to fulfil its functions the British civil service has three characteristics which were laid down in 1854 by the Northcote–Trevelyan Report:

Northcote-Trevelyan

- **permanence**
- **neutrality**
- **anonymity**.

A review of the civil service was commissioned in 1853 by William Gladstone, then Chancellor of the Exchequer. The terms of reference for Sir Stafford Northcote and Charles Trevelyan called for the 'revising and readjusting [of] the public establishments as to place them on the footing best calculated for the efficient discharge of their important functions, according to the actual circumstances of the present time'. The result was the permanent, neutral and anonymous civil service that remains at the heart of constitutional theory today.

Permanence

While ministers may come and go, civil servants remain. They do not change either when the minister changes or when the government changes. This system ensures that there is some degree of **stability** and **continuity** in government as the political personnel change. Officials are always there to brief an incoming minister on the decisions that have been made and those that need to be made. This enables the minister to take up the reins of office easily and allows the process of government to continue with as little disruption as possible.

Continuity and stability

In addition to knowledge of the issues and decision-making, civil servants build up a sound knowledge of how the department works and how policies can be implemented effectively.

Once the decision was taken to have a permanent civil service, this had obvious implications for the recruitment of civil servants. Before 1854 civil servants had been appointed through a system of patronage. This meant that jobs could be gained depending on political beliefs, family connections or the whim of politicians. Such a system was no longer appropriate after the Northcote–Trevelyan Report and it was replaced by recruitment based on merit. As the historian Peter Hennessy said: 'It

Meritocratic

Comparison

Until 1883 when the Pendleton Act was passed, the USA had a civil service based entirely on political appointments – the 'spoils' system. Since that date the main bulk of the administration has been permanent and appointed on a meritocratic basis. As in the UK, this brings continuity and stability to the administration.

In order to maintain control over the civil service, the higher layers are still filled by political appointees who are nominated by the President and ratified by the Senate. These political appointees can be dismissed at any time by the President.

---

worked. It created the country's first true meritocracy, a genuine aristocracy of talent' (*Whitehall*, Secker & Warburg, 1989).

Recruitment stages

A **meritocratic** civil service is recruited through a system of examinations and interviews, designed to select the best and the brightest. Today's higher civil servants are usually recruited from universities. Candidates complete a series of written examinations, known as the qualifying tests, and those who are successful take part in another series of interviews, simulations and written papers under the banner of the civil service Selection Board. Successful candidates then go forward to the final stage of interviews before the Final Selection Board.

'Oxbridge' predominance

Whether the British civil service is truly meritocratic has been the subject of considerable debate. In 1969 the Fulton Report was highly critical of the predominance of graduates from Oxford and Cambridge ('Oxbridge') among successful applicants.

The Fulton Report, 1969

The Fulton Report criticized the civil service for its 'amateurism', i.e. the tendency for higher civil servants to be 'generalists' or 'all-rounders', often educated in arts subjects without any prior knowledge of key issue areas. Nevertheless, they had the power to advise ministers on briefings prepared by specialists. This reflected the civil servants' idea that their specialism was administration.

The report also found that management skills were largely ignored in the service and it recommended the creation of the civil service College to improve training.

It suggested that recruitment to the service should be broadened and the dominance of Oxford or Cambridge arts graduates reduced in favour of a wider range of subjects and candidates with experience in the commercial and industrial sectors.

Finally, it recommended the abolition of the 'class' system in the service to allow greater mobility for talented administrators in the lower ranks.

While some of the report's recommendations were implemented, such as the abolition of the class sytem and the creation of the civil service College, the report itself was heavily criticized by the service as simplistic and some of its recommendations regarding recruitment were ignored.

The 'bias' towards Oxbridge would probably not have surprised the initiator of the Northcote–Trevelyan Report, William Gladstone. As his biographer H G G Matthew suggests, his aim was to ensure that 'a civil service appointed by patronage and influence would give way to a non-political administrative class educated in the moral values of a liberal education further developed by a reformed Oxford and Cambridge' (*Gladstone 1809–74*, Clarendon Press, 1986).

At the end of the nineteenth century it was not too difficult to justify Oxbridge predominance over other British universities, but today that is not so. In any case, it is questionable whether academic pre-eminence is sufficient to merit such success in civil service entrance examinations.

Neutrality

The need for neutrality comes from civil service permanence. If civil servants are to remain in office while governments change, they must be politically impartial. British civil servants should not allow their personal opinions to affect the way they serve their ministers. They are expected to offer impartial advice and implement ministerial decisions regardless of whether they agree with them.

Civil servants are thus required to be **non-partisan**. They are not allowed to take part in any party political activity, although they are allowed to vote in elections.

Non-partisan

> ## Comparison
>
> Neutrality is only appropriate for permanent civil servants who may be required to serve masters from a series of different political parties. Therefore political appointees in the US executive branch are not required to be neutral – in fact quite the contrary, they are expected to be loyal.
>
> The lower levels, staffed by permanent civil servants, are expected to be neutral and are prohibited from taking part in partisan political activity.

There has been some dispute over what the concept of neutrality actually means to civil servants. Some civil servants see themselves as servants of the Crown, which today is a symbol of the state rather than the monarchy. They believe, therefore, that their first loyalty is to the state, not to the government of the day. The danger of such an attitude is that civil servants might regard their professional morals as superior to those of the politicians or might even seek to influence their ministers in the direction of their own views. Indeed, the Labour politician Tony Benn believes that this is already the case:

Divided loyalty

'*The problem arises from the fact that the civil service sees itself as being above the party battle, with a political position of its own to defend against all-comers, including incoming governments armed with their philosophy and programmes.*' (*Arguments for Democracy*, Penguin, 1979)

The narrow dividing line between the desirability of a civil service conscience and the dangers of civil service independence was illustrated by the Ponting case in 1985. An employee of the Ministry of Defence, Clive Ponting, was tried for breach of the Official Secrets Act after having allegedly leaked information to a backbench Labour MP, Tam Dayell, regarding the sinking of the Argentine warship *Belgrano* during the Falklands War. He justified doing so by saying that the government had lied to Parliament regarding the circumstances in which the ship was torpedoed and that it was in the interests of the state to make public the information. Although Ponting was acquitted by a jury, the Secretary to the Cabinet and head of the home civil service, Sir Robert Armstrong, immediately restated the role of civil servants according to the Cabinet Office:

Ponting case

State and government

'*Civil servants are servants of the Crown. For all practical purposes the Crown in this context means and is represented by the government of the day ... The duty of the individual civil servant is first and foremost to the Minister of the Crown who is in*

*charge of the Department in which he or she is serving ... The determination of policy
is the responsibility of the Minister ... In the determination of policy the civil servant
has no constitutional responsibility or role, distinct from that of the Minister ... When,
having given all the relevant information and advice, the Minister has taken the
decision, it is the duty of civil servants loyally to carry out that decision ... Civil
servants are under an obligation to keep the confidences to which they become privy in
the course of their official duties.'* (Quoted in Peter Hennessy, *Whitehall*, Secker &
Warburg, 1989)

Anonymity

Civil servants are not elected and therefore should not have the power to make
political decisions. Decision-making is the responsibility of politicians and it is they
who should take responsibility for the successes or failures of departmental policy. For
this reason, civil servants are said to be **anonymous**. This might not mean that their
identity is secret, but it does mean that they should not be held publicly accountable
for their advice or for departmental policy.

Comparison

In the USA, permanent civil servants are generally not held accountable for their
advice. This is so as not to prejudice the advice they give and allow their political
masters to pass the buck.

For political appointees it is a different story. As they are not intended to be
neutral they can be blamed for policy failures. Nevertheless, even in the USA,
Presidents have held to the doctine of 'executive privilege' which allows dicussions
between the President and his or her closest advisors to be kept secret. This is
intended to allow the highest policy-makers to 'think the unthinkable'.

The civil service's power and influence

Despite the constitutional view that civil servants should not wield political power,
politicians from both left and right have accused the civil service of having
considerable influence over policy-making. Ironically, the main sources of this power
and influence are the functions and characteristics given to civil servants in the
Northcote–Trevelyan constitutional view of their position. As we saw above, Charles
Trevelyan intended to create a civil service made up of individuals 'possessing sufficient
independence, character, ability and experience to be able to ... to some extent,
influence those who are from time to time set over them'.

The nature of advice

Ministers have a large workload and limited time. They are responsible for their
department, general governmental responsibilities in Cabinet, parliamentary duties,

constituency business and party matters. As a result, they come to rely on civil service advice – and this puts the civil servant into a privileged and influential position.

Any adviser, in any walk of life, should have some influence. If not, there is little point in them being there. However, if ministers lack the time to weigh up civil servants' advice, there is a danger that they may become just a mouthpiece for *civil service policies*.

Ministerial dependency

The act of implementation

Once decisions have been taken it is left to the civil service to implement them. Again, this leaves room for civil servants to interfere in the political process by *delaying* or *obstructing* the implementation of policy. By seeking loopholes, creating difficulties or simply refusing to cooperate, policies can be undone. Some Labour ministers were quick to point to an uncooperative civil service when explaining the difficulties of the 1964–70 government. The creation of the Department of Economic Affairs was an attempt to sidestep an uncooperative Treasury. Ironically, the Treasury's refusal to work with that department was also cited as a reason for its demise. In another example, Barbara Castle, as Employment Secretary, used her diaries, published some years later, to accuse her civil servants of ambushing her bill to curb trade union power – a bill known as 'In Place of Strife' – by including controversial clauses that she had expressly deleted.

Obstruction

Bureaucracy

The German sociologist Max Weber believed that the **bureaucracy** would be one of the most powerful political forces in the twentieth century.

According to him, bureaucrats are professional administrators, recruited on merit rather than as political appointees. They work inside a hierarchical structure, following strict rules of procedure and decision-making and recording all of the decisions for future reference.

The advantages of bureaucracy are that it is efficient, consistent and gives advice on an objective basis, free from political bias. It also brings continuity to the system of government.

Bureaucracies are criticized for excessive red tape and form-filling and the danger that they might use their knowledge and expertise to subvert the governing role of their political masters.

The effect of permanence

Since civil servants are permanent and ministers are not, this potentially gives the former a great deal of power. Civil servants spend a substantial part of their working lives in the service and sometimes even within one department.

Ministers, on the other hand, have an average tenure of only two years. After that they can be expected to be promoted or demoted in a Cabinet reshuffle. Therefore, they have little time to get to grips with the issues.

Temporary ministers

Experience — In his diaries, the Labour politician Richard Crossman constantly expressed his concerns over his inexperience of housing issues compared with the vast experience of his Permanent Secretary, Evelyn Sharpe:

'She is really a tremendous and dominating character. She has worked with a great many ministers before me ... [she is] utterly contemptuous and arrogant, regarding local authorities as children which she has to examine and rebuke for their failures. She sees ordinary human beings as incapable of making a sensible decision.'

Departmental knowledge

H E Dale, a senior civil servant before World War II, described the role of a senior administrator:

'[He] knows the construction of the whole machine, the position of his own and other departments as wheels of the machine and their relations to the other wheels, and the general principles of operation which must be observed if the machine is to work smoothly. Finally, and perhaps most important of all ... it is the business of the high official to know the men who for the time being are, like himself, important parts of the central and controlling mechanism.'

Source: Quoted in Clive Ponting, *Whitehall: Tragedy and Farce*, Hamish Hamilton, 1986

A former head of the civil service, Edward Bridges, has summed up this advantage as the 'stock of departmental wisdom' that comes from 'the slow accretion and accumulation of experience over the years'.

Administrative knowledge — Of course, such wisdom is relevant not only to the issues but also to the workings of the department. The civil service has developed a great deal of control over the administrative process. Red tape, traditional procedures and set ways of doing things mean that it is very difficult for a minister to get anything done without civil service cooperation.

Links — Civil servants' knowledge of the ways of the bureaucracy is not limited to their own department. Their years in office enable them to make links with civil servants in other departments. The result can be a network of civil servants able to influence ministerial policy right across the civil service regardless of departmental boundaries. For civil servants in spending departments, such as Defence or Health, links with civil servants in the Treasury are particularly useful as the Treasury has a significant voice in decisions over spending plans.

Backgrounds — For many civil servants links are built very easily because so many senior members come from similar backgrounds. We saw above that the majority of successful applicants have an Oxbridge background. A H Birch goes further: 'Statistics published in the 1970s showed that most of the successful Oxbridge candidates had been educated at fee-paying schools, and were therefore members of the upper and upper-middle classes' (*The British System of Government*, Allen & Unwin, 1980). With its

146

culture and traditions which are slow to change, the civil service remains the bastion of the 'old school tie' network.

Links between civil servants across departmental lines are institutionalized through **interdepartmental committees**. Their purpose is to coordinate the work of government between departments and they shadow the work of Cabinet committees. Some observers argue that the committees give civil servants the opportunity to shape policy options before they are presented to ministers. In more extreme terms, they could enable civil servants to run a shadow government from behind the scenes. With this in mind, former Labour minister Peter Shore has referred to civil servants as 'permanent politicians'.

Interdepartmental committees

The effect of neutrality

The constitutional view expects civil servants to have, according to the ex-Conservative minister, Nicholas Ridley, 'a chameleon-like ability to identify with successive governments of quite different political complexion'. There is a danger that the expectation of political impartiality may become a cloak behind which civil servants can hide. If ministers expect civil servants to be neutral, they may be less vigilant regarding the advice they receive.

In 1987, in an interview on Channel 4 News, the former head of the civil service Lord Bancroft said: 'There are occasions when one looks at a manifesto … where a balloon comes out of one's head which says "Garbage! God!" and then it is a question of handling matters so that, somehow or other, the garbage is made into something edible.' The cloak of neutrality may mean that a minister is not aware that the policies are being made more 'edible'.

Cloak of neutrality

Labour politician Tony Benn was nothing if not vigilant during his time in office and he raises similar doubts about civil service neutrality: 'The deal that the civil service offers a minister is this: if you do what we want you to do, we will help you publicly to pretend that you're implementing the manifesto on which you were elected' (quoted in H Young and A Sloman, *No Minister: An Inquiry into the Civil Service*, BBC, 1982).

In this sense the shroud of neutrality is a threat to ministerial control. Supporters of this view look to the system of political appointees used in the United States to fill the highest offices of the civil service. The US President has the power to appoint around 4000 civil servants; they can be drawn from any walk of life and are likely to be his or her supporters.

US appointments

The effect of anonymity

Theoretically, civil servants do not take responsibility for departmental policy because they are not decision-makers. However, the logistics of minister–civil service relations means that this is sometimes not possible. The creation of 'super departments' such as the Department of the Environment has meant that full ministerial control of the department is virtually impossible.

In his biography of Michael Heseltine, Julian Critchley has pointed out that while at the Ministry of Defence:

Scale

'Michael Heseltine was in charge of an organization more than three times the size of the biggest private employer in the country. In 1983 £6 billion pounds were spent on new equipment … The scale of the problem facing Heseltine within the ministry can be demonstrated by one statistic: the enterprise was so vast that production orders worth less than £50 million did not go to ministers for approval.' (Heseltine: The Unauthorised Biography, Coronet, 1988)

Sources of civil servants' power

- Advice
  - time
  - information
- Implementation
  - delay
  - obstruction
- Permanence
  - knowledge
  - bureaucracy
  - links
  - background
- Neutrality
  - disguise
- Anonymity
  - size

The effect of ministerial weakness

While the constitutional position of civil servants has obvious advantages, it also carries dangers for the British system of government. Their functions and characteristics give them the opportunity to wield a great deal of influence over ministerial decision-making.

Civil service preference

However, civil servants and ministers have often claimed that undue civil service influence is largely the fault of weak ministers rather than overly ambitious civil servants. Labour politician Denis Healey has summed this up in the following terms: 'A minister who complains that his civil servants are too powerful is either a weak minister or an incompetent one.' We can also add the words of former Prime Minister Harold Wilson to this: 'If a minister cannot control his civil servants he should go.' This view has also been supported by Lord Croham, a civil servant who spent 30 years at the Treasury:

'Without any hesitation civil servants like strong ministers. They are much easier to deal with for a number of reasons … They are more likely to get their own views across and, therefore, if you work hard to do something for a minister it's not wasted. The other point is that if you're dealing with a minister and he doesn't like your advice, you know pretty clearly … He decides on his own line … which gives it the maximum

chance of succeeding ... and [he's] *most unlikely to turn round and blame the department if it doesn't work. Every civil servant I know likes strong ministers.'*
(Quoted in Peter Hennessy, *Whitehall*, Secker & Warburg, 1989)

Potential civil service bias

If civil servants do have some political power, how do they use it? The possible answers to this question take us into the realm of civil service bias. This is by no means a new accusation and in recent years has been as common from the Conservative party as it has from Labour.

Anti-Thatcherite views

Margaret Thatcher was very critical of some of the civil servants she encountered when she came into prime ministerial office. She felt that a number of senior civil servants did not have the right attitude towards government. She believed that they were negative and obstructive, often standing in the way of her policies. Her views were no doubt partly shaped by the reports of the head of her Policy Unit, John Hoskyns, who stated that joining a civil service team was 'like joining Napoleon's army just before the retreat from Moscow'. He had found that the civil service's approach to Britain's problems was the 'orderly management of decline'.

It could be argued that to Margaret Thatcher's mind, the civil service was insufficiently supportive of her policies and so was not really neutral when she came to office. Having spent their entire working lives in a political environment dominated by Keynesian economic thinking and the postwar political consensus (see page 53), it would be hardly surprising for civil servants to find it difficult to adjust to the new policies of Thatcherism. Therefore, any politicization she might have undertaken, she would have justified as attempts to correct the partisan balance.

Correcting the balance

Anti-Labour views

The question of whether the civil service is entirely neutral is certainly not new, but more often it has come from the political left than the right. Richard Crossman, Tony Benn, Barbara Castle and Peter Shore, all members of Labour governments in the 1960s and 1970s, accused the civil service of being negative towards Labour policies. Such a bias might be explained, according to Marxist political scientist Ralph Miliband, by the fact that the majority of civil servants are drawn from a privileged background, and they might seek to preserve this privilege against an onslaught by a socialist government committed to the removal of privilege. However, it is perhaps a little unlikely to believe that background should be the major determinant of civil service behaviour.

Backgrounds

An alternative explanation, associated with another Marxist, Nicos Poulantzas, suggests that civil servants are prisoners of the dominant ideology of the state. Britain is a capitalist state, the officials are servants of the state, and so if they wish to serve the system, administrators have no alternative but to be servants of capitalism. As a result, they are opposed to the socialism of the Labour party.

Servants of capitalism

149

Anti-radical views

Radicals Many of the criticisms of the civil service have come from the more extreme wings of both of the major political parties. Tony Benn, Richard Crossman and Barbara Castle might all be considered to come from the left of the Labour party. Of the Conservative critics, Nicholas Ridley and Margaret Thatcher could certainly be said to come from the right of the party.

Moderates It is possible to argue that the civil service is opposed neither to the Labour party nor to the Conservative party; rather it opposes radical change in either direction. This would also explain why Edward Heath, James Callaghan, Denis Healey and Harold Wilson did not have difficulties with civil servants – they were all from the mainstream of their parties.

Long-termism If there was anti-radical feeling in the civil service, this could be in line with its loyalty to the state rather than the government (see page 143). In the best interests of the state, civil servants might seek to steer a central course of moderate policies designed, in their opinion, for long-term benefit.

Civil service policies Tony Benn claimed to have identified such 'civil service policies' as civil servants prepare to welcome a new minister:

'They read the manifestos, then they prepare papers designed to show how part of them could be implemented and how part of them can't be implemented. They dress it up so that an incoming government will feel that there is a sympathetic civil service. In effect, what they do, however, is to write massive briefs, which are the most important documents to be found in Whitehall, in which – and it's the only time it happens – they actually set out civil service policy.' (*Arguments for Democracy*, Penguin, 1979)

On the other hand, the radical government of 1945–51 seemed to be well supported by the civil service.

Challenges to the constitutional position

Politicization

During Margaret Thatcher's premiership, a number of observers, politicians and officials began to voice concern over the constitutional position of the civil service. They argued that Margaret Thatcher's attitude towards the civil service – and many of the resulting reforms – had seriously damaged the constitutional masonry of the administrative branch of the executive.

One of us? The first characteristic to come under scrutiny in the 1980s was neutrality. Margaret Thatcher was accused of **politicizing** the higher civil service by putting her own supporters into key positions. Her famous maxim when considering recommendations for promotion was 'Is he one of us?' – meaning is the candidate on our side? If this were strictly applied, Margaret Thatcher might have seriously undermined the neutrality of the civil service.

Opportunities In the early years of her administration Margaret Thatcher certainly had the opportunity to politicize the higher civil service. Between 1979 and 1985, 43

Permanent Secretaries and 138 Deputy Secretaries left the civil service, of their own free will. This represents an almost total turnover of senior civil servants. However, only one example of the alleged politicization has ever been put forward to support the case of Margaret Thatcher's critics. In 1983 Sir Douglas Wass retired as Permanent Secretary to the Treasury and was replaced by Peter Middleton. As the historian Peter Hennessy has commented:

'*Certainly, some* [civil servants] *flew higher and faster because of her patronage. She has her favourites. Peter Middleton … was one. … Middleton was a convinced monetarist who had been crucial in putting together the government's medium-term financial strategy. Mrs Thatcher and those ministers who thought like her (as the Treasury team did) preferred dealing with Middleton rather than the ever-courteous but ever-sceptical Wass.*' (*Whitehall*, Secker & Warburg, 1989)

Comparison

In the USA the top layers of the administration are filled with political appointees. The head of each department is known as the Secretary and has a seat in the President's Cabinet. In many ways they fulfil the roles of ministers and junior ministers except that they are not elected, they meet only when the President requires it and they cannot outvote the president on any issue.

The aim of political appointees is to ensure loyalty to the President and to allow his or her influence to penetrate deeper into departments. They are nominated by the President and ratified by the Senate. They can be dismissed by the President at any time.

Margaret Thatcher's alleged politicization in civil service appointments was investigated by the Royal Institute of Public Administration in 1985, but no evidence of it was found. However, the report stated:

Investigation

'*To some extent, the appointment process has become more personalized in the sense that at the top level "catching the eye" of the Prime Minister (in a favourable or unfavourable manner) may now be more important than in the past … Downing Street communicates more opinions about the performance of civil servants, even down to quite junior levels, based on impressions made at meetings with the Prime Minister … However, we do not believe that these appointments and promotions are based on the candidate's support for or commitment to particular ideologies or objectives.*'

The danger of the need for 'catching the eye' of the Prime Minister is that ambitious civil servants might sacrifice some of their independence to seek the favour of their ministers. Peter Hennessy has quoted Lord Bancroft:

'Catching the eye'

'*The dangers are of the younger people, seeing that advice which ministers want to hear falls with a joyous note on their ears, and advice which they need to hear falls on their ears with rather a dismal note, will tend to make officials trim, make their advice what ministers want to hear rather than what they need to know.*' (*The Hidden Wiring, Unearthing the British Constitution*, Victor Gollancz, 1995)

As a result, Margaret Thatcher might not have politicized the civil service, but the impression that she did so was enough to achieve the same effect.

Defence
Individuals who were close to the Prime Minister at this time have also defended her against critics. Robert Armstrong, who headed the Senior Appointment Selection Committee, said:

'There is no question of political considerations entering into the choice. The Prime Minister is ultimately responsible for the appointments of permanent and deputy secretaries, and she takes a keen interest in them ... She is not concerned with, and I can vouch for the fact that she does not seek to ascertain, the political views or sympathies (if any) of those who are recommended. Nor do I. She wants, as I want, to have the best person for the job.' (Quoted in Peter Hennessey, Whitehall, Secker & Warburg, 1989)

Permanence threatened
Politicization could also undermine the permanence of the civil service because incoming Prime Ministers might seek to replace the appointees of the previous administration. Indeed, Neil Kinnock, as leader of the Opposition, hinted at his fears of politicization in a 1985 television interview:

'I don't know about the permanent secretaries. We obviously have to examine the degree of enthusiasm and loyalty that they are prepared to demonstrate in support of a Labour government and in the implementation of the policy of that government. I'm prepared to work on ... the conventional basis, which has stood us in good stead in Britain, about the way in which civil servants are prepared to work.'

Ongoing concerns
Despite Margaret Thatcher's departure from government, the debate regarding civil service neutrality and politicization has continued. In 1994 the minister for open government, William Waldegrave, dismissed one of his civil servants, Peter Kemp, because of difficulties in their working relationship. The minister, often referred to as the 'minister for the civil service', stated: 'When you put in a new policy which is controversial, it is quite difficult not to appoint people who are sympathetic to you to run it ... It is crazy to appoint people who are deliberately not going to do what you want.'

Civil service morale

Margaret Thatcher's attitude towards the civil service was sometimes negative. She was

---

Secrets trials

Between 1979 and 1986, 29 individuals were prosecuted for breach of the Official Secrets Acts. Important cases included those of Sarah Tisdall (1984), Clive Ponting (1985) (see page 143) and the *Spycatcher* affair (1986–88) (see page 187).

Sarah Tisdall was sentenced to six months in prison after leaking government documents concerning the strategy to head off opposition to the stationing of cruise missiles in Britain. She objected to the government's intention to make an announcement to Parliament only after the missiles had arrived.

concerned that the senior civil servants ('mandarins') were opposed to her policies and also were unduly pessimistic about Britain's future. Therefore, she attacked what she perceived as the complacency of the service. Between 1979 and 1992 the size of the civil service was reduced by 23 per cent, from 732,000 to 565,000. In 1981 she abolished the Civil Service Department, banned trade unions from Government Communications Headquarters (GCHQ), and held out against a 21-week strike for higher pay. These points, combined with her merciless hounding of those civil servants accused of leaking secret information, served seriously to undermine the morale of the administrators.

Efficiency and reforms

Margaret Thatcher was also extremely critical of the inefficiency of the civil service. She believed it was ignorant of management techniques, wasteful and showed little concern for the delivery of a public service. To combat these problems, she set up the **Efficiency Unit** as part of her office at 10 Downing Street in order to implant a private-sector mentality in the government administration.

The Efficiency Unit

In 1979, the Efficiency Unit was headed by Derek Rayner, who was the joint managing director of Marks & Spencer. He launched a series of investigations into departmental efficiency that resulted in annual savings which averaged £325 million by 1989.

Efficiency Unit

The unit, in conjunction with individual departments, also launched the Financial Management Initiative (FMI). The aim of the initiative was to foster a greater business awareness in civil service departments. Civil servants were encouraged to identify their objectives, along with means of measuring success; to accept greater responsibility for the use of resources; and to ensure that they had access to the necessary advice and training to enable them to perform effectively.

Financial Management Initiative

Individual departments often set up their own versions of FMI. Probably the best-known was Management Information System for Ministers (MINIS) which was founded by Michael Heseltine at the Department of the Environment.

Management Information System for Ministers

Efficiency and effectiveness in the civil service, 1982

A 1982 government white paper outlined the aims of the Financial Management Initiative regarding civil servants:

'... *a system in which managers at all levels have:*

a a clear view of their objectives; and assess and, wherever possible, measure outputs or performance in relation to these objectives;

b a well-defined responsibility for making the best use of their resources including a critical scrutiny of output and value for money;

c the information (particularly about costs), training and access to expert advice which they need to exercise their responsibilities effectively.'

Civil service reform

'The Next Steps' programme

'The Next Steps'

Derek Rayner was succeeded by Robin Ibbs who pushed the frontiers of civil service reform further than even the Fulton Report had been prepared to go in 1969. His report, *Improving Management in Government: The Next Steps*, was completed before the 1987 general election and recommended the most radical shake-up of the civil service since the Northcote–Trevelyan Report in 1854.

Executive agencies

The main element of '**The Next Steps**' was the suggestion that many of the functions of the civil service could be carried out more effectively and efficiently if they were the responsibility of **executive agencies**. These agencies were to be be discrete units given specific responsibilities under the leadership of a chief executive.

When considering the establishment of an agency, a department must first examine whether the function needs to be performed at all. If it does, the possibility of complete privatization or contracting out to a private business must be considered. If the function is to be retained by the public sector, civil servants analyse the extent to which ministers need to be involved in day-to-day decision-making, and whether the agency could function alone as a separate unit. It must have clearly defined functions and a strong management structure to deliver the service effectively and provide value for money.

Given that the potential for executive agencies was very wide, the intention was to be flexible in the way in which they were set up. All are based on a unique framework agreement drawn up by the parent department. This covers the role of the chief executive and the chains of responsibility, and specifies targets to be achieved by the agency. It is sometimes seen as almost a contractual relationship between the agency and its parent department against which its effectiveness can be assessed.

Improving delivery

The chief executives of the agencies are given, at least theoretically, a great deal of independence from the traditional departmental structures of the civil service. They are expected to be aware of management techniques and to strive constantly to improve the delivery of their services. A 1994 survey showed that chief executives were spending 25 per cent of their time trying to improve cost-effectiveness. Indeed in 1993, in line with private-sector policies, 50 per cent of the chief executives had received performance-related bonuses.

The Conservative government at the time believed that agencies would be more cost-conscious, more responsive to consumers in the delivery of their services, and more receptive to new management techniques to improve performance. Peter Kemp, one of the main architects of *The Next Steps* programme, described it as a means of 'getting the best of both worlds, filling a gap in the management armoury of this country … it's a public-sector owner, with broad public-sector rules with a private-sector approach to running businesses.'

Management principles

This was fully in line with the Thatcherite policies of bringing private-sector management principles into the running of government services. Margaret Thatcher believed that the public sector was often wasteful, bureaucratic and unresponsive; whereas, in order to survive and prosper, the private sector needed to be efficient, responsive and concerned with the quality of its services. This philosophy also underpinned her other key policies such as privatization of nationalized industries (see page 69) and allowing private firms to bid for the delivery of local authority services (see page 202).

Comparison

In the USA, the executive branch of government contains Independent Executive Agencies. The majority of these were created under the presidency of Franklin Roosevelt (1933–45) in an effort to give the chief executive greater control over certain aspects of the administration.

They are independent from departments, with their own staff and budgets – but less independent from the President because he or she appoints the heads of the agencies and can remove them from office at any time.

Examples of Independent Executive Agencies include NASA (the National Aeronautical and Space Administration) and the CIA (the Central Intelligence Agency).

In addition, the American system contains Independent Regulatory Commissions. They exist to regulate sectors of the private economy. They too are independent of departments and their heads are appointed by the President, but for a fixed term of office. Therefore they have security of tenure and greater independence than their colleagues in Executive Agencies. To an extent they are the equivalent of OFSTED, OFTEL and OFGAS in the UK.

The initial pace of reform along the lines suggested by Robin Ibbs was slow. However, the government of John Major continued the process, and by 1994 there were 97 executive agencies – including the Employment Service, the Inland Revenue, and Customs and Excise – and 64 per cent of civil servants (340,000) were employed by these agencies. By 1997 the process had virtually reached its conclusion, with 80 per cent of civil servants working in 170 agencies.

Extension of agencies

Market testing

At the same time as moving forward with *The Next Steps* in 1991, the government of John Major announced that it would expand the range of government activities to be subjected to **market testing**. Very simply this means that the government would test the relative cost of providing the particular service in-house or by the private sector. This had long been used in local government where it was known as **competitive tendering**, but now central government departments were forced to compete against the private sector to be able to deliver their services.

Tendering

Targets were set as follows: contracts worth £1.5 billion between April 1992 and October 1993, with a further £800 million to follow, were to be market tested, and savings of 25 per cent were sought. The project has seen only limited success. The in-house bids have won 75 per cent of the contracts, and savings have reached only the

Targets

20 per cent level. Certainly the exposure of departments of central government to the cold wind of private-sector competition have not matched the heights scaled by the National Health Service, schools and local government.

A new senior civil service

Five senior grades

Despite the advance of executive agencies, a core of around 20,000 higher civil servants remain to work closely with ministers. But even here there has been reform. In 1996 a new senior civil service was established. Five senior grades of civil servant were defined, with the Permanent Secretaries at the top and beneath them the Second Permanent Secretaries, the Deputy Secretaries, the Under Secretaries and Assistant Secretaries.

The new structure brought with it a new pay scheme. Permanent Secretaries have their pay determined by the Senior Salaries Review Body, and they are responsible for setting the pay of their subordinates according to performance.

This new structure is intended to open the way for more extensive recruitment of senior civil servants from outside the service, and to give greater flexibility in terms of changing senior personnel. Senior positions in the civil service have been opened to public competition for some time. By 1995 approximately 30 per cent of higher grade vacancies were open to outside competition and were advertised in the press, and in 50 per cent of cases external candidates proved successful.

Members of the senior civil service have new contracts which theoretically take incumbents up to retirement – and hence the permanent career civil service is maintained. However, the contracts are in fact made up of a series of short-term contracts which specify periods of notice required to remove the civil servant. It is believed that some former Conservative ministers, including Kenneth Clarke and Michael Heseltine, would have liked senior civil servants put on fixed-term contracts. As Peter Hennessy states:

'*... the nature of the deal is apparent. It is plain that ministers wished to go over completely to fixed-term contracts for the whole senior civil service, but were persuaded by their officials to settle for this kind of half-way house.*' (Peter Hennessy, *The Hidden Wiring: Unearthing the British Constitution*, Victor Gollancz, 1995)

The impact of reform

Constitutional position

All the changes made to the structure and functioning of the civil service under Conservative governments since 1979 have implications for the traditional constitutional position of the service. Like so many institutions, the civil service would appear to be in transition and the unwritten British constitution is taking time to evolve in order to cope with that transition.

Politicization

The most obvious threat to the traditional position of the civil service is politicization. As we know, the civil service should be neutral. Politicians making appointments to the administration for political reasons threaten to undermine that neutrality. Although Margaret Thatcher was accused of politicizing appointments of senior civil servants this was never proved and did not appear to take place on a large scale. However, whilst blatant politicization probably did not occur, more subtle versions may have occurred.

Firstly, Margaret Thatcher's personal interest in appointments and the apparent personalization of promotion through the principle of 'catching her eye' may have undermined civil service independence. Secondly, the fact that the Conservative party was in power for such a long time (18 years) must inevitably have led to civil servants becoming accustomed to that party's *modus operandi*. Concern over such gradual politicization arises when governments 'occupy the crease' for long periods.

In the traditional constitutional view of the civil service, there is an umbilical cord between civil service permanence and neutrality: a permanent civil service *needs* to be neutral. Of course, the relationship also operates the other way around: if neutrality is undermined then there is a danger that permanence will follow. Had the Labour party arrived in government concerned about civil service neutrality it could have completely changed the basis of the British civil service by making wholesale political appointments to ensure official loyalty, but Tony Blair does not appear to have done so.

Ironically, the structural reforms put in place by the previous Conservative administrations could have given the Labour party the capacity to make sweeping changes. The fact is that heads of executive agencies and senior civil servants have been given employment contracts that allow them to be removed under the pretext of poor

Openness of recruitment

Michael Howard v Derek Lewis

In January 1995, a number of prisoners escaped from Parkhurst Prison. An investigation followed and was published as the Learmont Report. This was highly critical of the Prison Service. Michael Howard, the Home Secretary, asked Derek Lewis, Head of the Prison Service – an executive agency – to resign over the issue. When Lewis refused to go voluntarily he was dismissed by the Home Secretary.

The resulting public conflict illustrated the difficulties associated with the division of accountablity between policy (the minister's responsibility) and operational matters (the civil servant's).

Michael Howard's view was that the breakout had been made possible by the ineffectiveness of Lewis. The latter countered that his job had been made impossible by continual *interference* from the Home Secretary, and that Michael Howard had in fact defined policy matters as any that were successful, while operational matters were any that involved Prison Service failure! Therefore the Home Secretary could take the credit when it suited him and pass the buck in the case of failure.

Whatever the rights and wrongs of this particular case, it illustrates clearly the *potential* for confusion surrounding the division of accountability between ministers and their civil servants. Indeed, the first Home Secretary of the new Labour administration in 1997 has resumed responsibility for both the policy and operational aspects of the Prison Service.

performance when in fact they might simply not suit the incoming administration. Furthermore the increasing openness of civil service recruitment allows a new administration to advertise vacancies and to appoint officials who will best fit their desired profile – political or otherwise.

Accountability

Perhaps the issue that has caused greatest controversy as a result of the Conservative reforms is that of **accountability**. Earlier in this chapter it was proposed that ministers are increasingly unwilling to resign in the wake of departmental errors. Indeed, Sir Robin Butler, in his evidence to the Scott Enquiry in 1995, has established the principle that ministers are responsible for policy decisions and should not take responsibility for departmental errors *if they are operational in their nature*. Unfortunately this does not help to establish clear lines of responsibility for departmental actions.

This state of affairs has been made somewhat worse by the creation of executive agencies and by the advent of market testing, as described above. If a minister is already having difficulty coping with the running of his or her department, surely that minister cannot be held accountable for the actions of executive agencies – and even private companies – carrying out market-tested work?

The situation at the moment is that, if a minister is asked a parliamentary question about an executive agency, he or she can pass the question to the agency's chief executive for a written response. However, there is no constitutional mechanism to hold an increasingly disjointed administration to account.

The civil service and 'New Labour'

Any party that has been outside the halls of government for many years has worries about the loyaly of the civil servants with whom it hopes to work. Some senior members of 'New Labour' (the term used to describe the Labour party since Tony Blair's arrival as its leader) were no exception to this.

Eighteen years of Conservative government would, they argued, have inevitably tainted the attitudes and beliefs of civil servants, even if they had been neutral to begin with. As Peter Hennessy has put it:

'There were problems ... associated with having an ideological government (by British standards) in office for so long. In part, these have to do with an increasing lack of familiarity with other kinds of thinking in the ministerial suites. For example if you joined the Department of the Environment after May 1979, you would be quite senior now. Yet you will not be able to recall a time when local government was seen by ministers as part of a solution rather than always part of the problem.' (*The Hidden Wiring*, Victor Gollancz, 1995)

There was talk of dismissal of senior civil servants suspected of having Conservative sympathies, and the introduction of personal advisers on a very large scale – perhaps akin to the ministerial Cabinets used in France.

Aware of these concerns, civil servants have made a particular effort to set Labour's fears to rest. By the beginning of 1997, while still only the official Opposition, all of Labour's shadow cabinet had met the Permanent Secretaries of the departments they shadowed, and Tony Blair's aids had made it clear that there would not be a 'bloodletting' or wholesale reform of the service.

Six months into the new Labour government's period of office, continuity and stability certainly appeared to be the order of the day. There had not been an exodus of higher civil servants, nor had there been any attempt at new reforms. However, this is perhaps not surprising. New administrations usually arrive in office with lengthy agendas of economic and social reforms. Whilst the current Labour government might not seem to have an agenda on the scale of that of its 1945 counterpart, or of Mrs Thatcher's new administration of 1979, its priorities are likely to be outward-looking rather than internal reform. Even a radical like Margaret Thatcher did not turn her attention to the civil service in earnest until her second and third terms of office. If Tony Blair achieves his aim of a second full term for the Labour party, the civil service might then expect some further scrutiny.

Continuity and stability

Having said that, the Conservative party in opposition has been quick to point to some low-key changes that have been made to the civil service. In October 1997 it was reported that five information or press officers had been moved from their departments owing to the dissatisfaction of their new bosses. Traditionally, departmental press officers are recruited from the Government Information Service, except for those for the Treasury and Foreign Office who are, equally traditionally, recruited from the service's high-fliers. It is possible, though by no means clear, that the practice of these two ministries might be used across the board in future.

The role of the Cabinet Secretary, currently Sir Richard Wilson, may come under scrutiny. The Cabinet Secretary is not only head of the civil service but is also potentially one of the Prime Minister's closest advisers – the position is thus a sensitive one.

Further perspectives on the civil service

The discussion in this chapter of potential or actual civil service power and bias possibly paints a picture of civil servants and ministers at loggerheads in an adversarial relationship. As in all other areas of politics, such a two-dimensional view is an oversimplification. The voices of those politicians who have had poor relationships with their civil servants have perhaps dominated the debate on the position of civil servants in British government, giving the impression that the civil service is a hidden, conspiratorial secret government. There are alternative points of view.

The government community model

Hugh Heclo and Aaron Wildavsky put forward the view that the core of central government is a small village (*The Private Government of Public Money*, Macmillan, 1981). Ministers and civil servants work together in the enclosed community of government administration. Both parties represent their department on the wider stage, and both are fighting for the well-being and advancement of that department. While they may disagree from time to time about the best way to further their cause, they are basically working together according to the agreed rules of the political game.

Agreed rules of the political game

It is from this perspective that civil servants often voice their desire for a strong minister to represent them with vigour in Cabinet, in Parliament and in public. Heclo and Wildavsky quote a civil servant as follows:

'*Civil servants hate a weak minister* [who] *reflects badly on the department. If he waffles in debate or is getting kicked about by his colleagues, it affects the department. His permanent secretary, when he goes to the Reform Club, will be embarassed and pitied by other permanent secretaries.*'

Sir Norman Fowler, a former Conservative Cabinet minister and Chairman of the Conservative party, has said:

'*The only situation in which the civil service is likely to initiate change is when there is a policy vacuum because ministers are not clear about what they want to do.*' (*Ministers Decide*, Chapman, 1991)

The bureaucratic expansionism model

Empire building

Another view, expressed by W Niskanen, is that civil servants, as bureaucrats, are always seeking to build their empires – either by expanding the scope of their department or by increasing the size of their budget (*Bureaucracy: Servant or Master?*, London Institute of Economic Affairs, 1973).

This view is similar to that expressed in economics – that company managers are often not seeking to maximize the profits of their company for the shareholders but to maximize the size of the company, because with that expansion comes power and prestige. Bureaucrats are in a similar position: by trying to increase the size of their budgets they may increase their own power and status without any thought for gaining value for money for the taxpayer and customer.

This view became popular among the right-wing of the Conservative party in the 1970s and 1980s and is the basis of many of the reforms that the Conservative administrations proposed between 1979 to 1997. By tackling the civil service regarding their attitudes – which, as we have seen, Margaret Thatcher often did not like – and their apparent inefficiency, the bureaucratic stranglehold on public policy-making could be broken.

Exercises

Short questions

1 **a** What recent changes have taken place in the practice of appointing senior civil servants?
b What are the implications of these changes?
(ULEAC, January 1992)

2 In what circumstances do ministers resign?
(ULEAC, January 1993)

3 **a** Define the convention of individual ministerial responsibility.

b How does it operate in practice?
(ULEAC, January 1995)

4 What principles govern the relationship of civil servants to ministers?
(ULEAC, June 1993)

5 Outline the case for the neutrality of civil servants.
(ULEAC, January 1994)

6 Outline the traditional features of the British civil service.
(EdExcel, January 1995)

Essay questions

1 State a case (a) for and (b) against the view that the civil service has too much power.
(ULEAC, June 1992)

2 Has the role of the civil service changed in recent years?
(ULEAC, June 1994)

3 Has the notion of a politically neutral civil service come under threat?
(ULEAC, June 1991)

4 'Civil servants may be civil, but do they serve?' Discuss this comment regarding the political relationship between ministers and civil servants.
(Cambridge, June 1994)

5 'The reforms of the 1980s have made the civil service more efficient but less accountable.' Discuss.
(Oxford, June 1994)

6 Explain why permanence, political neutrality and anonymity are regarded as important characteristics of the civil service.
(Oxford & Cambridge, June 1993)

7 Discuss the constitutional significance of recent changes in the civil service.
(EdExcel, June 1996)

8 How can ministers control their civil servants?
(EdExcel, January 1995)

Data response question

The following is taken from Peter Hennessy, *Contemporary Record*, Philip Allan, 1988.

'The place is St George's House in the shadow of Windsor Castle; the occasion, an Anglo-American seminar on bureaucracy; the time, the spring of 1984, well into Mrs Thatcher's second term; the speaker is a neat, precise, bespectacled Englishman in his forties, sporting a watch and chain.

"The British civil service," he declares, "is a great rock on the tideline. The political

wave, Labour or Conservative, rolls in, washes over it and ebbs. The rock is exposed again to the air virtually unchanged." He pauses. "But Mrs Thatcher has been applying sticks of dynamite to that rock."

The speaker was Clive Priestly, a former Whitehall Under-Secretary held in high esteem by the Prime Minister for the work he had done as a chief of staff to Lord Raynor of Marks & Spencer, her efficiency adviser. Mr Priestly's remarks were addressed to Mrs Thatcher as dynamiter of bureaucratic waste ... But there are observers in Parliament, the press and Whitehall itself who believe that more than one stick of dynamite has been applied by the demolition expert in No. 10, with damaging results to the constitutional masonry.'

1   What 'sticks of dynamite', other than the one referred to in the passage, have been applied to the British civil service by the 'demolition expert in No. 10'?

2   Discuss whether these 'sticks of dynamite' have produced 'damaging results to the constitutional masonry'.

3   What kind of work had Clive Priestly done as chief of staff to Lord Rayner?

4   How does this concern with civil service efficiency relate to the general context of the Conservative government's policies?

(ULEAC, June 1990)

8 The monarchy

Questions to be answered in this chapter

- What is the role of the monarch in contemporary society?

- What are the arguments for and against keeping the monarchy?

Terms to know

- Authority
- Civil List
- Constitutional conventions
- Constitutional monarchy
- Divine right of kings
- Head of state
- Meritocratic
- Non-partisan
- 'Reserve' powers
- Royal assent
- Unrepresentative

Introduction

New Labour's commitment to constitutional reform has not, as yet, embraced the monarchy. In fact, Prime Minister Tony Blair has seemed keen to foster a good working relationship with members of the Royal Family, especially the Prince of Wales. However, the untimely death of Diana, Princess of Wales, highlighted a great deal of popular unrest concerning the role of the monarchy. Whilst a wave of grief swept across the country, members of the Royal Family were criticized in some quarters for seeming too distant and out of touch with popular feeling. As a result, there seems to have been a conscious decision to give the Royal Family a more populist touch that, without Diana, had been lacking. If this can be achieved it is likely that the position of the monarch will be secured well into the next millenium.

The development of the constitutional monarchy

The institution of the monarchy in Britain dates back to the ninth century. It has continued with only one interruption since. Theoretically, the throne is handed down on an hereditary principle to the eldest son, or to the eldest daughter if there are no male children. However, at times, there have been departures from this principle, as kings and queens have been brought in from abroad to fill vacancies.

Originally, the monarch was extremely powerful, holding legislative and executive powers. However, the monarch's power was always exercised in consultation with the

Magna Carta

barons. The Magna Carta, signed by King John in 1215, was intended to be a confirmation of the monarch's relationship with the barons rather than a new departure. It was signed by the king in order to prevent a civil war with barons from the north and east.

Great Council

During the thirteenth century the barons continued to be uneasy about the power of the king. In 1258 there were demands for the monarch to hold a Great Council. It met in 1264 and is widely considered to be the origin of Parliament. The Council met more regularly at the end of the century as Edward I requested funds for his campaigns to pacify the Scots and Welsh. By this time it was beginning to be called Parliament.

Finance

The reason for the extension of Parliament's power was the king's need for money. The monarch's normal sources of revenue were insufficient to fight extended wars, and so additional taxation was required. In view of this, the composition of Parliament had to be broadened in order to include the rich merchants whose support the monarch needed. Increasingly, merchants and knights met separately from the lords and clergy and Parliament began to develop two *houses* – the Commons and the Lords.

It is from the end of the thirteenth century that Parliament's function of controlling finance originates and from this function many significant battles between king and Parliament would unfold.

Tudors and Stuarts

Tudor monarchs consulted Parliament about finance and, increasingly, about making laws. As they did so, they gave Parliament legitimacy and helped to establish its **authority**. The power and legitimacy of Parliament became an important issue under the Stuart monarchs. James I dissolved Parliament over a dispute concerning finance. When he recalled it ten years later, he rapidly dismissed the members again, believing that they were exceeding their power.

The idea that Parliament was becoming too powerful and encroaching on the power of the monarch came to a head during the reign of Charles I. Charles believed in the **divine right of kings**. According to this theory, the king was given his authority by God and so all institutions were subordinate to the monarch and their powers were derived from him.

Civil War

Once again, under Charles, king and Parliament could not agree about finance and the king viewed its members' intransigence as a challenge to his authority. Parliament was dissolved for eleven years until 1640, but then recalled. The new Parliament, known as the Long Parliament, ordered the arrest and execution of Strafford, one of the king's ministers, passed laws that limited the power of the monarch, and attempted to insist that the king's ministers should be approved by Parliament. This was too much for the king and the war between royalists and parliamentarians broke out in 1642. Charles I was executed in 1649.

Glorious Revolution

After a short period of republican government, the monarchy was restored in 1660 when Charles II assumed the throne. Nevertheless, conflict between the monarch and Parliament broke out again under James II, who believed in the divine right of kings and was also a Catholic. The religious issue caused considerable division, and in 1688 James was forced to flee to France. He was replaced on the English throne jointly by William of Orange and Mary.

The accession of William and Mary was a crucial turning point in the relationship between monarch and Parliament. In 1689 both monarchs signed the Bill of Rights which confirmed the supremacy of Parliament. As a result, **constitutional monarchy** was born, and since 1689 the power of Parliament has never been in doubt.

At the beginning of the eighteenth century, George, Elector of Hanover, became king when Anne died without an heir. George I's command of English was poor and he seemed to care little for England. Therefore, he left much of the day-to-day running of his government to Sir Robert Walpole, his chief minister – later to be known as the Prime Minister.

Walpole

For a short time, George III tried to bypass the Prime Minister and Cabinet by attempting to manipulate voting in Parliament. However, this was short-lived and with the 1832 Reform Act the dawn of democratic government had arrived. By this time, the power of the monarch to dissolve Parliament and to choose the Prime Minister had largely passed to the latter, the Commons and the electorate.

The power of the monarch

The 'reserve' powers

Traditionally, the monarch had the power to summon and dissolve Parliament, to appoint the Prime Minister and to grant the **royal assent** to Acts of Parliament. Although the monarch retains these powers, in practice they have passed to the Prime Minister or the Commons as a whole or, to some extent, the people.

A monarch who refused to give the royal assent to a bill would be likely to face the threat of abolition from Parliament. The first-past-the-post electoral system (see page 22) engineers such majorities in the House of Commons that it is usually quite clear who should become Prime Minister, and that minister is normally given a general election when it is requested.

Realities of power

However, it is perhaps too easy to discount the powers of the monarch. As the extract from Peter Hennessy's article in *The Economist* (on pages 168–69) shows, there are circumstances in which the power of the monarch would be extremely important. In addition, there are no rules about how these powers should be used. However, if the powers were used, the monarch would be put into a political situation.

The fact that the monarch could still, in a constitutional democracy, become involved in a political situation disputes the common belief that the monarch is now above politics. It is true that, since Queen Victoria, monarchs have been required to be **non-partisan**, but they can become embroiled in political controversy.

Non-partisan

'The right to be consulted ...'

The constitutionalist Walter Bagehot believed that the monarch had 'the right to be consulted, the right to encourage and the right to warn'. These rights are based on the non-partisan nature of the monarch. The Prime Minister meets the monarch every week to give a brief on the affairs of state, and can take advantage of any advice

Bagehot

the monarch wishes to give. In this way, the monarch can act as a check on politicians.

By early 1995, Elizabeth II had seen ten Prime Ministers come, and nine go, and so had a great deal of experience of government. The historian Peter Hennessy quotes the queen as saying:

'They know that one can be impartial. I think it's rather nice to feel that one's a sort of sponge and everybody can come and tell one things. And some things stay there and some things go out of the other ear and some things never come out at all.'

The authority of the monarch

Although, under most circumstances, the powers of the monarch are exercised on the advice of ministers, monarchs derive authority from their position in the British political system.

Head of state

Ambassador

As **head of state**, the monarch performs many ceremonial functions both at home and abroad. While the political head of government is the Prime Minister, the monarch can take advantage of their non-partisan position to unite the country and to build relationships with foreign leaders independently of the political process. This has been particularly important in the Commonwealth. While Margaret Thatcher was Prime Minister, there were often divisions between Commonwealth leaders over, for example, the American invasion of Grenada in the West Indies, and the issue of sanctions against South Africa.

Symbolic role

The monarch also has a symbolic role. Many officials of the state see themselves as loyal to the state rather than to the government of the day. This might be true of civil servants or members of the armed forces. The monarch provides a focus for such loyalty.

Tradition

As the longest surviving political institution in Britain, the monarchy is a symbol of the history and tradition of the British political system. In this role the monarchy also becomes a symbol for continuity and stability. Critics argue that this even extends to the class system, which the monarch heads. As long as the monarchy survives, they argue, so will the British class system.

Arguments for and against the monarchy

Class system

The monarch, as head of the class system, represents the feudal system of medieval England and not the classless society that modernizers would like to see. This criticism comes not only from the left of British politics. Liberals, too, believe in equality of opportunity and upward mobility in society. They believe in a **meritocratic** system in which people are appointed and promoted according to talent rather than birthright. The monarch is not identified with these ideals.

The fact that the monarch is not elected and stands apart from partisan politics allows the monarch to act as a unifying force in British politics and society. The military take an oath of allegiance to the monarch and many civil servants see the monarch, the symbol of the state, as the focus of their loyalty. Also, as we have seen, the non-partisan position of monarchs allows them to give independent advice to the Prime Minister.

Unifying force

Not only are monarchs **unrepresentative** as head of the class system, they are also unelected. If the queen's role were purely ceremonial, say critics, this might be tolerable. However, we saw above that Queen Elizabeth II does have the power to become involved in politically sensitive issues, such as the appointment of a Prime Minister or the dissolution of Parliament. Critics also question whether an unelected individual should have the power to become involved in politics since they consider it to be out of step with the rest of Britain's political system.

Undemocratic

The vagueness that surrounds the monarch's **'reserve' powers** is typical of the vagueness of many of Britain's **constitutional conventions**. However, ideas such as the monarch's ability to act as a check on the power of politicians in order to safeguard constitutional propriety or to prevent the abuse of power is a misleading fiction. In reality, the monarch does not have the power to check the politicians. If a monarch attempted to do so, he or she would run the risk of being ignored or the monarchy abolished. Therefore, to suggest that the monarch could act as a check is to give the British constitution an additional safeguard that does not really exist.

Constitutional check

Finally, critics point to the high cost of keeping the monarchy. The money to finance members of the Royal Family is provided from the **Civil List** and in the 1990s amounts to almost £8 million per year. Some suggest that this is far too expensive, especially the amount of money that is given to peripheral members of the family who, according to the argument, perform no useful function. It is argued that a president would be much cheaper and adhere more closely to the principles of democratic government.

Expense

The alternative view is that the pomp and ceremony surrounding the monarchy is a tourist attraction and as such earns a large amount of revenue for the British economy.

Tourist attraction

Ultimately, as the Duke of Edinburgh pointed out in an interview with *The Daily Telegraph* in 1994, the monarchy should survive only so long as the British people wish to see it survive. In a *Guardian*–ICM poll of 1000 people conducted in January 1995, 28 per cent stated they would like to see the monarchy abolished and 34 per cent stated that they were 'not especially keen' on the monarchy, but supported it because it is 'better than the alternatives'. Only 36 per cent of respondents described themselves as strong supporters of the monarchy, compared with 90 per cent ten years earlier. In 1996, a Gallup poll found that the Royal Family had gone down in the estimation of 57 per cent of respondents. Nevertheless, in a telephone poll taken by Granada Television in 1997, 66 per cent of respondants were in favour of retaining the monarchy.

Exercises

Short questions

1 Distinguish between the power and authority of the monarch.

2 Outline a case for and against the retention of the monarchy in Britain.

Essay questions

1 Does the monarchy still have a significant role to play in the British political system?
(Cambridge, June 1994)

2 Is it any longer possible to justify an hereditary monarch and an unelected House of Lords within a modern democratic system of government?
(Oxford & Cambridge, June 1993)

Data response question

The following is taken from Peter Hennessy, 'The throne behind the power', *The Economist*, 24 December 1994.

The powers of the monarch

'... *from overt and covert sources, through discreet conversations over lunch, in the interstices of chats about entirely different matters, as is the British way, I have distilled the following details of the monarch's "reserve powers" as they are thought to exist by those in a position both to know and, if circumstances require it, to advise on the basis of that knowledge:*

- *Only the monarch can dissolve Parliament, causing a general election to be held.*

- *Only the monarch can appoint a Prime Minister.*

- *After an indecisive election, the monarch is required to act only if the incumbent Prime Minister resigns before a queen's speech is presented to Parliament, or after failing to win a majority for that legislative programme in the House of Commons.*

- *The overarching principle at such delicate times is that the queen's government must be carried on and that the monarch is not drawn into political controversy by those politicians competing to receive her commission to form a government.*

- *Normally, an outgoing Prime Minister is asked to advise the monarch on the succession, but it is for the monarch to ask for that advice, and, if given, it is proffered as informal advice that can be rejected, not formal advice that must be acted upon.*

- *After an inconclusive election result, if the Prime Minister resigns, the monarch will normally offer the first chance to form an administration to the party leader commanding the largest block of seats in the Commons.*

- *A Prime Minister can "request" but not "demand" a dissolution of Parliament, and the monarch can refuse. Circumstances in which this might happen are, in the words of a former Cabinet secretary, Lord Armstrong, "improbable", but the power to withhold consent is a check on any "irresponsible exercise" of a Prime Minister's right to make such a request.*

The circumstances in which a royal refusal could be forthcoming are, in the words of the late Sir Alan Lascelles, former private secretary to George VI and Elizabeth II, if "the existing Parliament was still vital, viable and capable of doing its job" or if the monarch "could rely on finding another Prime Minister who could [govern] for a reasonable period, with a working majority in the House of Commons".'

1   What effect might reform of the electoral system have on the role of the monarch?

2   How far do Peter Hennessy's arguments suggest that Britain is in need of a written constitution?

9 The judiciary

Questions to be answered in this chapter

- How is the judiciary organized in Britain?
- To what extent are judges independent of politics?
- What is the role of the judiciary in the UK?
- Should the power of the judiciary be increased?
- How adequately are civil liberties protected in Britain?

Terms to know

- Bill of rights
- Civil rights
- Collective rights
- Common law
- Freedom of speech
- Human rights
- Inalienable rights
- Individual rights
- Judicial creativity
- Judicial discretion
- Judicial independence
- Judicial inquiries
- Judicial restraint
- Judicial review
- Law Lords
- Lord Chancellor
- Natural rights
- Non-partisan
- Political rights
- Politicization
- Precedent
- Rule of law
- Separation of powers
- Treaty of Rome
- *Ultra vires*
- Unelected
- Unrepresentative

Introduction

Theoretically, or constitutionally, judges should not be involved in politics. In practice they are. The very nature of their role brings them into the political arena to an extent that is unavoidable. On top of this, the activities of judges can add to their politicization. Contacts with the media, a desire to use their creative powers and, allegedly, a biased application of those powers, can all combine to bring judges to the centre of politics and, sometimes, controversy.

To an extent the politicization of judges comes with their power. To increase their power would automatically increase their political involvement. Therefore any decision to improve protection of human rights in Britain, probably through the introduction of a bill of rights, would increase judicial power – and, in turn, the political involvement of an unrepresentative and unaccountable group.

Judges and the constitution

Traditional liberal constitutional theory states that the three main branches of government should be separate. Each should have their own functions and their own personnel. This idea is known as the **separation of powers** and is usually traced back to the eighteenth-century French philosopher Montesquieu. Heavily influenced by John Locke, he believed that liberty could only be preserved and tyranny avoided if the doctrine of the separation of powers was adhered to. Without it there 'could be no liberty' and there would be 'an end to everything'.

In line with this doctrine, each branch of government has its own functions. The legislature makes the law, the executive implements the law and the judiciary applies the law.

The process of applying the law involves interpreting the laws made by Parliament and applying them to particular cases. As they carry out their functions, judges should not be subjected to political interference. If politicians were to be involved in the judicial process, they might be tempted to influence the way that judges apply the law. In doing so, the impartiality of the law would be impaired and individuals might not be treated equally and fairly. Political opponents, hostile groups, different classes or races might not receive equal treatment at the hands of a politically motivated judiciary. The opportunities for political influence are, as John Locke said, 'too great a temptation to human frailty'.

Maintaining judicial independence

The British constitution contains a number of provisions to ensure that judges remain independent of politicians.

- Judges should be selected in a **non-partisan** manner. Those to lower courts are appointed by the **Lord Chancellor**, who also advises the monarch on appointments to the High Court. Appointments to the Court of Appeal are made by the monarch on the advice of the Prime Minister. However, political matters should not be considered when these appointments are being made.

- Judges should have security of tenure; in other words, they are permanent. They cannot be changed when there is a new government and do not have to shape their decisions in order to hold on to their jobs.

Once appointed, judges of the High Court hold office 'during good behaviour' and can only be removed by the monarch following a vote in both houses of Parliament. Only one judge has been removed in this way since 1701. Sir Jonah Barrington, a judge in the High Court of Admiralty in Ireland, lost his position in 1830 for taking money paid to the court.

Judges in lower courts can be removed by the Lord Chancellor on the grounds of incapacity or misbehaviour. In 1983, Judge Campbell was dismissed after being caught smuggling cigarettes and alcohol into Britain.

- Judges' salaries are relatively high in order to prevent corruption and to reflect the responsibility of their positions. In addition, their salaries are paid from the Consolidated Fund. This means that Parliament does not vote on the appropriation of money for judges' salaries and so they do not become subject to party political debate. In 1995, the most senior judge in the criminal courts, the Lord Chief Justice, earned a salary of £118,179; a judge of the Court of Appeal was paid a salary of £108,922.

Debate
- Judicial decisions or matters awaiting a judicial judgement are not discussed in Parliament. This is a parliamentary convention to prevent the work of the judiciary becoming part of political debate.

Non-partisan
- Judges do not take part in partisan political activity. They are not allowed to join political parties, although they are allowed to vote.

Kilmuir rules
- Traditionally, judges do not make any public comments on matters of party political debate. This convention was clearly stated in 1955 by Lord Chancellor Kilmuir in a letter to the director-general of the BBC, in which he stated that it was 'undesirable for members of the judiciary to broadcast on the wireless or to appear on television … [because] … every utterance which he makes in public, except in the course of the actual performance of his judicial duties, must necessarily bring him within the focus of criticism' (see page 178).

Preserving judicial independence does not mean only that judges should be protected from interference by politicians. It also means that judges should be prevented from entering political debate.

Political and judicial decisions

Political decisions
As part of the drive for judicial independence, political thinkers have attempted to make a distinction between political and judicial decisions. Political decisions are policy-making decisions involving choices between alternative courses of action. They should be made by elected politicians and so, to an extent, are biased according to the political outlook of the governments of the day.

Judicial decisions
Judicial decisions are procedural or mechanistic decisions based on the laws already laid down by Parliament. Therefore, they are merely concerned with applying the law, not with making the law. They are limited in scope and should be politically unbiased.

The rule of law

Rule of law
The need for **judicial independence** is reinforced by the doctrine of the **rule of law**. This is usually associated with A V Dicey and has become a central pillar of the British constitution. According to Dicey, the concept can be divided into a number of parts:

- All citizens should be limited by the law.

- The government should be limited by the law.

- Everyone should be treated fairly by the normal courts of law.

The doctrine of the rule of law

In 1885, A V Dicey wrote *Introduction to the Study of the Law of the Constitution*. He divided the doctrine of the rule of law into three components:

- 'The absolute supremacy of regular law as opposed to the influence of arbitrary power and excluding the existence of arbitrariness, of prerogative or even wide discretionary authority on the part of the government ... a man may be punished for a breach of the law, but for nothing else.'

- 'Equality before the law, or the equal subjection of all classes to the ordinary law of the land administered by the ordinary law courts.'

- 'The constitution is the result of the ordinary law of the land.'

The aim of the rule of law is to create 'a government of laws not men'. This means that laws will be applied in a predictable manner by neutral judges and all citizens can rely on equal treatment from the courts. If a person is arrested they should know which law they are accused of breaking and should expect to receive specified treatment at the hands of the law. The treatment will include access to a lawyer, trial by jury, and the right to be considered innocent until proven guilty.

Government of 'laws not men'

The rule of law is designed to avoid a situation in which politicians might try to apply laws according to their mood, particularly against their political opponents. Furthermore, the government itself is subject to the law and cannot act outside the law.

The judiciary and politics

Although judges should not be involved in politics, to a greater or lesser extent they are. Constitutionally, judges are expected to make mechanistic decisions with little or no room for their own opinions, but this is impossible. The nature of their political involvement is partly attributable to the nature of their position, but to some extent they have been brought further and further into politics over recent years both by their own actions and by those of the government.

The Lord Chancellor

The Lord Chancellor is an institutionalized infringement of the separation of powers. Although head of the judicial branch of the government, the Lord Chancellor is also a member of the executive and the legislature – and so crosses the dividing lines laid down by Montesquieu.

Separation of powers

The Lord Chancellor, as a member of the legislature, presides over the House of Lords. The Lord Chancellor acts as Speaker of the Lords but, unlike the counterpart in the Commons, he or she is not a neutral referee but a government spokesperson.

Legislature

As a member of the executive, the Lord Chancellor is appointed by the Prime Minister and is a member of the Cabinet. He or she presides over a department of approximately 12,000 staff with an annual budget of around £2500 million. The main

Executive

responsibility is to supervise the running of the English legal system, and so the Lord Chancellor must also be be responsible for judicial reform. It is not the Lord Chancellor's role to offer legal advice to the government – that is the province of the Attorney-General.

Judiciary

In a judicial capacity the Lord Chancellor heads the judiciary and regularly liaises with other senior members of the judiciary. He or she is also able to sit as one of the **Law Lords** to hear appeal cases.

'Constitutional buffer'

Although the Lord Chancellor's roles are obviously an infringement of the doctrine of the separation of powers, many holders of the office have attempted to justify the act of straddling all three branches of government by viewing the position as a 'constitutional buffer'. This was most clearly expressed by former Lord Chancellor Hailsham:

'*In the absence of a paper constitution, the separation of powers is the primary function of the Lord Chancellor, a task which he can only fulfil if he sits somewhere near the apex of the constitutional pyramid armed with a long barge pole to keep off marauding craft from any quarter.*' (Lecture to the Holdsworth Club, quoted in Joshua Rozenberg, *The Search for Justice*, Hodder & Stoughton, 1994)

Appointments

In Lord Hailsham's view, the Lord Chancellor is acting to *preserve* the separation of powers, rather than undermining it. However, the appointment of judges is one area where there is a danger of such a breach. As we have seen, judges should be independent of politics and should be unbiased. The fact that a member of the government is responsible for making judicial appointments potentially puts judicial neutrality at risk.

Politicization

In 1992, Lord Chancellor Mackay made, or recommended, 1300 appointments and so had ample opportunity to make political appointments had he so wished. However, evidence of **politicization** is hard to find. It is widely believed that the Labour government of 1974–79 stood in the way of Lord Donaldson's promotion to Master of the Rolls because he had held office as president of the National Industrial Relations Board, a body set up under the Conservative government of Edward Heath (1970–74). Lord Donaldson was promoted only when a Conservative government came to power in 1979.

Secrecy

The secrecy surrounding judicial appointments does not help to reduce the fear of politics playing a part in the judicial arena. There are no job descriptions; the higher appointments are not advertised, and there is no interview process. As David Pannick has written:

'*Judges are appointed by a process that resembles a pre-1965 Conservative party leadership contest or a Papal Conclave rather than the choice of law-makers in a modern democracy.*' (David Pannick, *Judges*, Oxford University Press, 1987)

In 1986, Lord Hailsham published a guide to appointment policies and procedures in order to 'dispel any lingering sense of mystery or obscurity'. His successor, Lord Mackay, published his own version in 1990, but the terms of reference continue to be vague.

The Law Lords

As well as being part of the legislature, the House of Lords is the highest court in the land. As such, it acts as a court of appeal and cases are heard by a panel of senior judges appointed to the Lords for this purpose. These are the Law Lords.

In 1994 the following were the Law Lords, shown in order of precedence, with their ages in brackets:

Lord Keith of Kinkel (71)
Lord Templeman (73)
Lord Goff of Chieveley (67)
Lord Jauncey of Tullichettle (68)
Lord Brown-Wilkinson (63)
Lord Mustill (62)
Lord Slynn of Hadley (63)
Lord Woolf (60)
Lord Lloyd of Berwick (64)
Lord Nolan (65)

Precedence in the Lords is based on the order of appointment.

Over half of the Law Lords have been appointed since 1991. Lords Brown-Wilkinson, Mustill, Slynn and Woolf are all considered quite liberal, while Lords Lloyd and Nolan are believed to be less obviously liberal, but nonetheless committed to overturning miscarriages of justice. It was Lord Lloyd who presided over the final appeal of the 'Birmingham Six' in 1991, when he overturned the conviction of six men for the bombing of a pub in Birmingham in 1974. Lord Nolan presided over Judith Ward's appeal in 1992. Judith Ward had been convicted of the murder of twelve people who died when a bomb exploded on a coach. Her conviction was overturned owing to the unreliability of the evidence given by the police forensic scientist, Dr Frank Skuse, who had also been involved in the Birmingham Six case.

Judicial law-making

The main function of a judge is to apply law. According to constitutional theory, law is made by Parliament and judges decide how the law should be applied to a particular case. The implication of this is that a judge's decisions are mechanical and straightforward – the judge picks up a law and applies it to a case almost like completing a multiple-choice question paper. However, this could not be further from the truth. No law is so straightforward that it can be interpreted in such a mechanical way.

Mechanistic decision-making

As H L A Hart wrote: 'All rules have a penumbra of uncertainty where the judge must choose between alternatives' (*The Concept of Law*, Clarendon Press, 1961). In effect, the judge must decide what the law actually means in order to apply it to a case. It is at this stage that there is room for **judicial discretion** or **judicial creativity**. The judges must choose between different interpretations of the law, and in doing so they are

Judicial creativity

Judicial decision-making interpreted

Lord Templeman describes the Law Lords at work:

'One of the five will say: "Looks to me as though the Court of Appeal got it quite right." ... And somebody else will say: "Oh, I'm not at all happy about the way they argued this point." ... And at that we'll go up and listen to the argument. And in the course of the argument, we'll argue amongst ourselves: when a Law Lord makes a point to a counsel, he's asking for the answer from the counsel, but he's also pointing out to his colleagues the way his mind is working. And then another Law Lord, who at that stage takes a slightly different view, comes in. Well then, of course, we have lunch. And at lunch, as we're going down, we'll have a sort of mild discussion and at the end of the day we'll have a mild discussion, and then the first serious discussion comes when counsel have finished. We throw everybody out, the doors are shut and the five of us sit in our horseshoe – five of us rather like the forward line of Manchester United. And the outside left who's the junior, he gives his opinion; he says he would dismiss this appeal for the following reasons, and we each do the same in turn. If we're agreed, then the presiding judge asks one of us, usually an expert in the particular field, to write the first judgement. If we're not agreed, we have a further discussion and then we all write separate judgements.

The next thing that happens is that whoever drafts a judgement circulates it to all the others. And even if we're agreed on it, each goes through and criticizes it, each asks for amendments. And so even if there's one judgement, it's a concerted team effort.

If we're not agreed, we might have lots of discussions. Although people don't believe this, it is a fact that one changes one's mind in the course of a case, if it's one of those knife-edge cases, in deference to the views of the other Law Lords. Sometimes I have said: "Well, I'm not convinced you're right, but I think it would make for unease and uncertainty if I dissented on this particular point, and therefore, I'm not going to dissent, although I have my doubts."'

Source: Hugo Young, *The Judges*, BBC Radio 4, 13 April 1988

creating law – this is known as **common law**. Judicial interpretation of statute law is unavoidable, but nevertheless, it puts judges in a political position because they are, in effect, making law.

Precedent

The extent to which judges are willing to make use of opportunities to use their judicial creativity varies between courts and between individual judges. To a large extent, judges tend to follow judgements made in previous cases; i.e. **precedent**.

Traditionally, judges' attitudes have been conservative and they have often been unwilling to depart from precedent, preferring to leave law-making to the politicians. It was not until 1966 that the House of Lords changed its procedures to allow the Law Lords to depart from precedent. Since then the Law Lords have been prepared to move away from precedent in civil cases, but have been much more reluctant to do so in criminal cases.

Nevertheless, there are a number of well-known examples of judges interpreting law, and in so doing they have become involved in controversial policy areas. In *Gillick v West Norfolk and Wisbech Area Health Authority* [1987], Victoria Gillick sought assurances from her area health authority that contraceptives would never be prescribed for her children, below the age of 16, without her consent. This case embroiled the Law Lords in a controversial area of social policy concerning the degree of control parents may exercise over their children. The Lords ruled that, if a doctor believed that the prescription of contraceptives was in the interests of the child, parental consent was not required.

Gillick case

A similar area of controversy was marital rape. Traditional common-law interpretation of the 1976 Sexual Offences (Amendment) Act was that unlawful sex meant sex outside marriage, and that a husband could not be convicted of raping his wife because the woman was said to have given her consent during the marriage ceremony. A series of decisions in the lower courts that eroded this exception to the crime of rape finally culminated in *R. v R.* [1991] before the House of Lords. In this case, the Law Lords ruled that the exception of marital rape should be overruled – and in doing so were making policy in a controversial area.

Marital rape

When judges decide to *reinterpret* the wording of statute law, they tend to follow the wording of the parliamentary statute quite closely. As Lord Diplock said in *Duport Steels Ltd v Sirs* [1980]:

'Parliament makes the laws, the judiciary interpret them ... The role of the judiciary is confined to ascertaining from the words that Parliament has approved as expressing its intention, what that intention was, and giving effect to it. Where the meaning of the statutory words is plain and unambiguous it is not for the judges to invent fancied ambiguities as an excuse for failing to give effect to its plain meaning because they themselves consider that the consequences of doing so would be expedient, or even unjust or immoral.'

Such an interpretation of the role of judges can be considered conservative or one of **judicial restraint**. Judges following such a line are reluctant to have the judiciary become politically involved to a greater extent than is necessary.

Judicial restraint

Some judges, notably the former Master of the Rolls Lord Denning, have argued that judges should be free to be much more active, in that they should be able to examine not only the words of a statute but also the motives of the law-makers lying behind the statute. This would involve examining the records of parliamentary debate in Hansard as well as any Law Commission reports that may have preceded the law. Lord Denning, in *Davis v Johnson* [1979], commented:

Lord Denning

'Some may say – and indeed have said – that judges should not pay any attention to what is said in Parliament. They should grope about in the dark for the meaning of an Act without switching on the light. I do not accede to this view ... And it is obvious that there is nothing to prevent a judge looking at these debates himself privately and getting some guidance from them.'

The danger of this attitude is that judges could be accused of 'usurping the role of the legislature'.

Judges and the media

Kilmuir rules

Traditionally, judges have been encouraged to keep their opinions and attitudes to themselves. The Kilmuir rules, laid down in 1955, were designed to prevent judges speaking their minds on radio and television (see page 172). In 1987, Lord Mackay abolished these rules as one of his first acts on taking office. Since then, judges at all levels have spoken for and against government policies. Lord Chief Justice Taylor, for example, has spoken out against government policy on legal aid, in favour of the incorporation of the European Convention on Human Rights into British law and against the Government's Criminal Justice Act of 1994.

Judge Pickles

Lower down the judicial hierarchy, Judge Pickles achieved notoriety by appearing regularly on television and radio and in newspaper articles, even before the abolition of the Kilmuir rules. His comments included the suggestion that young women might become pregnant in the interval between arrest and sentencing, in an attempt to avoid prison.

While it is possible to argue that judges have a right to give their opinions on legal matters and even matters of opinion, such pronouncements do little to reinforce the separation of the political and judicial branches of government.

Judicial attitudes and background

The fact that judges make law through their interpretations and that some have become outspoken in their comments regarding government policies means that judges' attitudes are a cause for concern.

John Griffith

In 1977, Professor John Griffith of the London School of Economics first argued that British judges could be viewed as an homogeneous group who share a set of views and attitudes. He described them as having 'a unifying attitude of mind, a political position, which is primarily concerned to protect and conserve values and institutions' (*The Politics of the Judiciary*, Fontana, 1977). In fact, Griffith went further and argued that 'the judicial conception of the public interest ... is threefold. It concerns, first, the interest of the state (including its moral welfare); secondly, the preservation of law and order, broadly interpreted; and, thirdly, the promotion of certain political views normally associated with the Conservative party.'

Issues

Griffith identified a number of areas which illustrate these shared attitudes. They include race relations, industrial relations, and public order issues. Of the three, industrial relations has probably been the most controversial area for judges. The industrial relations measures introduced by the Conservative governments of 1970–74 and 1979 until now have forced judges to become involved in a highly political area.

Social background

It can be argued that judges' perceptions of the national interest are a result of their backgrounds. From a Marxist point of view, the background of judges can be considered to be indicative of their likely attitudes. Hugh Collins, the legal academic, stated:

'*From* [a] *materialist perspective, ideas, knowledge and motivation were neither arbitrary flights of the imagination nor the product of research into the recesses of the*

178

mind, but were constructed in response to practical experiences.' (*Marxism and Law*, Oxford University Press, 1982)

Judges are generally male and white. They are usually from the middle/upper-middle classes, with a public-school background and are graduates of either Oxford or Cambridge University. Of the Law Lords listed on page 175, eight attended 'Oxbridge'. As John Griffith has said:

Education

'Judges have by their education and training and the pursuit of their profession as barristers, acquired a strikingly homogeneous collection of attitudes, beliefs and principles, which to them represent the public interest.'

In 1995 there were no black or Asian judges among the 124 judges of the Appeal or High Court, while only four of the 487 judges on the Circuit bench were from ethnic minorities. There was only one woman, Lord Justice Butler-Sloss, in the Court of Appeal, seven in the High Court, and only 28 on the Circuit Bench.

Race and gender

However, Griffith's argument is not completely watertight. The fact that the majority of judges come from a particular background does not necessarily indicate their belief systems and the ways in which they behave. Almost half of Labour Cabinet ministers between 1964 and 1979 were Oxbridge-educated, and almost a third had attended public school; nevertheless they were committed to socialist policies.

Griffith is also concerned that judges 'do not regard their role as radical or even reformist'. However, it is by no means clear that judges should see themselves as reformers. Given that they are **unelected**, perhaps they should confine their activities to applying the laws made by the legislators. From this position it is difficult to behave in a radical way.

Conservatism

This argument may be taken one step further. Marxists argue that every nation state has a dominant ideology. The function of the ideology is to lay down the belief system of a society. It shapes the formation of political institutions, the relationships between institutions and individuals, and the relationships between individuals. The laws of the state are designed to preserve the ideology. The dominant ideology in Britain is liberal and capitalist. Therefore, the laws are designed to preserve the system. Judges, as an arm of the British state, are required to uphold these laws and in turn to uphold the ideology. According to this view, it is unrealistic to expect judges to act in a way that is contrary to the dominant ideology of the society.

Marxism

Controversial law

Judges should apply the laws made by legislators, and as they do so they may be drawn into the middle of heated political debate. If the government, via Parliament, is passing laws that concern controversial areas of policy, it is only to be expected that judges will be called upon to apply these laws.

The Conservative administrations of 1979–90 illustrate very well the effect on the judiciary of controversial laws and the manner in which government chose to enforce them. Although the Official Secrets Act dates from 1911, Prime Minister Margaret Thatcher used the Act to hunt civil servants leaking information. The Ponting case

Margaret Thatcher's administrations

(1985) (see page 143) and the *Spycatcher* case (1986) (page 187) are examples of this. Although it was the government that chose to pursue the civil servants, it was the judges who were perceived to be in favour of the Official Secrets Act. Similarly, it was the Conservative government of 1979–90 which initiated legislation to limit the power of trade unions, but it was the judiciary that was called upon to apply the law and so became labelled anti-trade-union.

Judicial inquiries

Governments have also drawn the judiciary into the political debate by taking judges out of the courtroom and asking them to head **judicial inquiries** into a variety of incidents and issues. In 1994, Lord Justice Scott chaired the 'arms to Iraq' hearing in which government ministers were accused of breaking their own code of conduct by exporting weapons to Iraq. Lord Justice Taylor investigated the Hillsborough disaster of 1989 in which 93 people were killed and 200 injured in the crush inside a football stadium. Lord Nolan reported in May 1995 on his inquiry into the standards of ethics expected of MPs.

Perhaps the most controversial of judicial inquiries in recent years was headed by Lord Scott into the sale of arms to Iraq. This inquiry was a spin-off from the Matrix–Churchill case (see below) and involved a 'who's who' of the most senior civil servants and Conservative politicians from the governments of the 1980s giving evidence. Appearances by Margaret Thatcher and John Major topped the bill.

All these areas are controversial and potentially political. The judges' reports are always eagerly awaited and often form a basis for future government policy. Obviously, the reason for asking judges to chair such inquiries is their experience in dealing with a wide range of evidence and opinion. Nevertheless, from a constitutional point of view they may threaten judicial impartiality because judges are asked to draw conclusions on debatable matters.

Lord Scarman and the Brixton riots

Perhaps the most outstanding example of a government placing a judge at the head of a politically controversial inquiry occurred in 1981 when Lord Scarman was asked to look into the causes of the Brixton riots. During one weekend in April, riots broke out in the Brixton area of London. At the height of the disturbances 279 police officers and many members of the public were injured and 28 buildings were damaged or destroyed. Margaret Thatcher's government was heavily criticized for the unemployment and social deprivation that many believed had been the cause of the riots, while the Prime Minister herself believed that social deprivation could never justify criminal behaviour. Lord Scarman, a moderate judge, was asked by the Home Secretary, William Whitelaw, to produce a report. To take on such a politically explosive task put Lord Scarman in a very delicate position and, as Hugo Young said: 'Almost all that Scarman had to say about strengthening the police, and almost nothing he had to say about social reform, was put in train with Whitelaw's blessing' (Hugo Young, *One of Us*, Macmillan, 1989).

Judicial review

Judicial review concerns the ability of courts to review the action of other branches of government in order to determine their legality and constitutionality. It is an important element of the separation of powers as it offers a means to prevent the abuse of government power. It is most clearly illustrated in the USA where the Supreme Court, at the head of the judicial branch of government, has the power to check the other branches of government. It can do this by declaring acts of Congress and action by the President unconstitutional. Such decisions take the courts into controversial areas of governmental power and often require the judges to make political decisions.

In fact the activities of judges in the area of judicial review increased substantially in the 1980s and 1990s. In 1985 there were a little over 1000 applications for judical review; by 1990 this had doubled, and by 1994 the number had reached 3208.

In Britain the power of judicial review is limited by the fact that there is no codified constitution and by the doctrine of parliamentary sovereignty. Traditionally, in Britain any act of Parliament is, by definition, constitutional and is not subject to review by the courts. However, the judiciary does have the right to review the actions of the executive branch and local government.

Parliamentary sovereignty

Ultra vires

The basis for the review of the executive and local government is administrative law. Every action by central or local government must be based on law. If it is not, that branch of government is said to be acting beyond its powers, or ***ultra vires***.

The courts can declare an action *ultra vires* if it is contrary to the 'express terms' or the 'implied terms' of a statute. The former relates to terms specifically outlined in the statute, while the latter is concerned with the spirit of the statute. Both principles are illustrated by *Bromley LBC v Greater London Council* (1983), also known as the 'Fares Fair' case.

'Fares Fair' case

In this case the Greater London Council (GLC) was taken to court over its policy towards fares on London Transport facilities and their impact on ratepayers. The GLC proposed to reduce the fares on public transport, in line with election promises, even though this would cause an increase in the bill facing ratepayers. The House of Lords ruled that in doing so the council was acting *ultra vires*. By not trying to run public transport along traditional business lines it was acting contrary to the express terms of the Transport (London) Act 1969. The Lords also ruled that the GLC was acting outside the implied terms of the GLC's remit in that the council had a duty to ratepayers not to spend their money recklessly. The increases in rates were said to be contrary to this commitment.

More recent examples of the executive branch being checked by the judiciary have attracted a great deal of attention. They include Lord Rees-Mogg's case against the government's power to ratify the Maastricht Treaty (July 1993); Home Secretary Kenneth Baker being found in contempt of court for failing to comply with court instructions regarding an individual seeking political asylum (1993); and the Pergau Dam affair of 1994. In the latter, the courts ruled that the Foreign Secretary, Douglas Hurd, had acted *ultra vires* by linking the distribution of foreign aid to orders for British products. In this particular case, the Foreign Office granted aid to the Malaysian government to build the Pergau Dam in return for which the Malaysian government placed an order for British arms which was worth millions of pounds.

Pergau Dam

181

Judicial review and the EU

Since Britain became a member of the European Community, now known as the European Union (EU), the powers of judicial review available to British courts have increased.

Treaty of Rome

According to the **Treaty of Rome** (see page 213), which Britain signed to become a full member of the Community, EU law is supreme and takes precedence over the legislatures and laws of individual nation states. Although the treaty itself had no validity in British law, an Act of Parliament – the European Communities Act (1972) – brought it into effect domestically.

As a result of this Act, European law is now supreme in Britain and British law must adhere to its provisions. For the first time since the establishment of parliamentary sovereignty there is now a body of law against which British statute law can be judged. If a parliamentary statute contravenes EU law it must be repealed or amended by Parliament. If Parliament decided not to do so, it would, in effect, be tantamount to leaving the European Union.

Factortame case

The best-known case illustrating the supremacy of European law is *R. v Secretary of State for Transport, ex parte Factortame Ltd (No. 2) (1991)*, which is also known as the Factortame case. The House of Lords judged the 1988 Merchant Shipping Act to be unlawful because it contravened EU law, and suspended it. The attitude of the judiciary to the EU was summed up by Justice Hoffman in *Stoke-on-Trent County Council v B&Q Plc (1991)*:

'*The EEC Treaty is the supreme law of this country taking precedence over Acts of Parliament. Our entry into the EEC meant (subject to our undoubted but probably theoretical right to withdraw from the Community all together) Parliament surrendered its sovereign right to legislate contrary to the provisions of the Treaty on matters of social and economic policy.*'

By giving up much of its sovereignty as a result of the European Communities Act, Parliament has allowed the courts greater power of judicial review, so bringing them further into the political arena.

Judicial power

Despite the fact that membership of the EU has extended the powers of judicial review, many observers believe that the British judiciary should be given still greater powers by increasing judicial review.

In order to give the courts wider powers of judicial review, Britain's unwritten constitution would have to be replaced by a codified constitution together with a **bill of rights**. Such a document would give the courts an authority, higher than parliamentary law, against which to scrutinize the actions of the government.

Parliament restrained

This would have a considerable impact on certain branches of government. However, the body responsible for such regulation would be the unelected and **unrepresentative** judiciary. As a result, several observers have argued against giving such enhanced powers to the courts. Some of these issues are discussed more fully in Chapter 1, but the political implications for the judiciary are examined here.

Judicial review and policy-making

We saw above that the power of the judiciary to interpret law gives the courts considerable opportunity to make law. This would be much greater if the power of judicial review was extended. The implications of such a change in Britain can best be seen in the USA where the Supreme Court has the power to interpret not only law but also the constitution. Naturally, this is a broad, and in some cases vague, document so the court has considerable scope in its interpretations.

US Supreme Court

Comparison

'The Federal Constitutional Court is a major policy-making institution in Germany's sytem of government. ... this tribunal has evolved into the most active and powerful constitutional court in Europe. Its pivotal character in the German political system stems from its role as a judicial law-making body created for the specific purpose of deciding constitutional disputes under the Basic Law (formal name for the German constitution). In deciding such disputes – that is in interpreting the language and spirit of the Basic Law – the Constitutional Court has influenced the shape of Germany's political landscape, reaching deep into the heart of the existing state, guarding its institutions, circumscribing its powers, clarifying its goals and, in some instances, instructing its politicians to adopt given courses of action.'

Source: Donald P Kommers (the foremost American expert on the German Constitutional Court) 'The Federal Constitutional Court in the German political system', *Comparative Political Studies*, January 1994

The policy-making power of the US Supreme Court is well illustrated by the issue of abortion. Until 1973, individual state governments were free to determine their own policies on the legality and availability of abortions in their state. 'Jane Roe', a resident of Texas, wanted an abortion in order to avoid the social stigma of single parenthood and the economic hardship it would involve. However, abortion was outlawed in her state. She took the case to the Supreme Court. The justices ruled that it is a woman's right to make her own decision about whether to have an abortion. Therefore, the court overruled the laws of many states and set up a constitutional right to have an abortion.

Abortion

This case, known as *Roe v Wade*, shows the extent of the Supreme Court's ability to interpret the constitution and to make policy without reference to elected politicians. If the power of judicial review were extended in Britain, with the adoption of a written constitution, British judges would have similar power to make policy.

Judicial review and other branches of government

Greater powers of judicial review would have a considerable impact on the other branches of government. Parliamentary sovereignty would be restrained because no longer would Parliament's word go unchallenged. When Lord Rees-Mogg challenged

183

the government' ability to ratify the Maastricht Treaty in 1993, the Speaker of the House of Commons issued a terse statement reminding the judges that, since the Bill of Rights of 1689, Parliamentary sovereignty has been the order of the day and so Parliament could not be challenged by the courts. The introduction of a written constitution and greater powers to the judiciary would necessarily bring this to an end.

It can be argued that to bring parliamentary sovereignty to an end would be no bad thing. With the quality of Parliament's performance coming under serious scrutiny (see Chapter 5) the courts could provide an extra layer of scrutiny to perhaps prevent bad law.

In addition, greater power to the courts would provide a more effective check on the executive. Whilst the judiciary does have the power to declare the executive to be acting *ultra vires*, the main responsibility for checking the executive currently lies with Parliament. Arguably its ability to do so is seriously undermined by large government majorities combined with strong party discipline. This led Lord Hailsham to term British government an 'elective dictatorship' because within our pyramid system of government power was becoming increasingly concentrated at the top with the executive and more specifically with the Prime Minister. The courts would give an extra layer of defence against an overpowering executive branch of government.

Politicization

Appointments
The American experience also suggests that the more power the courts possess, the more interested politicians become in the appointment of judges. If judges have considerable policy-making power, there is obviously an incentive for politicians to harness that power. In the USA the nine justices of the Supreme Court are appointed for life by the President, with Senate ratification. Many Presidents have appointed judges who share their political beliefs and attitudes in order to shape the composition of the court and so influence its decision-making. Presidents Reagan and Bush were in office for twelve years and during that period appointed five justices. As a result the court moved to the right as its decisions reflected the views of its new members.

We have already seen that it is desirable for the judiciary to be independent of politics. Political interference in the appointment of judges brings it to the very centre of the political world and puts judicial independence at risk.

Civil liberties

Natural rights
Liberties, or rights, are entitlements and freedoms. **Natural rights**, sometimes called **human rights,** are considered to be liberties to which we are entitled solely because we are human beings. There is often wide disagreement about which rights may be considered human rights. The European Convention on Human Rights (1951) includes rights as wide as the right to life (Article 2), the right to peaceful enjoyment of possessions (Protocol No 1, Article 1), the right to marry and build a family (Article 12), and freedom from torture or inhuman or degrading punishment.

Inalienable rights
Human rights are often termed **inalienable** because they can never be removed or given

up. Of course, this does not mean that every individual in every state is benefiting fully from their human rights.

In each nation state citizens are granted certain rights, known as **civil rights**. They vary widely from one state to another. In 1973, General Augusto Pinochet came to power in Chile, ending 40 years of democracy and civil rights. All democratic institutions were closed; the security forces murdered, imprisoned or tortured thousands of citizens; and freedoms of association, speech and the press were withdrawn. In the USA, on the other hand, citizens' rights are outlined in the Bill of Rights and are preserved, at least theoretically, by the courts and politicians who respect the citizens.

Civil rights

Even within democratic states, such as Britain or the USA, there is disagreement about which civil rights should be guaranteed to citizens. Those on the right of the political spectrum tend to emphasize **individual rights** and **political rights** – for example, the right to a fair trial, the right to take part in elections, and the right to own property. Those on the left tend to stress **collective rights**, or the rights of the group, along with economic rights – for example, freedom of association, including membership of a trade union, the right to education, and the right to work.

Disputes over rights

A further distinction can be made between negative and positive rights. The former involve freedom from government restriction, while the latter involve the freedom to reach one's full potential, perhaps with the assistance of the state. Liberals or conservatives tend to emphasize an individual's freedom from government interference and regulation, while socialists tend to favour government intervention to enable individuals and groups to achieve their full potential.

Civil rights in Britain

As Britain has an unwritten constitution, there is no codified document to list the rights and liberties of citizens. The Bill of Rights of 1689 was written in the wake of the Glorious Revolution and was designed to limit the power of the monarch in relation to Parliament rather than to outline the rights of citizens. Therefore, all of the rights available to British citizens rest in statute or common law. In other words, our rights are derived from Parliament or from the decisions of judges. Often our liberties are not explicitly spelt out, rather they need to be extracted from the tangle of restrictions: those things not restricted are our rights (see Table 9.1, page 186). As Geoffrey Robertson said: 'Liberty in Britain is a state of mind rather than a set of legal rules' (*Freedom, the Individual and the Law*, Penguin, 1993).

Bill of rights

Given the sources of our rights, it follows that it falls mainly to Parliament and to the courts to protect civil liberties in Britain. In Parliament it is the responsibility of MPs and Lords to scrutinize proposed legislation carefully and to decide if it unduly threatens civil rights. Similarly, in the courts judges should ensure that individuals are treated equitably by the law. However, as both Parliament and judges take into consideration civil liberties in Britain, they are also required to balance the preservation of one person's liberties against the rights of others, because frequently liberties conflict. Decision-makers search for the greater good either of individuals or of the country as a whole.

Parliament and rights

Table 9.1 Searching for British civil rights

Rights	Explanation
Freedom of speech	The freedom of speech can be interpreted widely to include the rights to speak, publish and broadcast without government interference. There is no right to freedom of speech in Britain. The law places restrictions on the freedom of expression, anything outside these restrictions is lawful. Legal restrictions cover obscenities, racial taunts, libel, slander and official secrets.
Freedom of the person	These rights concern the rights of the individual *vis à vis* the police, e.g. freedom from unlawful arrest, the right to a lawyer, *habeas corpus* and the right to silence. These rights rest largely on statute law, e.g. the Police and Criminal Evidence Act 1984.
Freedom of association and assembly	The freedom of association refers to citizens' entitlement to form groups, for example political parties and trade unions. The freedom of assembly concerns the people's right to gather together, e.g. to demonstrate or to organize a procession. British law does not give a citizen any absolute right of association or assembly. The law places restrictions on these rights, e.g. to prevent a breakdown of public order or to prevent incitement of racial hatred.
Freedom of movement	This freedom concerns the citizens' right to move freely around their country without restriction. Although British citizens have no legally enforceable right to freedom of movement there are relatively few restrictions. The police are able to restrict travel to demonstrations, and the Prevention of Terrorism Act allows the authorities to prevent those suspected of sympathizing with terrorism from entering the mainland from Northern Ireland.
Freedom of religion and thought	Although Britain has an established religion, the Church of England, there is freedom of worship in Britain. Religious meetings are protected by law from disturbance. Since 1677 Britain has had a law against blasphemy which prevents remarks or the publication of material that is insulting to the Christian religion. The law only applies to Christianity; hence Salman Rushdie could not be prosecuted by Muslim groups for the authorship of *The Satanic Verses*.
Property rights	This includes the right to possess property and to use it as one sees fit. A great deal of British statute and common law is designed to preserve property rights. However, the government has contravened the right through nationalization and compulsory purchase orders.
Right to privacy	This concerns citizens' rights to respect for their private life. Telephones should not be 'bugged', correspondence should not be opened, and individuals should not be harassed by the media. There is no right to privacy in Britain, although the law does protect citizens from trespass, nuisance and breach of confidence.
Right to equal treatment	Citizens have a right to expect equal treatment before the law, in their employment and in terms of political rights. The law upholds the right to vote, equality before the law, and should prevent discrimination according to race or gender.

The conflict between different civil liberties is illustrated very simply by the issue of **freedom of speech**. Although this freedom is desirable and necessary in a democracy, for it to be unrestrained would damage the right of others to be free from slanderous, blasphemous or discriminating remarks.

The ability, and desire, of Parliament to maintain rights adequately has been seriously questioned. In February 1997, *The Economist* stated:

'Traditionally, Parliament is supposed to be the champion of liberty. But in recent years it has been more of a threat to liberties than their champion, and it has done a miserable job of balancing individual rights with the competing claims of public order and efficient government ... In the absence of a bill of rights, there exists no legal restraint on the powers of the executive. Even a government with a small majority has the power to ram ill-considered legislation through Parliament. ... As the powers of government have grown, the ability of Parliament to hold its actions up to detailed scrutiny have failed. ... In recent years, the courts have tried to make up for Parliament's failures through reviews of government actions. But without a bill of rights or written constitution, Britain's judges can only examine the procedures by which a decision was reached, not its merits. British courts also have to uphold the law as determined by Parliament, even if this conflicts with Britains international human-rights obligations.'

Some commentators in the UK have argued that the balance between individual liberty and the rights of the wider society has been upset by the Conservative administrations of 1979–97.

Freedom of speech

We have already seen that there are a number of restrictions on absolute freedom of speech, including laws. However, since 1979 the government has acted to reinforce restrictions on a number of occasions.

The Official Secrets Act

Throughout Margaret Thatcher's period as Prime Minister, the Official Secrets Act (1911 and a new Act in 1989) was enforced with vigour. Civil servants, past and present, were taken to court on a number of occasions to prevent them making their views public, or to punish them for having done so. For example, Sarah Tisdall (1984) (see page 152) and Clive Ponting (1985) (page 143) were two of 29 prosecutions under the Official Secrets Act in Margaret Thatcher's first seven years in office. Both civil servants believed they were acting in the best interests of the state by making information public, but the government – through the courts – showed its displeasure. Sarah Tisdall received a prison sentence, while Clive Ponting was found not guilty.

In 1986, former MI5 agent Peter Wright was taken to court in order to prevent the publication of his memoirs (the *Spycatcher* case). Despite the fact that much of the information was dated, the government was determined to use the law to gag Wright (see also page 119).

Spycatcher

The Sinn Fein broadcasting ban

In 1988, the government ordered that no interviews with representatives of Sinn Fein (the political wing of the IRA), or of any other Irish organizations that supported the use of violence, could be broadcast on television or radio using the actual voices of the interviewees. The justification for the ban was that many viewers would be outraged by such interviews and that their access to the broadcast media might also give the groups a degree of respectability.

This was an example of political censorship that would appear to be contrary to the freedom of speech provision of the European Convention on Human Rights. As such, it removed the opportunities for the public to judge the acceptability of politicians, and their beliefs, for themselves.

Freedom of association

GCHQ

There is no absolute freedom of association in Britain and the government is able to ban organizations if it can justify its actions. In 1984, the government decided to ban trade unions at the Government Communications Headquarters (GCHQ) for reasons of national security. The ban was initially overturned in the High Court on the basis that the trade unions had not been adequately consulted before the action was taken. However, in the Court of Appeal the government convinced the court that national security was of paramount importance because the centre had been affected by a strike two years earlier. The Labour government elected in 1997 has since removed the ban.

The Criminal Justice and Public Order Act of 1994 also reduced the freedom of association in the UK. In 1997, the Court of Appeal ruled that the Act had removed any right to hold a demonstration on a public highway, even if this demonstration was not causing an obstruction. This is due to the powers the police have been given to crack down on public protests under greater anti-trespass powers.

Freedom of movement

Miners' strike

The British police have the power to restrain people who are likely to create public disorder that will lead to a 'breach of the peace' – damage to persons or property. These powers were used controversially in 1984 during the miners' strike when the police intercepted miners travelling across the country to picket other pits. The miners were turned back several hundred miles from their destination.

A great deal of violence had occurred during the miners' strike and there was some sympathy with the police's desire to prevent further incidents. The courts agreed with this attitude. However, the line between crime prevention and infringement of civil liberties is narrow.

The right to silence

Traditionally, the police have been required to caution an arrested person before beginning an interview: 'You do not have to say anything unless you wish to do so, but what you say may be given in evidence.' The caution was the embodiment of the 'right to silence' which means that no one should be required to incriminate themselves. A person is innocent until proven guilty and it is the responsibility of the prosecution to prove guilt, if necessary without the assistance of the accused.

Some observers objected to the right to silence on the grounds that if the accused is unwilling to answer questions they are obstructing justice and so may have something to hide.

In 1988, the government abolished the right to silence in Northern Ireland where failure to answer police questions can be given an adverse connotation by the court. This was followed by the Criminal Justice and Public Order Act in 1994 which removed the right to silence in the remainder of the UK. The Act makes it legal for juries to decide to find an individual guilty on the basis of a refusal to give evidence. In fact, the United Nations Committee on Human Rights found that this revision of the Act was contrary to the right to a fair trial as laid down by the United Nations Covenant on Human Rights.

Abolition

The courts and civil liberties

The judiciary in Britain has only limited ability to preserve civil liberties. It does not have the power to review the actions of Parliament, so any statute law that might be considered to include infringements of civil liberties – such as the Criminal Justice Act – is beyond the reach of the courts.

However, the courts do have the power to review the actions of the executive branch of government, so here the judiciary has more discretion in preventing the infringement of civil liberties.

As a result of their limited power, judges often appear to be inadequate guardians of civil liberties. Furthermore, as we have seen, in recent years judges have found in favour of the government as a series of civil liberties has been eroded, giving the impression that they share the government's conception of the national interest. However, it would be unfair to accuse all judges of failing to protect civil rights.

The Matrix–Churchill case (1992) clearly illustrates a judge's willingness to protect civil liberties. In 1991, Paul Henderson, managing director of Matrix–Churchill, a Coventry-based engineering company, was arrested by customs officials. He, and two colleagues, were accused of exporting £70 million of arms to Iraq between 1987 and 1990, in the face of a ban on such exports. It was alleged that they had deceived the Department of Trade and Industry (DTI) by claiming that the exports comprised engineering equipment.

Matrix–Churchill

Prior to the case coming to court, defence lawyers requested certain documents from a number of civil service departments. In September 1992, four government ministers – Kenneth Clarke, Tristan Garel-Jones, Malcolm Rifkind and Michael Heseltine – all signed 'public interest security certificates'. The purpose of these was to prevent the release of the documents for reasons of national security.

Under these circumstances, the presiding judge was required to decide if some or all of the material should be released. Judge Smedley released some of the papers. They showed that the Matrix–Churchill executives had informed the DTI of the nature of the exports and that a government minister, Alan Clarke, had encouraged the executives to avoid the restrictions on military exports to Iraq by hiding their true purpose. As a result of these revelations, the trial collapsed and the government set up the Scott Inquiry into Britain's export of arms to Iraq.

The European Convention on Human Rights

European Court of Human Rights

The European Convention on Human Rights was designed to improve the observance of human rights by governments throughout Europe. Britain ratified the Convention in 1951 but did not incorporate it into domestic law. Therefore, British citizens who feel that their human rights have been infringed cannot appeal on the basis of the Convention to British courts. They can, on the other hand, take their case to the European Court of Human Rights (ECHR) in Strasbourg.

ECHR decisions against the government have included the treatment of suspected terrorists in Northern Ireland, the banning of newspapers publishing extracts of Peter Wright's *Spycatcher* memoirs (see page 187), and the use of corporal punishment in schools. In fact, the British government has been taken to the ECHR more than any other signatory of the treaty – 43 times by 1997.

A bill of rights

Supporters of a bill of rights in Britain include former Lord Chief Justice Taylor, the pressure groups Charter 88, Liberty, and many members of the major political parties. Indeed, Prime Minister Tony Blair has committed the Labour party to the incorporation of the European Convention on Human Rights into domestic law. This would in effect give Britain a bill of rights and enable cases to be brought in domestic courts rather than in the European Court of Human Rights in Strasbourg.

The basis of the supporting argument is that nowhere are the rights and liberties of British citizens clearly outlined in a single document. Therefore, it is unclear what rights citizens can expect. Governments, MPs, judges and citizens themselves would all benefit from the clarity that such a document would bring.

Contents

Opponents of a bill of rights believe that even the initial stage of drawing up the document would involve political conflict. As we have seen, there is some disagreement between parties of the left and right about the type of rights to which citizens should be entitled. Therefore, far from clarifying the situation a bill would become the object of political dispute.

Judicial power

If a bill of rights were created, it would be enforceable by the judiciary. This would lead to an increase in the power of the courts at the expense of Parliament. The principle of parliamentary sovereignty would be ended to ensure that statute law could no longer infringe on civil liberties. Therefore, the courts would be better equipped to protect freedoms and rights.

Judicial bias

The difficulty of abandoning parliamentary sovereignty and increasing the power of the judiciary is that a democratically elected assembly would be subordinated to a panel of unelected and unrepresentative judges. This is of particular concern given John Griffith's view that judges hold a particular set of attitudes which reflect their backgrounds (see page 178–79).

The operation of a bill of rights in the USA illustrates both the advantages and the dangers of such a document. The Supreme Court has used the Bill of Rights to preserve the rights of citizens. In *Brown v The Board of Education, Topeka, Kansas* (1954) the court ruled racial segregation unconstitutional. In *Miranda v Arizona* (1966) the court established the procedure of the accused being read their rights as they are arrested. Judgements such as these are particularly important for minority groups which might not receive full protection from the legislature as they have a limited impact on election results.

USA

Cases such as *Miranda* and *Brown* are well known. However, less well-known are cases such as *Plessy v Ferguson* (1896) and the Hirabayashi case (1943). The former ruled racial segregation constitutional, and the latter allowed Japanese Americans to be held in internment camps for the duration of World War II. Therefore, despite its powers the Supreme Court has not always acted to preserve the liberties of citizens, as we perceive them today.

The assumption that a bill of rights and courts with greater powers would automatically preserve civil liberties is simplistic. Courts cannot initiate cases; they must wait for cases to be brought before them. They cannot enforce their decisions – for this they rely on the other branches of government and, ultimately, courts are effective only if politicians are willing to abide by their decisions. Therefore, the effectiveness of courts depends on the constitutionalism of the politicians.

Limits on courts

Exercises

Short questions

1 What justifications might there be for limiting freedom of expression?
(ULEAC, June 1992)

2 Outline, with examples, judges' attitudes towards the issue of official secrecy.
(ULEAC, January 1993)

3 a Define 'open government'.
b To what extent do judges uphold this idea?
(EdExcel, June 1996)

4 a Define one civil liberty.
b How adequately do judges protect this liberty?
(EdExcel, January 1996)

Essay questions

1 Discuss the problems involved in drawing up a written constitution for Britain.
(ULEAC, June 1994)

2 How adequately do judges protect civil liberties?
   (ULEAC, June 1993)

3 Discuss the view that demands for a bill of rights are a result of Parliament's failure
   to protect civil liberties.
   (Oxford & Cambridge, June 1992)

4 Discuss the problems in drawing up a written constitution for Britain.
   (EdExcel, June 1994)

5 Discuss (a) a case for, and (b) a case against the introduction of a bill of rights.
   (EdExcel, January 1996)

Data response question

The following is adapted from Lord Taylor, *The Judiciary in the Nineties*, BBC
Education, 1992.

'*In short, it is suggested that judges are too stuffy and remote; that they are out of
touch with society today, with its lifestyle and its standards; that they are all in the
same mould – white, male, public school, Oxbridge …*

*It is true, until recently, barristers and therefore judges tended to be drawn from the
middle class upwards … But the idea that judges should be more representative would
be taken too far if judges were not drawn from those trained in the law, experienced in
the courts and best suited for the job …*

*The suggestion that judges are biased towards the Establishment does not stand up to
examination. For example, in a recent case a judge ordered disclosure of government
documents and thereby enabled three defendants to be cleared of criminal charges.*'

1 According to the passage, why might judges be regarded as unrepresentative of
   society?

2 Is it important that judges should be representative?

3 State an argument supporting the view that judges are not biased towards the
   Establishment.

(ULEAC, January 1995)

10 Local and regional government

Questions to be answered in this chapter

- What is the function of local government?
- What are the functions of local councillors?
- How is local government structured?

- How is local government financed?
- What is the relationship between central and local government?
- What is the future of regional government in the UK?

Terms to know

- Capping
- Centralization
- Community charge
- Competitive tendering
- Corporatism
- Council tax
- Councillors
- Devolution
- Enablers

- Grant Related Expenditure Assessment (GREA)
- Internal market
- Marketization
- Metropolitan authorities
- Municipal socialism
- Ombudsmen
- Politicization
- Poll tax

- Privatization
- Providers
- Rate support grant
- Tax-raising powers
- Two-tier structure
- Uniform Business Rate (UBR)
- Unitary
- 'West Lothian' question

LOCAL GOVERNMENT

Introduction

Since 1979, local government in Britain has undergone considerable transformation. The Conservative administrations of 1979 to 1997 saw local authorities as a possible hinderance to the full implementation of their national policies. The 18-year period saw increasing centralization of government and the diminution of the role of local authorities as quasi-governmental bodies, and private companies became responsible for the delivery of a growing number of services. The result has seen local government in its weakest and most subordinate position in relation to central government since 1945.

Why have local government?

Functions Local government fulfils two major functions: democratic and administrative. The former allows members of the local community to participate in local affairs, both by standing as **councillors** and by voting in local elections. Although the turnout in local elections is significantly lower than in general elections (40 per cent compared with 70 per cent), and the quality of councillors has often been criticized, the system does allow local people to have a voice in local affairs.

Non-partisan competition Traditionally, individuals have been able to take part in local politics independent of political parties. A great deal of local competition was non-partisan. The advantage of this was to allow individuals to put forward their point of view for the benefit of the community without having to follow a party line. In the 1970s, however, local politics became more partisan and political parties now dominate local elections as they do at national level.

Politicization Many observers have mourned the passing of the independent councillor, but wherever there are elections, political parties will follow. Their rise in the 1970s can probably be attributed to the polarization of national politics. The breakdown of the postwar political consensus and the emergence of adversarial politics made electoral competition at all levels of great importance to the parties. Local politics became particularly important as Margaret Thatcher's governments pushed the national political agenda to the right. The Labour and Liberal parties saw local government as a means to oppose the advance of Thatcherism; and when the Conservative administrations began to reassess the role of local government, the other parties saw the need to defend local democracy. Events such as the abolition of the **metropolitan authorities** in 1986 were seen as overtly political, as they were all Labour-controlled, and this gave further impetus to the **politicization** of local democracy.

The results of politicization have been changes in the nature of representation at local level, along the lines of those that have already occurred at national level. Councillors, like Members of Parliament, no longer represent only their constituents; they must consider the party line as well.

Local conditions Administratively, local government allows policies to be given a local flavour. Although laws are made at Westminster and many policies are determined by central government, local authorities have the freedom to shape policies to suit local conditions. In addition, local government allows services to be delivered to the community in a sensitive and responsive manner, which means that people receiving important services, such as policing or housing, are able to take up any difficulties or complaints with local bodies rather than with a vast bureaucracy in London.

The role of local councillors

Election Councillors are elected locally from constituencies known as wards which they represent on the council. In order to stand for election, an individual must be at least 21 years old. The Commission for Local Democracy reported that in the 1990s 80 per cent of councillors are in fact aged over 45, and only 25 per cent are women. This has led to charges that councillors are unrepresentative of the population. In fact, local councils are no more unrepresentative than the House of Commons, where, for example, only 9 per cent of MPs in the last Parliament were women – although this has now risen to 18 per cent.

The role of local councillors differs significantly from those of MPs (see Chapter 5). Local authorities are not local legislatures: they cannot make law, other than local bylaws. Councils fulfil an executive role, not a legislative role, in that they implement policies that have been made by central government, perhaps putting a local perspective on the *delivery* of these policies. Therefore, their responsibilities are purely local. Since local councils perform an executive function, they are under the supervision of Parliament and so councillors are subordinate to MPs.

Role

Within the authorities most business is carried out via committees that specialize in policy areas and have authority that has been delegated to them by the full council. The chairpersons of council committees are powerful. They determine the agenda, make many of the decisions regarding policy and finance, and liaise with the chief officer of the council.

Committees

The chief officer or chief executive of the council heads the local authority's permanent staff, who fulfil a similar role to civil servants at central government level. They are expected to implement local authority policy and provide information for relevant committees.

The structure of local government

The structure of local government in Britain was set up by the Local Government Act of 1972 which was based, to some extent, on the Redcliffe-Maud Report of 1968. This report had found that Britain had too many local authorities, the majority of which were inappropriate for dealing with the problems faced in their areas. Some were too small to provide the required services economically; others were based on electoral boundaries that no longer reflected demographic realities; and the **two-tier structure** was confusing for the population.

Redcliffe-Maud Report

Maud recommended that the two-tier structure be replaced by a **unitary** (one-tier) system which would provide all of the services for a given area. The population of these areas should be between 250,000 and one million people and boundaries should be redrawn to reflect movements in the population. Finally, it was recommended that metropolitan counties should be created to coordinate the services and cope with the special problems of the large conurbations such as Birmingham, Liverpool and Greater Manchester; London already had the Greater London Council (GLC).

Recommendations

The 1972 Local Government Act adopted some of Maud's proposals. It distinguished between the conurbations and areas that combined urban and rural areas by setting up metropolitan counties in Greater Manchester, Merseyside, Tyne and Wear, the West Midlands, West Yorkshire and South Yorkshire. However, it retained the two-tier structure for the non-metropolitan areas. In fact, if parish councils are included, the non-metropolitan counties have a three-tier structure.

Local Government Act 1972

The adoption of the tier system reflects the difficulties faced by central government in creating a workable structure for local authorities. On the one hand, many services can

Two-tier structure

Table 10.1 Local government in England after 1986

Area	Tiers of local government	Functions
Metropolitan areas	*Unitary* 36 metropolitan districts and 33 London boroughs created when the metropolitan counties were abolished in 1986 Cover large urban areas and provide most services in that area	Education Social services Housing Roads Refuse Leisure
Non-metropolitan areas	*Top tier* Shire counties or county councils 39 in England covering large areas and providing 'big budget' services	Police Fire Major roads Refuse disposal Social services
	Second tier Shire districts or district councils 296 in England They are subdivisions of the shire counties	Housing Planning Refuse collection Local roads Leisure
	Third tier Town and parish councils 11,000 in England Cover very small areas	Footpaths Lighting Local amenities

be provided only on a large scale. Economically and logistically, services such as the fire service and the police force need to be delivered by a body that is sufficiently large to give an overview to the service. However, the large-scale local government that this requires conflicts with the need for local democracy. The larger the units of local government, the more bureaucratic and less accessible they are likely to be and the less responsive to the needs of the local community. The two-tier structure was an attempt to solve this conflict. Table 10.1 shows the tiers of local government in England and the services for which they are responsible.

County councils

The *top tier* of the non-metropolitan structure includes the shire counties or county councils. They are responsible for the 'big-budget' services that require coordination on a large scale and are expensive to provide. Their responsibilities include major roads, policing and education.

District councils

The *second tier* – shire districts or district councils – is responsible for delivering the services that are less expensive and need to be attuned to the needs of local people. Its responsibilities include housing, planning and refuse collection.

Banham Committee

The confusing nature of the two-tier system was a problem. In 1992, Michael Heseltine, during his second term at the Department of the Environment, initiated a review of local government organization, under the leadership of Sir John Banham, former Director-General of the Confederation of British Industry (CBI). The intention of the government was to abandon the two-tier system in favour of a unitary system. However, Sir John Banham's independent commission turned out to be just that – independent. Its early proposals in 1993 included a unitary council for the Isle of Wight; the division of Cleveland into four unitary counties, and the replacement of Avon, Gloucestershire and Somerset with eight unitary councils. The commission, however, refused to propose a unitary solution to every local situation, and recommended the retention of two-tier authorities for some areas. This stance was supported by many local authorities at both county and district levels – both of whom were anxious to preserve their status or even their very existence.

Owing to the differences of outlook between Sir John Banham and the government, he was replaced in 1995 by Sir David Cooksey, the former head of the Audit Commission. The result was the extension of unitary authorities across a greater part of England. In 1997/8 the total number of unitary authorities had reached 46.

In fact, a unitary system is already in place in the metropolitan districts. In 1986, the metropolitan counties were abolished and replaced by metropolitan districts and the functions of the GLC were incorporated into the London boroughs. Margaret Thatcher's government believed that the metropolitan counties were bureaucratic, wasteful and were abusing their positions by using taxpayers' money for political ends. These were alleged to include anti-government propaganda and the promotion of left-wing ideas, such as 'nuclear-free zones' and police monitoring units.

Metropolitan counties

Even in the metropolitan districts, the need for an overview of some services is recognized. For example, police and fire services are provided by specialist authorities which are made up of representatives from the districts or boroughs of the area.

In recent years these metropolitan areas have also attracted interest owing to proposals to introduce directly elected mayors in many towns and cities. Mayors are currently elected by local councillors and fulfil mainly ceremonial functions. A number of politicians, including Michael Heseltine and Tony Blair, have favoured greater executive powers for mayors along the American model. As a result, mayors would have more prominent leadership, policy-making and implementation powers.

Top of the list for a directly elected leader is London. The Labour government is currently considering direct elections for a mayor of London, possibly backed by a directly elected local assembly.

The central–local relationship

The constitutional position

Constitutionally, local government is in a very weak position compared with its central counterpart. Britain is a unitary state and at the centre of the system is a Parliament with sovereign power. This means that there is no countervailing power to that of Parliament. Statute law is supreme in this context, and local authorities derive their powers entirely from Parliament. It follows that what Parliament gives, it can also take away.

Unitary state

Ultra vires   One aspect of the sovereignty of Parliament – and therefore of central government – is that the courts have the power to review the actions of local government. If a local authority exceeds the authority given to it by Parliament, the courts can declare it to be acting *ultra vires*, or beyond its powers.

Comparison

The USA has a federal system of government. This means that state governments have constitutional powers that cannot be removed by the central (federal) government. Divorce, capital punishment and alcohol consumption all come under the remit of state governments. It would be fair to say that over the last century the federal government has become more dominant owing to the extent to which it has begun to interfere in a broader range of policies; nevertheless, it is not able to undermine the constitutional position of the states.

Famous cases of local authorities exceeding their powers have included the 'Fares Fair' case (1983), in which the courts ruled the GLC's public transport fare cuts were illegal (see page 181), and *Hazell v Hammersmith and Fulham London Borough Council* (1991), in which the House of Lords declared that the council's speculation on option swaps on the London money market was illegal. (Option swaps involve swapping a loan with a fixed rate of interest for a loan at a variable rate of interest. Under certain conditions, the market rate of interest will fall and the speculator will be better off.)

Tameside decision   The courts do not always find against local authorities. In 1976, Tameside Metropolitan Borough Council decided to abandon comprehensive education, despite government policy to the contrary. The minister of education, Shirley Williams, issued a directive to the council in an effort to force it to comply with government policy. The council refused. The courts found in favour of the local authority, explaining that the government had acted beyond the powers given to it by the Education Act of 1944. Like local authorities, the central executive is subject to judicial review in the light of parliamentary statutes. However, the government was quickly able to pass a new Education Act which gave it the power to prevent other local authorities following Tameside's example.

Comparison

Local government in the USA is subordinate to state governments. Whilst the country has a federal system, individual states do not – they are unitary. Therefore local government has as much or as little power as the state government wishes.

Other controls   In addition to statute law and judicial review, the central government has a wide range of methods to control local authorities. Apart from financial intervention (see page 201), central government can launch an inquiry into local authority affairs. An example is the Widdicombe inquiry into the conduct of local authority business, which recommended the banning of, among other things, political advertising by local authorities and the employment of political advisers. In 1972, central government set up **ombudsmen** – commissioners for local administration – to investigate complaints against local authority actions. Central government can also organize systems of inspection over local authority services, such as schools and the police force.

Changes in centre–local relations

Given the constitutional weakness of local government, the stimulus for the nature of the centre–local relationship tends to come from the dominant partner, central government. It has three options:

- It can treat the local authorities as partners in a single governmental system, both levels of which have common aims for delivery of services to the public.

- Central and local government can see themselves as independent units bargaining with each other for power.

- Central government can view the local authorities as merely agents through which to carry out its own policies.

The political scientist R A W Rhodes incorporated the above options into his analysis of changes in the nature of centre–local relations since 1970 ('Local government', in B Jones and L Robbins (eds) *Two Decades in British Politics*, Manchester University Press, 1992). Between 1970 and 1974, the tone of centre–local relations was one of partnership. According to Rhodes, 'Consultation was the "normal" style of central–local relations throughout the postwar period until the mid-1970s. For most of this time, local service spending was buoyant, and the numbers of local government employees grew fairly regularly.' Such an approach recognizes the democratic credentials of local government and attempts to build an effective relationship through consensus rather than confrontation.

Consultation

Under the Labour government of 1974–79, local authorities were caught up in the **corporatism** of government at the time. Like trade unions, local authorities were co-opted into government decision-making. The government set up the Consultative Council on Local Government Finance which allowed the local authorities and the Treasury to negotiate over the financing of local government.

Corporatism

Since 1979, the relationship between central and local government has changed – some might say beyond recognition. The era of consensus and cooperation came to an end with the Conservative administrations which tended to adopt a confrontational approach to local government. Margaret Thatcher did not accept the democratic qualifications of local government, because the turnout in local elections is so low (see page 194), whereas she believed her government had a national mandate to carry out their economic and social policies. Therefore, the period 1979–97 saw the ever-greater centralization of policy-making and the rise of the view that local authorities were simply agencies for the delivery of those policies.

Confrontation

Centralization under Margaret Thatcher

The Conservative party came to power in 1979 with an agenda and a leader with sufficient conviction to see those policies implemented. Margaret Thatcher was not a supporter of consensus and would countenance no opposition.

Thatcherism

The main aims of what became known as Thatcherism were the control of inflation and the limiting of the role of the state in an effort to free the marketplace for private competition. For Margaret Thatcher, these basic aims would lead to efficiency, consumer choice, economic prosperity and a healthier democracy. To achieve these aims, the Conservative government needed to reduce government spending, both to bring down inflation (according to monetarist theory – see page 53) and to reduce the size of the state to leave more room for private industry.

Margaret Thatcher believed that local authorities – at least some of them – stood in the way of reducing public expenditure. At the time, local authorities were spending almost 13 per cent of Britain's gross national product (GNP), accounting for 28 per cent of all government spending. From the point of view of local authorities, such expenditure was necessary given the extent of their responsibilities, the rise in wage costs, and increases in the population. However, Margaret Thatcher was determined to reduce local authority expenditure.

Spending controls

The Conservative government's first attempt to control local authority spending was the 1980 Local Government, Planning and Land Act. This sought to exert tighter control over local authority spending as a whole and particularly on capital expenditure.

Rate support grant

Until 1980, central government had given financial assistance to local government via the **rate support grant** which was, at least partially, calculated according to how much local authorities intended to spend. The government could vary the rate support grant only as a total figure; it could not alter the amount received by individual authorities. This scheme was replaced by a system of block grants which was intended to give central government greater control of the overspending of specific authorities. Under the new system, central government calculated what it believed each authority should be spending – the **Grant Related Expenditure Assessment** (GREA) – and compared this figure with the local council's estimated spending for the year. The greater the excess of the local authority's estimates, the more the block grant to that authority was reduced.

The government took the provisions of the 1980 act a step further in 1981 by introducing targets and penalties for council spending. The targets were separate from the GREAs. For example, in 1980 local authorities were told to cut 5.6 per cent from their 1979 expenditure figure for the new year or to face reductions in their block grant as a penalty.

Rate rises

The government's intention was to discourage high spending by forcing local councils to make up any shortfall in their budget from local taxation – the rates. It anticipated that the local electorate would be disgruntled by the spiralling rates bill and would vote against the sitting council at the next election. Therefore, not only would local spending come under control, but local accountability would also be improved. Not all observers believed the government's motives to be so high-minded – most of the high-spending authorities were under Labour control.

The 1980 Act also introduced controls on local authorities' capital expenditure. Councils undertook a great deal of expensive projects, such as the maintenance of school premises and housing construction. By introducing the need to seek central government permission for such spending, between 1979 and 1983 local authority capital expenditure fell by 60 per cent.

Capital controls

Although central government's contribution to local government financing had fallen from 60 per cent in 1979 to 48 per cent in 1983, local government spending had not decreased significantly and rates had risen dramatically. Therefore, in 1982 the Local Government Finances (No. 2) Act removed the councils' right to levy an extra rate in the middle of the financial year. This was followed in 1984 by the Rates Act which enabled the government to cap the level of rates to be charged by an authority. The decision to cap was to be taken by the Secretary of State on the basis of an assessment of whether spending in that authority had been excessive.

Rate capping

As a result of these spending restrictions, many local councils ran into serious financial difficulties. For example, Liverpool City Council set a budget that would see them through only nine months of the year. Many other councils turned to 'creative accounting' and imaginative financial deals. These included selling council properties in order to raise money and then renting the property back from its new owner. We saw above how the London Borough of Hammersmith and Fulham engaged in illegal trading on the London financial markets in order to raise money.

Abolition of the metropolitan authorities

Considerable opposition to Margaret Thatcher's attempts to control local authority spending came from the metropolitan authorities that were responsible for the large conurbations. The GLC in particular had been determined, under the leadership of Ken Livingstone, to confront the government.

GLC

The metropolitan authorities were controlled by the Labour party. Their control of key local authorities was seen as an opportunity to present alternative policies to Thatcherism. This is often referred to as **municipal socialism**. The councils believed that they had a local mandate for their policies and were committed to protecting their vision of local democracy.

Municipal socialism

Margaret Thatcher believed that the metropolitan authorities were irresponsible, out of touch with the public, bureaucratic, and wasteful. The Local Government Act of 1985 abolished the metropolitan authorities, including the GLC, and replaced them with metropolitan districts and London borough councils.

Local authorities and the free market

Perhaps the main element of Thatcherism was the nurturing of the free market economy in Britain. Margaret Thatcher wanted to create a democracy in which consumers could own shares, own their homes, and have choice in the field of education, and could expect local authorities to deliver such services of a high standard at the right price. She intended to do this through the **marketization** of the public sector.

Marketization

Privatization and housing policy

Privatization

Privatization first came to local councils in the Housing Act of 1980. They were forced to make local authority housing available for purchase to tenants of three years' standing or more. This was extended in 1984 by the Housing and Building Control Act, and again in 1992 by the Housing, Land and Urban Development Act. In addition, the 1988 Housing Act enabled tenants of derelict council housing to vote to replace the local authority as landlord by a landlord of their own choice. The Act also created Housing Action Trusts (HATs) that could take over dilapidated estates, improve and sell them into private ownership. The aim of all of these policies was to remove the stock of public housing from local authority control and put it in private-sector hands.

Consumer sovereignty and education

National curriculum

Since the 1944 Education Act, local authorities had been given a virtually free hand in deciding the school curriculum. This came to an end in 1988 with the Education Reform Act. For the first time, central government had the power to lay down a national curriculum. In addition, the Act weakened, and even ended, local authority control over schools, colleges of further education and polytechnics. Parents were given the opportunity to vote on whether their child's school should opt out of local authority control. If they did so, the responsibility for staffing and budgets was to be transferred to the head teacher and the board of governors, with finance coming directly from the central government.

League tables

The introduction of mandatory testing at a range of ages and league tables of school examination results were further steps towards the marketization of education. The government's intention was to increase the power of parents as consumers. If a school's examination results were poor, parents would be able to move their child elsewhere. As a result, all schools would be encouraged to maintain standards. Critics of the system argued that the emphasis on examination success was too great and that it, in effect, recreated a two-tier education system with the academically talented students being accepted at high-calibre schools and the less-gifted being relegated to poorer-quality schools.

The marketization of services

Competitive tendering

The 1988 Local Government Act forced local authorities to accept the practice of **competitive tendering**. This entailed a fundamental revision of the role of local authorities. No longer would they necessarily be the **providers** of the service; they might only be the **enablers**; that is, local authorities would ask private firms to bid for the opportunity to provide services. For example, many leisure facilities and sports halls are no longer managed by the local authority, but by a private firm employed to do so by the council.

The government believed that this would encourage a higher standard of service at a more competitive price. Local authority departments were allowed to bid for the contracts against private competitors, and the government hoped that this would provide sufficient incentive to keep costs down and standards high. If the delivery of service was unsatisfactory, the firm, local authority or private company could be replaced.

There was also a drive to create an **internal market** within local authorities, so that departments within the authority had to charge *each other* for the services they provided. This was an attempt to make authorities more efficient and cost-conscious, and to create fair competition for private firms. Before the internal market, many authority departments were able to win contracts because their costs could be kept artificially low – many of the services they received, for example, accountancy and legal advice, were provided free of charge by other council departments.

Internal market

Quangos and the avoidance of local authorities

In its desire to inject more private enterprise into the local economy, the Conservative government occasionally ignored the local authorities, turning instead to quasi-governmental bodies ('quangos'), such as Training and Enterprise Councils (TECs).

There were 82 TECs in England and Wales designed to build up the level of skills within the British workforce. They were private limited companies run by businesspeople from the private sector with funding from central government. Local authorities were bypassed because the government felt that businesspeople would shape the curriculum to suit the needs of the local business community in a way that the local authorities would not.

TECs

In education, while local authorities lost control of grant-maintained schools, sixth form colleges, further education colleges and the former polytechnics, central government reinforced its dominance through the Funding Agency for Schools, the Further Education Funding Council, the Higher Education Funding Council, and the Qualifications and Curriculum Authority.

Education

The Conservative government's extensive use of quangos came even after their pledge to wage war against them in 1979. The number did indeed seem to fall, but Charter 88 (a pressure group seeking constitutional reform) claimed at one point that there were no fewer than 5521 quangos, in one guise or another.

Numbers

Considerable controversy surrounds the use of quangos because, critics argue, they are not accountable to any elected authority. Many of the functions carried out by quangos were once the responsibility of *elected* local authorities, which allowed citizens opportunities to influence the policies adopted and the services provided. Other functions were carried out by civil service departments in Whitehall, and so ministers were accountable to Parliament for the performance of these functions.

Accountability

All quangos are directly responsible to central government, so *ultimately* ministers are responsible for their performance. However, John Stewart, professor of local government at Birmingham University, argued in 1994 that, since ministers cannot realistically be held accountable for the whole range of matters under their *direct* control, let alone for quangos, the doctrine of ministerial responsibility was placed under immense strain.

Ministerial responsibility

In addition, technical checks on the performance and financial affairs of a quango are less stringent than those on local government. The Audit Commission checks the works

Checks on quangos

of local authorities and NHS trusts, but is not responsible for other significant quangos. In addition, quangos do not have to keep a register of members' outside interests (in case a conflict of interest should arise), and their members are not personally liable to be financially charged for misuse of public funds. Of all the quangos, only the NHS trusts are required to make their meetings open to the public. Local authorities are subject to all of these controls.

Personnel   Controversy also surrounds the appointment of personnel to quangos, most of which are made on the recommendation of ministers or the Cabinet Office's Public Appointments Unit. In 1994 the Nolan Committee on Standards of Public Life expressed concern about the standard of the appointees and governments' practice of making senior appointments to those who supported their policies. Since July 1996 the appointments made by ministers (about 8000) are supervised by the Commissioner for Public Appointments, through a code of appointment that stresses merit. However the Labour government approaches quango appointment, there was certainly concern that the Conservative government had used this extensive power of patronage to reward its friends. Sir Derek Barber, former chairman of the Countryside Commission, wrote in the CC's newsletter in 1991:

'I became chairman … as a consequence of sharing a cab with a stranger. Another chairman was appointed following a pheasant shoot at which the secretary of state was a fellow gun; the subsequent chairman of a water authority bumped into a Cabinet minister while birding on a Greek island. It is a splendidly capricious and British way of doing things.'

Financial reform

The 'poll tax'

Rates   The rating system had long been considered unfair and inadequate as a system of local taxation. It was a property tax which could fall on families or individuals, old or young, regardless of income. In other words, it was a regressive tax.

Accountability   In view of its regressive nature, many were exempted from payment and only about one-third of the electorate paid the full amount. Businesses accounted for a great part of the revenue from the rates, but had no vote in elections. These two factors undermined the accountability of local authorities and enabled them to continue increasing rates in the face of the central government's spending controls (see page 200).

In 1985, the rateable value of properties in Scotland was reassessed – resulting in a 50 per cent increase in some cases. A review of rateable values in England was due and it had been postponed since 1973. The outcry that resulted from the increase in rates in Scotland persuaded the government to look seriously at an alternative local tax.

Community charge   Alternatives considered included a local income tax and a local sales tax, but in 1988 the Local Government Finance Act introduced the government's solution – the **community charge**. There was a great deal of hostility to the charge, resulting in a backbench revolt of 38 Conservative MPs, and the bill passed through the Lords only when the government called up its 'backwoodsmen' (see page 79).

The community charge was a flat-rate tax to be paid by every adult, i.e. a **poll tax**. Some people were exempted from full payment of the tax, including 18-year-olds at school, those in nursing homes, and those in prison (unless imprisoned for non-payment of the charge). The level of the tax was to be set by district councils.

Poll tax

Businesses could not pay a poll tax and so were subject to the **Uniform Business Rate** (UBR), which was based on property values but set and collected nationally and redistributed to councils through government grants. The system of grants was simplified into one payment, the level of which was set by central government according to its assessment of the finance needed to provide a standard level of service (Standard Spending Assessment – SSA).

Uniform Business Rate

The government retained the right to cap the poll tax by setting an upper limit to the level of tax. In order to be capped, an authority originally needed a budget of over £15 million, but this qualification was soon dropped. In addition, its spending estimates had to exceed the SSA by 12.5 per cent and £75 per resident. In 1990, 20 local councils were capped. However, the Secretary of State's use of his **capping power** seemed to be biased against Labour-held councils. For example, the London Borough of Brent, a Labour-controlled council where spending rose by 1.4 per cent, was capped, but Conservative-controlled Berkshire Country Council, where spending rose by 20.6 per cent, was not. The courts ruled that capping was legal, but that the Secretary of State should make clear the circumstances under which a council could be capped.

Capping

The government had announced that the average annual poll tax bill was expected to be £276. It soon became clear that this would not be the case. Businesses in the south were unhappy at the level of the UBR, and many people demonstrated against the unfairness of the poll tax.

Dissatisfaction

Objections were mainly based on its regressive nature. Like the rates which it replaced, this new local tax took no account of the ability to pay. It was also an expensive and difficult tax to collect – twice as expensive as the rates. The register of taxpayers was difficult to keep up to date and easy to avoid. As a result, councils lost revenue.

Local authorities also complained that the new system concentrated power and control in the hands of central government. According to many, this had been Margaret Thatcher's aim since 1979.

The council tax

Amid fears that the Conservative party would lose the next general election, Margaret Thatcher was replaced as the party's leader in November 1990. During the campaign to choose her successor the poll tax became an issue and all candidates committed themselves to a review of the tax.

On his election to Conservative party leader, John Major became Prime Minister and appointed Michael Heseltine, a long-time critic of the poll tax, as Secretary of State for the Environment. In March 1991, the government announced an across-the-board reduction in poll tax bills of £140 in order to defuse the poll tax crisis. However, by September 1991 the poll tax had been abolished – to be replaced by the new **council tax**.

Reform

The council tax combined a personal tax with a property tax. Local authorities set the level of this council tax (which was still subject to capping), a proportion of which would be paid by each household; how much depended on the valuation of their property. Properties were graded into bands related to the capital value of the property: the higher the grade, the higher the proportion of council tax to be paid. It was hoped that linking the council tax to property values would remove the most regressive elements of the tax.

Since its introduction in 1991 the council tax has become widely accepted and has never been plagued by the political controversy that surrounded the community charge.

The status of local government today

Local government has probably never been at such a low ebb as it is today. Conservative administrations from 1979 onwards showed considerable hostility to local government and sought to remove power from local authorities and transfer it to central government.

However, as important for local authorities is their changing role in the governmental system. The Conservative governments had moved local authorities away from their traditional function as provider of local services to a new function as purchaser of those services. Therefore, local government had become an agent of central government rather than a policy-maker and service provider in its own right.

REGIONAL GOVERNMENT
Introduction

Perhaps it is surprising that a book dealing with the politics of the UK should include a section on regional politics. Britain is, after all, a unitary state. The doctrine of parliamentary sovereignty means that anything Parliament says goes, whether it concerns local, regional or national affairs. Therefore what place is there for regional politics? Exactly what position regional government might occupy within the constitutional system of the UK is still relatively unclear; but the very fact that it is being discussed means that the regions are firmly on the political agenda, and as Britain enters the new millenium the details of their constitutional position are likely to become clear.

Devolution   **Devolution** of power to Scotland became an issue in the 1970s. In 1972, direct rule was returned to Northern Ireland. The Scottish National party began winning seats in a 1967 by-election following the lead of the Welsh Nationalists, Plaid Cymru, in 1966. A referendum was granted on the issue of devolution in Scotland and Wales in 1979 as part of the Labour government's plans for survival. However, the required majorities were not achieved in either region and plans did not go ahead.

The 1997 general election campaign made clear the renewed importance of regional politics. During the campaign the Labour party made devolution a major plank of its policy platform, promising regional assemblies for Scotland and Wales following referendums. The Conservative party, as it had done in 1992, made preservation of the union a main plank of *its* policy platform – portraying devolution as the first step on the slippery slope to the disintegration of the UK.

In the general election, the Labour party won an overall majority of votes in Wales (55 per cent), the North (61 per cent) and North West (54 per cent) of England, and in Yorkshire and Humberside (52 per cent). It came close to doing so in Scotland (46 per cent) and in London (49 per cent). The Conservative party won no seats in either Scotland or Wales and performed best in the South East (41 per cent), East Anglia (39 per cent) and the South West (37 per cent).

Labour's success in these regions makes devolution high on its political agenda, both as a reward for its supporters and to ensure the future loyalty of those regions.

States and nations

The positions of England, Scotland, Wales and Northern Ireland within the union of the United Kingdom encapsulates the distinction between a nation and a state. A state is a geographical, legal and political entity. It is geographical because it occupies given boundaries. It is political because within these boundaries citizens are governed by a particular political system. It is legal because a state has a legal identity before international law and is subject to international law as laid down by the United Nations.

A nation is an historical, cultural and emotional identity. People within a particular geographical area feel loyal to their area for historical reasons, owing to common experiences and often to a common language. Not only do those people feel a loyalty towards each other; they feel different from their neighbours.

National identity

States and nations do not necessarily coincide. In Spain, a football fixture between Barcelona and Real Madrid means much more than a match between two great football clubs. The fixture symbolizes the conflict between the region of Catalonia, of which Barcelona is the capital, and the national state of Spain, of which Madrid is the capital. Even within the UK a match between England and Scotland embodies the turbulent history of the two nations.

Britain is a unitary state, with power emanating from the centre. In the regions, local government has as much or as little power as the Parliament in London wishes. Furthermore, Parliament can take any power back from the regions.

Unitary state

Comparison

In many countries, regional differences are incorporated into the political system through federalism. The USA was created from thirteen individual colonies which then became individual states before being incorporated in the United States of America. As a result, individual states in the US have a great deal of power and the central government cannot interfere with these powers. Divorce, alcohol, transport, education are all covered by state laws in the USA, and as one drives across state boundaries the laws change.

Federation

The historical composition of the United Kingdom

Strictly speaking the term 'Britain' refers to England, Wales and Scotland. Wales was incorporated with England in 1536, Scotland in 1603 (the monarchs) and 1707 (the parliaments).

Stormont

The United Kingdom refers to Britain plus Northern Ireland. Ireland was formally brought into the union in 1801 but had been dominated by England for centuries prior to this. In 1921 Ireland was divided into North and South. The latter was a free Irish state, governed from a Parliament in Dublin. The North was given its own parliament, Stormont, and its own Prime Minister. However, Westminster reimposed direct rule on Northern Ireland in 1972.

The governance of the United Kingdom

During the twentieth century, to a greater or lesser extent, all of the regions have been governed from the centre – Westminster. However, a degree of administrative independence has always been allowed.

Scotland, Wales and Northern Ireland all send MPs to Westminster. In fact all three are over-represented in the House of Commons. Scotland, for example, sends 72 MPs whereas only around one-fifth of that number would be merited by its population size. Each region has its own administrative office in the government. The **Scottish Office**, the oldest of these, was established in 1885, the **Welsh Office** in 1964 and the **Northern Ireland Office** in 1972 (with the re-establishment of direct rule).

Each Office is headed by a Cabinet minister who, in some limited respects, functions as the 'prime minister' of that region. However, they are based within the Cabinet of central government and so their political room for manouvre is limited.

Regional government offices

For many years the English have seemed to view their nation as synonymous with the larger state. This attitude, combined with a lack of nationalist feeling within English regions, has meant that there has been little effort to give greater power to the regions. However, during the 1992–97 Conservative administration some effort was made to give greater coherence to the English administrative regions by creating regional government offices. The new offices, set up in 1994, included the North East, the North West, the West Midlands, and the South East.

Progress towards devolution

Centralization

The eighteen years of Conservative government from 1979 to 1997 saw a trend towards greater **centralization** within the UK. The powers and freedom of action of local authorities were reduced, regional economic planning councils were abolished (except in Scotland), and the National Health Service was removed from regional control. Conservative governments were adamant that the regions would gain more economically from remaining within a centralized structure. They argued that taxes would be lower and the inflow of investment funds would be greater.

Culturally, the Conservative governments did make some concessions to the regions. The Stone of Scone was returned to Scotland after 700 years in England, and greater resources were made available for Scottish scholarship. However, such concessions were not forthcoming in Wales.

Administratively, Scotland and Wales were given some executive agencies to deal specifically with their problems. For example, in 1993 the Scottish and Welsh Higher Education Funding Councils were established.

Proponents of devolution viewed these changes as mere tinkering with the system and pressed harder for constitutional change. The Scottish Constitutional Convention (SCC) was created in 1989 and reported its findings in 1990. Made up a broad range of opinion in Scotland, it proposed an assembly with **tax-raising powers** elected on the basis of proportional representation. The Labour party's proposals built on these recommendations.

Constitutional change

Referendums were held in September 1997 in both Wales and Scotland. The latter generated a great deal of enthusiasm for a Scottish Parliament with tax-raising powers. The campaign in Wales was rather more low-key, but nevertheless the required majority was achieved for a Welsh assembly. Devolution in both regions will move forward on the basis of an assembly elected according to proportional representation.

Proportional representation

It is likely that some degree of devolution to the English regions will then follow. Plans are already afoot for the recreation of a London-wide authority, be it simply a directly elected mayor and/or an assembly. The regions in the north of England are likely to be the first to follow.

Constitutional issues surrounding devolution

The main issue facing all devolved assemblies will be that of their constitutional position and security. If the principle of parliamentary sovereignty remains in place, the constitutional position of the assemblies will be no better than that of local government. Power can be given and taken away at the will of the Westminster Parliament. The 'independence' of these assemblies can only be secured if Britain adopts a written constitution. This would mean the end of parliamentary sovereignty and clearly defined powers and duties for the regional assemblies.

Written constitution

The **'West Lothian' question** remains on the agenda. This issue – named after the Scottish constituency of MP Tam Dalyell, who repeatedly raised the question – refers to the apparent contradiction of Scottish MPs in the Westminster Parliament having the right to vote on 'English issues', whilst English MPs will not be able to vote on matters that have been devolved to the Scottish Parliament. This possible difficulty remains to be resolved, as does the issue of Scottish and Welsh representation at Westminster. As pointed out earlier, both regions are currently over-represented at Westminster. Will this remain the case after devolution?

'West Lothian' question

Exercises

Short questions

1   **a**   What was the community charge (poll tax)?

b Why was it introduced?

c Outline a case against it.

(ULEAC, June 1990)

2 Can local government be considered democratic given that participation at local level is often extremely limited?

3 **a** What are the main functions of district councils?

b How has the manner in which these functions are performed been affected by changes since 1987?

(ULEAC, January 1992)

4 **a** What are the functions of the metropolitan district councils?

b Is the distribution of functions to such authorities administratively rational?

(ULEAC, June 1990)

Essay questions

1 To what extent can local government act independently of central government?
(ULEAC, June 1993)

2 How far, and by what means, has the role and power of local government been changed in recent years?
(Cambridge, June 1994)

3 How and why does central government attempt to control local government expenditure?
(Oxford, June 1992)

4 How true is it that central–local government relations in recent years have been characterized by increasing central control and a consequent enfeeblement of local democracy?
(Oxford & Cambridge, June 1992)

5 'Local authorities are mere agents of central government.' Discuss.
(EdExcel, June 1996)

6 Discuss the main factors affecting the relationship between central and local government.
(EdExcel, January 1995)

7 Has the role of local government been reduced or strengthened in recent years?
(EdExcel, January 1996)

Data response question

The following is adapted from *Local Government Since Widdicombe*, Joseph Rowntree Foundation, November 1990.

Councils 'put party interests above the public's'

'*Councillors throughout Britain are increasingly putting party loyalty above the interests of their constituents, according to a new survey of 407 local authorities in England, Wales and Scotland, which found that most important decisions were taken in private political group sessions at which councillors were told how they should vote at public council and committee meetings.*

So formalized had the position become that in half of all councils the chief executive officer now attended meetings of the ruling party group to advise on policy. The result was that meetings attended by the public were rendered virtually meaningless because the outcome of every debate had already been decided behind closed doors.

The report by Professor Ken Young of London University and Mary Davies of the Institute of Local Government Studies at Birmingham University found that councillors were also taking a bigger part in appointing middle-ranking council officers, especially in the big cities. "Partisan conduct is rapidly becoming commonplace with members of both major parties increasingly bound by group decisions and with more consistently partisan voting in both council and committee meetings," the report said. While Labour councils remained more politically partisan than those under Tory control, figures showed that Conservatives are rapidly catching up.'

Consider the view that the problem of local government is the dominance of party political control exercised not at central government level but rather within each locality.

(AEB, June 1992)

11 The European Union

Questions to be answered in this chapter

- What is the history of the European Union (EU)?
- What are the relationships between the institutions of the EU?
- What effect has membership of the EU had on British sovereignty?
- What are British political attitudes to the EU?

Terms to know

- Committee of Permanent Representatives (COREPER)
- Common Agricultural Policy (CAP)
- Delors plan
- European Free Trade Area (EFTA)
- Exchange Rate Mechanism (ERM)
- Factortame case
- Federalism
- Group of six
- Luxembourg compromise
- Maastricht Treaty
- Single internal market
- Social Chapter
- Sovereignty
- Supranational
- Treaty of Rome

Introduction

Since the 1950s the European dimension to British political life has been taking on greater proportions. Controversy at first surrounded the possibilities of membership. In the 1970s, the debate was about confirmation of Britain's full membership of the European Community. In the 1980s, political upheaval centred not on membership but on the extent of integration.

Aside from the political controversies that membership of the Euoprean Union has brought, it has also had an impact on British political institutions, in terms of workload and power.

The history of the European Union

Origins   Between 1800 and 1945, major European nations had taken part in four major wars, two largely confined to Europe (the Napoleonic Wars and the Franco-Prussian War) and two taking on a more international character (World Wars I and II). It was in the light of this intra-European conflict that the idea of a European 'community' was born. The French, in particular, felt that Germany was a naturally aggressive nation that would go to war once more if not controlled. This was understandable since France had been attacked by Prussia or Germany three times in less than 100 years.

In 1946, Winston Churchill called for a United States of Europe in order to entwine the political and economic future of the European nations so closely that Germany would be unable and unwilling to turn on its neighbours again. However, he did not believe that Britain should play a role in such a body.

Two French politicians, Jean Monnet and Robert Schuman, were the moving forces behind the early stages of European cooperation. In 1950, they suggested that France and Germany should combine their coal and steel industries under a **supranational** authority. In 1951, France, Germany, Italy, Belgium, the Netherlands and Luxembourg signed the Treaty of Paris which set up the European Coal and Steel Community (ECSC).

European Coal and Steel Community

Soon after the formation of the ECSC, two more European communities were proposed: the European Atomic Community (Euratom) and the European Economic Community (EEC). The former was concerned with the development of nuclear energy; the latter was intended to further economic integration.

Euratom and EEC

The **Treaty of Rome**, setting up the EEC, was signed by the six members of the ECSC in 1957. The treaty set up a customs union in which the six member countries would trade freely with each other, without any tariffs. They also set a common tariff (Common External Tariff – CET) against non-member countries to enable them to trade as a bloc with the rest of the world. In addition to the trade provisions, the treaty also committed the members to the creation of a common regional policy and agricultural policy (**Common Agriculture Policy** – CAP). The ultimate aim was to coordinate the economic and monetary policies of the membership to such an extent that the EEC could be managed as a single economy.

Treaty of Rome

The EEC was designed not only to increase economic cooperation and integration, but also to bring greater political union, and in the late 1960s the institutions of Euratom, the ECSC and the EEC were merged to create the institutions of the European Community (EC).

Britain and the EEC

Britain did not become involved in the early stages of European cooperation. Its links with the Empire and the USA persuaded Britain's leaders that greater union with Europe would undermine Britain's position in the world. Of all the European nations Britain was in a unique international position and considered itself to be a world power with a global, rather than European, perspective on events. The difference in attitude was clearly illustrated by the issue of tariffs. Britain was in favour of global free trade and viewed the creation of a European customs union as bad for the world economy.

Furthermore, the internal upheaval created by the postwar Labour government's nationalization of key industries and the creation of the National Health Service meant that Prime Minister Clement Attlee decided to shun what he perceived to be 'European experiments'.

Sovereignty

A conclusive reason for Britain's reluctance to welcome the EEC was the threat to Britain's **sovereignty**. British politicians believed that European cooperation, the creation of supranational institutions and the aim of greater European union would undoubtedly limit Britain's national sovereignty.

European Free Trade Area

In the late 1950s, under the leadership of Harold Macmillan and a Conservative government, Britain's attitude towards Europe began to change. The disintegration of the Empire, the uncertainty of the special relationship with the USA and the fear of being excluded from the European markets led Britain to look more seriously at European cooperation. As a result, Britain was instrumental in creating the **European Free Trade Area** (EFTA), consisting of Britain, Denmark, Austria, Sweden, Switzerland and Portugal, which was a much looser organization than its EEC counterpart.

Application for membership

By 1961 there had been a further revision of Britain's European policy, as it was decided that Britain's future lay inside the EEC rather than with a number of minor European countries, outside the **group of six**. Therefore, in 1961 Harold Macmillan announced that Britain would seek EEC membership. A year later the French President Charles de Gaulle vetoed the British application.

The Labour government of 1964 did not continue the overtures towards Europe until 1967 – when Charles de Gaulle again used the French veto to exclude Britain, and it became clear that Britain would not be admitted until he had left office. The French President resigned in 1969 and Britain was encouraged to reapply.

Edward Heath and EEC membership

The Conservative party came to power in 1970 led by Edward Heath, who had been Harold Macmillan's envoy to negotiate EEC membership. As Prime Minister, Edward Heath enthusiastically pursued membership of the EC. The European Community Act was finally signed in 1972 and Britain became a member of the EC in 1973.

Referendum on Europe

However, the issue of EC membership continued to be a thorny one when Labour was returned to power in 1974. While Prime Minister Harold Wilson was committed to Europe, many of his party were not. Faced with a divided Cabinet and unable to enforce collective Cabinet responsibility (see page 106), he declared that such an important constitutional issue as continued EC membership should be put to the British electorate through a referendum in 1975. At that time a unique event in British politics, the referendum campaign created unusual partnerships as Labour left-wingers, such as Michael Foot, spoke on the same platform as Conservative right-wingers, like Enoch Powell. The electorate voted 65:35 in favour of continued membership.

Developments in Europe

In the 1980s, the EC moved towards a new stage of European integration. First, the net of integration was widened as the number of states involved in the EC increased. The Republic of Ireland and Denmark had entered the EC with Britain in 1973. They were joined by Greece in 1981 and Spain and Portugal in 1986.

Second, the level of integration was intensified under the presidency of Jacques Delors.

Members initiated the creation of a single internal market, the European Monetary System (EMS), and changes to the methods of voting in the Council of Ministers.

The objective of a **single internal market** was adopted by all members of the EC in 1985. The aim was to ensure the free movement of goods, capital and labour within the EC by 1992. Remaining internal barriers to free movement were abolished and members moved to adapt their laws and regulations to a common European standard. Parliament confirmed British commitment to Europe by passing the Single European Act in 1986.

Single internal market

The 1986 Act also amended the Treaty of Rome to allow the Council of Ministers to make decisions on the basis of support of a majority of members rather than on the unanimous voting that had effectively given each member a veto over EC policies. This was considered necessary owing to the expansion of the EC to twelve members. The **Luxembourg compromise** of 1966 is still in force, which gives individual states the power to veto a policy if they feel that their national interest is threatened by it, and the Community remains committed to seeking consensus on the major issues concerning its development, such as extension of membership, the powers of the community, tax and treaties.

Majority voting

Pressure for greater economic integration has included greater coordination of European monetary policies. The first stage of this process was the creation of the European **Exchange Rate Mechanism** (ERM) within which the currencies of EC countries were partially fixed relative to each other. The ultimate aim is to create a single European currency controlled by a European central bank that would also control a Europe-wide monetary policy. The result of all of these policies would automatically be a greater correlation of economic policy.

Exchange Rate Mechanism

Alongside the drive for greater economic integration has been a move to coordinate the social policies of the member countries. The **Social Chapter** – the brainchild of Jacques Delors – is an attempt to develop common policies on areas such as employment law, trade union representation on companies' boards of directors, and hours of work.

Social Chapter

The moves towards greater integration were formalized at the Maastricht summit in 1991. Here the members of the EC adopted the **Delors plan** for greater integration. Divided into three stages, the plan envisaged an independent European bank and the ECU (European Currency Unit) becoming the currency of the community by 1999.

Maastricht Treaty

As the EC, now known as the European Union, moves towards greater integration, its route seems likely to be complicated by the addition of new members – Austria, Sweden and Finland joined on 1 January 1995 – and by the uncertain commitment of some of its current members, including Britain.

Margaret Thatcher, John Major and Tony Blair

Like Charles de Gaulle before her, Margaret Thatcher was highly suspicious of supranational institutions. At the beginning of her term of office she made the reduction of Britain's contributions to the EEC budget a main priority. In fact, in 1980 and 1981 she gained rebates worth £1.4 billion, with a further instalment in 1982.

EEC budget

Believer's

Margaret Thatcher's scepticism

Following this move, she set about resisting, in her opinion, the continual interference in British affairs by Brussels' bureaucrats. She did not approve of the Social Chapter and often referred to it as the 'socialist chapter' because she saw it as 'socialism through the back door'. Nor was Margaret Thatcher happy with the idea of the ERM. She, and her economics adviser, Alan Walters, believed that sterling should be able to float freely. This issue led to the resignation of the Chancellor of the Exchequer, Nigel Lawson, in 1989, although Britain subsequently joined the ERM in 1990.

Ultimately, Europe was a major factor in Margaret Thatcher's downfall. Her Deputy Prime Minister, Sir Geoffrey Howe, resigned in 1990 and later cited the Prime Minister's unconstructive attitude towards Europe as a major reason for his decision.

John Major

John Major came to power with a more positive attitude to Europe, being a supporter of the ERM and a believer in negotiation rather than confrontation. However, his premiership was beset with difficulties rooted in the European question: how far should Britain go down the road of European integration?

British opt-out clause

At the Maastricht summit in 1991, John Major negotiated an 'opt-out' clause for Britain with regard to the third stage of the Delors plan, leading to a single European currency. He also persuaded the other member nations not to include the Social Chapter in the **Maastricht Treaty**. The Social Chapter is a separate protocol of the treaty, to which Britain at that time did not give its support. The 'opt-out' clause led to concern over an inner and outer circle of the European Union.

ERM problems

John Major's European difficulties were heightened in 1992 when Britain was forced to withdraw from the ERM. The Prime Minister had committed Britain to continued membership at the high exchange rate of 2.95 deutschemarks to the pound sterling, fixed by Margaret Thatcher. However, the financial markets felt that this was too high, and after a period of heavy selling of sterling, Chancellor of the Exchequer Norman Lamont was forced to announce Britain's withdrawal from the ERM.

So-called 'Black Wednesday' – when Britain was forced out of the ERM – probably returned to haunt the Conservative party in the general election of 1997. The images of economic mismanagement were so strong that they perhaps undermined the public's confidence in the Conservative party's ability to manage the British economy successfully. This was a lack of faith and trust that opened the door for the revitalized Labour party.

Euro-rebels

Ratification of the Maastricht Treaty, the prospect of rejoining the ERM and, more recently, increases in Britain's contribution to the EU budget, provoked serious divisions in the Conservative party. With barely a working majority after the 1992 election, John Major by early 1995 had been able to hold the parliamentary party together only with threats of a dissolution if defeated in Parliament. Indeed, in November 1994 the party whip was withdrawn from nine Conservative MPs who abstained in the Commons vote on Britain's contribution to the EU budget.

Tony Blair arrived in 10 Downing Street in 1997 promising to bring Britain into the centre of European decision-making. This was a claim that John Major had made himself, but Blair's ability to deliver on such a claim was reinforced by the 'feel-good' factor that seemed to permeate through Britain and even into European neighbours. Blair was fêted as the new power in Europe during his initial meetings with European colleagues, particularly at the Amsterdam summit in 1997.

In addition, the new government signed up to the Social Chapter and declared its enthusiasm, in principle, for a single European currency – although membership has been ruled out during the lifetime of the 1997–2002 Parliament. The fact that it has been ruled out is probably due to the Labour party's commitment to a referendum on membership of the single European currency. At the time of writing, a 'yes' vote would not by any means be certain. Delaying such a move until after the next general election could enable the Labour party to make a manifesto commitment of joining the single currency.

The institutions of the EU

The institutions of the European Union were established in the late 1960s when Euratom, ECSC and the EEC were merged. The range of institutions, including the Council of Ministers, the European Council, the European Commission, the European Parliament and the European Court, all reflect the dual concerns of the supranational organizations – the national interests of the members and the general interest of the Community.

The Council of Ministers

The Council of Ministers is the main policy-making body of the EU. In fact, there is not one single council but a series, all operating at different levels. The senior council is known as the General Council and is made up of the foreign ministers of the member countries. Below it are the Technical Councils which deal with specific areas of policy and are composed of the relevant ministers from each state.

Councils

There is also a **Committee of Permanent Representatives** of each state – the ambassadors to the EU. This is known by the French acronym COREPER.

COREPER

> **Voting in the Council of Ministers**
>
> Votes in the Council of Ministers are distributed as follows: Germany (10), France (10), Britain (10), Italy (10), Spain (8), Belgium (5), Greece (5), Netherlands (5), Portugal (5), Austria (4), Sweden (4), Finland (3), Denmark (3), Ireland (3), Luxembourg (2).
>
> A simple majority is required on procedural matters.
>
> A qualified majority (61:86 majority) is necessary for issues like the completion of the internal market, discrimination and the free movement of capital.
>
> A unanimous vote is required to enlarge the Community, extend the EU's powers, make changes to laws regarding training, changes in treaties and harmonization of taxation systems.

Working groups All of these levels are supported by a series of working groups made up of civil servants. It is in these groups that proposals from the European Commission are first discussed and passed on to COREPER for agreement. If agreed at COREPER level, the Technical Councils are likely to concur.

Traditionally, the Council of Ministers has endeavoured to avoid taking a vote on issues, in order to determine policy via a consensus. However, as the membership has increased and the emphasis has begun to move away from national interests towards the well-being of the Community, voting has become more common.

The European Council

Since 1974 the heads of government of the member states have met twice a year at a summit meeting. The purpose is to discuss and decide on the main strategic issues facing the EU. Matters for discussion have included the creation of the ERM, the expansion of membership and budget issues.

The European Commission

The Commission was created by the Treaty of Rome and was intended to be the most 'European' of all the institutions. It is composed of bureaucrats from each of the member nations, all of whom are required to be loyal to the Commission rather than to their parent states.

Jacques Delors The Commission is headed by the President – until 1994 Jacques Delors – who coordinates the work of the Commission and has the opportunity to give direction to the Commission. Hence, the plans for development of the EU to the end of the century are known as the Delors plan. In January 1995 Jacques Santer succeeded Jacques Delors as President of the European Commission.

Commissioners Below the President are seventeen commissioners with specific areas of responsibility. Each is nominated by a member state, two from the larger states, one from each of the smaller states. The commissioners are usually former politicians of considerable stature. The commissioners serve a four-year term of office that can be renewable.

The Commission is responsible for initiating the legislative proposals of the EU which are put before the Council of Ministers for approval. In addition, it administers those policies once they have been approved.

Bureaucracy Over recent years, the Commission has been the focus of much British criticism of the EU. It is an unelected body with a great deal of power to 'interfere' in the affairs of the member states. In addition, it has often seemed to be beset by the problems of a bureaucracy: red-tape, lack of common sense, and high costs.

The European Parliament

Powers The European Parliament is *not* the legislature of the EU. Treaties, laws and policies are all drawn up by the Commission and approved by the Council of Ministers. The Parliament merely has the right to be consulted on most, but not all, issues. It has the power to suggest amendments to Commission proposals, but not to impose them on the Commission. It does have the power to reject the annual budget of the EU, but in a direct confrontation with the Council of Ministers is likely to lose. A final power, which has never been used, is the right to dismiss the Commission.

The Parliament is made up of 626 directly elected Members of the European Parliament (MEPs). In 1997, the allocation of seats was as follows: Germany, 99; Italy, UK and France, 87; Spain, 64; Netherlands, 31; Belgium, Greece and Portugal, 25; Sweden, 22; Austria, 21; Denmark and Finland, 16; Ireland, 15; Luxembourg, 6.

Composition

Within the Parliament, the party representatives from each member state have tended to join supranational party groupings. The Labour party participates in the socialist grouping, which is the biggest in the Parliament; while the Conservatives are part of the most nationalist grouping, the European Democratic Group.

The European Court of Justice

The European Court is made up of thirteen judges appointed by the member states for fixed terms of office. Their role is to apply Community law and decisions, regulations and directives of the Commission. Community law is derived from the treaties on which the EU is based, while all the decisions of the Commission and the Council of Ministers also have the force of law. The Court hears cases against the member states and against the Commission itself.

European Union law

The role of the European Court has serious implications for all of the member states because Community law takes precedence over domestic law. Domestic law, therefore, has to be in line with European law or face being struck down by the court. This occurred for the first time in the UK when the **Factortame case** (1991) declared the Merchant Shipping Act (1988) to be contrary to European law (see page 182). As with all courts, the greater their power the more likely they are to become law-makers rather than simply law-enforcers. The European Court is no exception, and its power to interpret the treaties of the EU gives it the opportunity for judicial creativity.

Supremacy of EU law

However, it is important for the European Court, as for all courts, to keep in touch with public opinion. If it fails to do so, it is in danger of losing the respect of the member states. For example, when France refused to allow Britain to export lamb freely, the court ruled in Britain's favour, but France refused to accept the decision and complied only after considerable negotiation.

The European debate

Since 1945 the 'European question' has caused divisions in British society. Initially, the conflict was based on whether Britain would be better off throwing in its lot with the Europeans or with the Empire and with the USA. As the Empire changed into the Commonwealth and the USA turned its attention away from Europe towards Asia, many felt that Europe was the only option if Britain wanted to maintain its position as a trading nation with full access to European markets. However, as the trading argument seemed to have been won and Harold Macmillan's government sought membership of the EEC, the argument shifted away from trade towards sovereignty.

The attitudes of British politicians can perhaps be divided into three groups:
- those favouring withdrawal
- those favouring caution
- those urging progress with integration.

The anti-Europeans

Conservative critics

During the referendum campaign in 1975, the most vociferous anti-European groups were from the left of the Labour party. Michael Foot, Tony Benn and Peter Shore all feared the loss of British sovereignty to a supranational government in Brussels. More recently, the anti-European focus has shifted to the right of the Conservative party – Bill Cash, Sir Teddy Taylor and even Margaret Thatcher herself have been strident in their criticism of the EU. The power of the unelected Commission, the bureaucracy and inefficiency of rule from Brussels, interference in 'the British way of life' and the dominance of the Franco–German alliance within the Community have all provoked harsh criticism of the EU.

Centralization

The organization of the EU and many of the aims of its former President, Jacques Delors, have been fundamentally contrary to those of the Thatcherite right of the Conservative party. Margaret Thatcher believed that she had worked hard to decentralize decision-making, to reduce the regulation of British markets, and to pull down the structures of socialism, as she saw them, in the UK. She did not wish to have those 'evils' reimposed by Brussels.

Sovereignty

Thatcherite objections have focused attention on the loss of sovereignty involved in membership of the EU. We have already seen that European laws and regulations are superior to domestic law and can be enforced by British courts as well as by the European Court of Justice. No longer can the British Parliament be considered sovereign because it is constrained by European laws. As a result, British governments might be forced to follow policies that are contrary to those on which they were elected. Therefore, legal and political sovereignty has been lost.

Their concern over Britain's loss of sovereignty has led some to label the Thatcherites as 'little Englanders', with a narrow, nationalistic perspective on policy-making. In fact, this is an exaggeration. Few members of the Conservative right have actually called for Britain's withdrawal from the EU. At the 1994 Conservative party conference, the former Chancellor of the Exchequer, Norman Lamont, raised eyebrows by calling for discussion of withdrawal from the EU, but few have taken up his theme.

In fact, elements of the philosophy of the EU are very appealing to the right. The creation of a single European market and free competition between nations is equivalent to deregulation in the Thatcherite mould. While Prime Minister, Margaret Thatcher was not so much anti-European as in favour of a different conception of Europe. She was strongly in favour of the expansion of membership of the EU to include the newly independent states of eastern Europe, and even Russia. She was equally strongly opposed to the idea of a United States of Europe, set up along federal

> **Federalism**
>
> **Federalism** involves a group of independent states giving up some of their power to a central government.
>
> Many Euro-critics fear that further European integration will lead to a United States of Europe. Under these circumstances many, but not all, policies would be determined by a central government in Brussels.

lines, preferring instead a confederal Europe with all of the member states joined in a loose organization.

In 1996 a new anti-European force entered British politics – the Referendum party. Created by Sir James Goldsmith, a millionaire financier, its aim was to force a referendum on Britain's membership of the European Union. In the 1997 general election, candidates were fielded in constituencies in which the incumbent MP was a committed pro-European. It has been estimated that Sir James Goldsmith committed £20 million to the party's election campaign.

The Referendum party polled 811,827 votes but failed to win any seats. Probably the biggest impact of the party was on the Conservative party. Many Conservatives felt that Goldsmith's candidates could tap into a fundamental anti-European sympathy in the British electorate that might make the difference between the Conservative party winning or losing marginal seats. As a result many took a more fervently anti-European stance than the Conservative leadership.

The cautious Europeans

The 'anti-Europeans' are probably more accurately described as extremely cautious Europeans. The more moderate version includes the majority of the Conservative party and perhaps the left of the Labour party.

In recent years the Labour party seems to have overcome the divisions of the 1970s and has been united in its support for the EU. However, some commentators argue that while in opposition the party has been happy to unite against the Conservative party which is deeply divided over the future of the EU. It is also true that the Labour party's unity over Europe is a triumph of public relations over reality – or at least in comparison with the appalling public relations of the Conservative party on this issue. In the spring of 1996, while the Conservative government was adopting a policy of 'wait and see' over entry into the single European currency, 40 Labour MPs published a document calling for their own leadership to rule out membership.

Labour party

John Major's approach to Europe was generally enthusiastic, while keeping one eye firmly on Britain's national interests. He sought to prevent interference from Brussels in the social policy of the UK by persuading the other member states to sign the Social Chapter as a separate protocol rather than as a part of the Maastricht Treaty. He also attempted to provide a voice and a point of focus for those members of the Community who were less enthusiastic about the idea of a federal Europe. Many of his

John Major

critics claimed that John Major was seeking a 'two-tier' Europe – with a hard core of federal European states subscribing to all elements of EU policy, while the outsiders, including Britain, would only join up for selected elements of EU policies.

Pro-Europeans

Illusion of sovereignty

Many of the pro-Europeans are found at the centre of British politics. The left of the Conservative party, the right of the Labour party and the Liberal Democrats all support a strong EU with Britain at its core. They argue that Britain's economic future lies inside Europe and that arguments about the loss of sovereignty are merely 'red herrings'.

They suggest that true national sovereignty is an illusion in the contemporary world. Multinational companies, advances in telecommunications, and the interdependence of financial markets mean that, metaphorically at least, Britain is no longer an island. Therefore, whether inside or outside the EU, Britain is not in control of its own destiny and so would be better served by being at the centre of the decision-making process rather than sitting on the sidelines.

Ultimately, however, legal sovereignty resides with the British Parliament. Although the Treaty of Rome does not include any detail about how countries can withdraw from the EU, the British Parliament could repeal the 1972 European Communities Act and so resign its membership at any time. This would involve a breach of the country's treaty obligations, but it could be done.

Exercises

Short questions

1   a   Define sovereignty.
    b   Outline the effect of membership of the European Union on the sovereignty of Parliament.
    (ULEAC, June 1993)

2   Give *two* arguments for and *two* arguments against further integration of nation states within the European Union.

3   a   What is meant by a two-tier or two-track Union?
    b   Give arguments for and against such a proposal.

Essay questions

1   In what ways might Britain's membership of the European Union undermine the sovereignty of Parliament?
    (ULEAC, January 1992)

2   Assess the impact upon domestic government and politics of Britain's membership of the European Community (Union).
    (Oxford, June 1992)

3   Discuss the impact of European institutions on the British system of government.
    (EdExcel, January 1996)

Data response question

The following is from *The Economist*, 21 May 1994.

'*What is Europe for? That simple question is a vital one for an entity so liable to disunity among the nation-states that compose it, to becoming mired in the technical details of the Union's bureaucratic, commercial and legal affairs, and to dreaming up structures before sorting out foundations. Should Europe have a single currency, admit new but poorer members, narrow its democratic deficit, increase its fiscal transfers, or forge a common security policy? Answers to such questions can be found, and agreed upon, only once the prior question is answered. And it is on that question that there is the most disagreement and disillusion.*

The broadest – and best – answer came from the Community's founding fathers in the 1950s. To such as Jean Monnet and Robert Schuman, Europe's primary aim was to end the continent's ancient rivalries by replacing them with a sense of mutual interest. It followed that the motive for ceding sovereignty to European institutions was the same that leads individuals in a nation-state to agree to give powers to their own governments: the idea that some things can be done better together than separately. Only when that is thought to be the case should powers be transferred.'

1   To what extent has membership of the European Union undermined the
    sovereignty of the British Parliament?

2   Do you believe that the European Union has brought an 'end to the continent's
    ancient rivalries'?

3   What effect has membership of the European Union had on the rivalries within the
    Conservative party in Britain?

12 Pressure groups

Questions to be answered in this chapter

- What are pressure groups?
- Why are some groups more powerful than others?
- What factors determine the power of groups in society?
- Are pressure groups a good or bad influence in society?

Terms to know

- Access points
- Corporatism
- Direct methods
- Elite pluralism
- High profile groups
- Indirect methods
- Insider groups
- Interest groups
- Low profile groups
- Oligarchy
- Outsider groups
- Pluralism
- Pressure group
- Prisoner groups
- Promotional groups
- Sectional groups

Introduction

Pressure groups have experienced a fairly uneven press over the last forty years. During the 1950s and 1960s they were seen as the saviours of the democratic process, allowing general participation on a whole range of issues. In the 1970s and 1980s they fell from favour as the activities of some of the more powerful groups were believed to distort the political process as they pursued their own self-interest. Nevertheless, pressure from groups such as companies, trade unions, Friends of the Earth, or the British Medical Association, are very much a part of everyday political life.

As well as examining the role and value of pressure groups in the polical process, this chapter also looks at the comparative power of pressure groups and why some groups have greater influence than others.

What are pressure groups?

Definition A pressure group can be defined as a group of like-minded people who are organized with a view to influencing the formulation of government policy. Unlike political

224

parties, they do not put forward candidates for election to government office and so they do not seek to become government, only to influence the outcome of government decisions. The aims of pressure groups are usually relatively narrow as they tend to concentrate on a limited range of issues. Unlike political parties, they do not put together a manifesto covering a broad spectrum of policies.

Despite the differences between pressure groups and political parties, the distinction between them can often become blurred. Some parties are so small that they can never hope to form the government. Instead, they must try to influence the government. The Ulster Unionists, Plaid Cymru (the Welsh Nationalists) and the Scottish Nationalists are all small parties at Westminster and so can only hope to affect policy in Northern Ireland, Wales or Scotland by influencing the government or the Opposition.

Influence of small parties

In the past, pressure groups like trade unions had such close links with political parties that they were virtually indistinguishable. The trade union movement was the basis for the Labour party's formation, and once provided the bulk of its funding and dominated the direction of party policy. While this link has grown weaker in the 1990s, the unions control 50 per cent of the total votes cast at the party's annual conference, and 33.5 per cent of the votes for choosing a party leader. Union funding of candidates in elections, called 'sponsoring', has been abolished, however, and contributions are now made to local parties rather than the central Labour party.

Ties with parties

Large pressure groups, such as the Confederation of British Industry (CBI) and the trade unions, are concerned with a wide variety of issues. The CBI speaks on behalf of much of British industry, and is therefore interested in all the policy areas that affect industry – from employment to the environment and from education to exports.

Range of issues

The Confederation of British Industry

The Confederation of British Industry (CBI) was created in 1965 to represent the interests of a wide range of firms. In fact, the broad spectrum of firms under its banner has undermined its influence for it has been difficult to unite them behind a single line.

Its influence has waxed and waned since the 1960s. Its high point was probably in the 1970s when it was consulted regularly by the Edward Heath and Harold Wilson governments. Since 1979 it has largely been excluded from government deliberations, although after 1990 it regained a little influence.

The classification of groups

The traditional means of classifying pressure groups is to distinguish between groups according to their aims and the issues they represent. The most common distinction is between promotional and sectional groups.

Sectional groups act on behalf of a particular part of society. They are also known as 'protectional' groups and **'interest' groups** because they protect the interests of a section of society. Therefore, they are sometimes referred to as 'self-interested' groups.

Sectional groups

Examples include the British Medical Association (BMA), the CBI, and the Trades Union Congress (TUC).

Promotional groups

Promotional groups endeavour to promote a particular cause, and for this reason are sometimes called 'cause' groups. They are not self-interested in that they promote an idea or cause to further the general good. Examples include the Campaign for Nuclear Disarmament (CND), Greenpeace UK, Shelter, and Amnesty International.

Short and long term

Pressure groups can also be classified according to their potential lifespan. Interest groups are likely to be long-term groups, unless the section of society that they represent disappears, whereas promotional groups may be short lived because their aims are finite. A promotional group knows when its goals have been achieved because, for example, the fifth runway at Heathrow Airport has or has not been built or nuclear weapons have or have not been destroyed. Of course, this is not true of every cause. Some may be ongoing issues; for example, it may never be clear whether whales or the rain forest are actually safe.

Insider and outsider

In *Pressure Groups, Politics and Democracy in Britain* (Philip Allen, 1989), Wyn Grant – a political scientist – established a classification of pressure groups based on their status and methods rather than their aims. He called them insider and outsider groups.

Direct methods

Insider groups have strong links with decision-makers and are regularly consulted. This may be because these groups are acceptable to the government or helpful for the consultation process. The fact that insider groups are part of the consultation process enables them to use **direct methods** in order to exert influence. This means that they can gain direct access to decision-makers and put forward their case face to face. An example of an insider group under Margaret Thatcher was the Institute of Directors. Insider groups tend to be very powerful and long-term. It is more common for interest rather than promotional groups to be insiders, although this is by no means always the case.

Indirect methods

Outsider groups do not participate in the consultation process, either by choice or because they are excluded by government. In the 1980s, CND was excluded from any consultation process with the government because its aim was unacceptable to the Conservative government. An extreme example of an outsider group is the Irish Republican Army (IRA) which seeks a united Ireland but has been considered an illegitimate organization by the British government. It was considered anti-constitutional because its violent **indirect method** – terrorism – is unacceptable in a democratic country.

Types of insider

Wyn Grant takes the division between insider and outsider groups a step further by distinguishing between different types of insider and outsider group. He divides insiders into high-profile, low-profile and prisoner groups. **High-profile groups** have good contacts with decision-makers, but also choose to build a high public profile. They may do this by gaining exposure through the media. A **low-profile group** has good contacts with decision-makers and chooses to concentrate on these as a means of gaining influence. The CBI was traditionally seen as a low-profile group, working quietly behind the scenes. However, in the 1980s, perhaps as its influence with government declined, it turned to a more high-profile strategy.

Prisoner groups have insider status not by choice but by necessity. Public-sector groups, such as the Consultative Council on Local Government Finance, are part of the governmental process and so must consult regularly with government. To fail to approach such consultation in a constructive manner might result in the loss of finance or the cancellation of a favoured project.

Outsider groups can be divided into potential insiders, outsiders by necessity, and ideological outsiders. Potential insiders seek insider status. In order to achieve this, they use discreet, acceptable methods in the hope that they will be seen as sufficiently legitimate to gain insider status in the future. Their ability to reach insider status depends on the group's political skills. Groups that do not possess the necessary abilities to become insiders are doomed to remain 'outsiders out of necessity'.

Types of outsider

Ideological outsider groups remain outside the consultative process because their beliefs are beyond the realms of normal political acceptability. The Animal Liberation Front has used violent techniques and so its presence in negotiations has generally been seen as unacceptable.

The Trades Union Congress (TUC)

The TUC is the umbrella organization of the trade union movement. It consists of over 70 unions with a combined membership of almost 8 million.

In the 1970s it spoke for labour in trilateral meetings with the government and the CBI, but since 1979 has lost influence. Recently, it attempted to revive its fortunes through a process of modernization, and to some extent it shed the ideological paraphernalia that hindered its progress in the 1980s.

All of the unions retain their independence within the TUC and there are serious divisions – similar to those that beset the Labour party – between the traditionalists and the modernizers.

Groups can move easily between insider and outsider status. Between 1974 and 1979, the TUC was very much an insider group, representing trade unions as a whole in negotiations with government over economic, industrial and employment policy. Meetings at 10 Downing Street were regular events. However, in 1979 when Margaret Thatcher came to power, the trade unions were excluded from all discussions and became an outsider group. As a result, they turned to indirect methods – marches, demonstrations and rallies – in an effort to influence public opinion.

Determinants of the power of individual groups

Pressure groups attempt to influence decision-makers in the hope that their favoured policies will be adopted. In order to do so, they must be able to attract the attention of the decision-makers and be able to compete against other pressure groups. The resources, whether economic or political, of any government are limited. However, there is almost an infinite number of groups which seek to benefit from those resources. Therefore, competition between groups can be fierce. How powerful an individual group becomes depends partly on the nature of the group itself and also on the nature of the government it seeks to influence.

The nature of the group

The power of an individual group depends on a variety of characteristics of the group. They include membership, wealth, knowledge, and importance in society.

Membership

Size — Although often the most obvious characteristic of a pressure group, the size of its membership is by no means the most important. Mass membership is extremely useful if a group wishes to make an impact in the media. Large-scale demonstrations, marches or even strikes are newsworthy and may catch the public imagination, but they do not necessarily lead to influence. In fact, the use of indirect methods, such as demonstrations, can be interpreted as a sign of weakness rather than strength. If such a group had the ear of the government, these types of action would be unnecessary.

Social background — Other characteristics of a group's membership can be at least as important as size. The social background of members could be extremely important. A membership with middle-class, public-school, university backgrounds could be very important in building contacts with members of the civil service or the government. This is perhaps one of the reasons for groups like the BMA and the Bar Association maintaining insider status over a long period of time. Similarly, in 1994 87 per cent of the members of the Friends of the Earth had senior managerial, administrative, professional, educational, technical or scientific occupations.

Knowledge

Credibility — Pressure groups must know the issues *and* the political system because a great deal of their influence depends on the credibility they can build with the decision-makers.

Information — MPs, ministers and civil servants turn to pressure groups for information. To build a steady relationship this information must be reliable. If it is, a pressure group may be able to achieve insider status.

Not only must a pressure group be a source of reliable information, it should also have a sound grasp of the British political system. A well-informed group will be aware, for example, of the limited power of MPs and will use them to ask questions of ministers, propose amendments to legislation and perhaps introduce private members' bills. It will also be conscious of the fact that ministers rely on civil servants for their advice and so a civil servant is an excellent target for pressure group activity.

Wealth

Lobbyists — Obviously the wealth of a pressure group will be partly determined by the nature of its membership. The trade union movement's members are not particularly wealthy. However, their numbers make the movement relatively rich. The wealth of a group can be used to finance indirect campaigning, contributions to political parties and the

> **Lobbyists**
>
> Lobbyists are professional 'influence peddlers'. They act as agents for their clients, putting across their message to decision-makers, helping to plan their strategy and gaining publicity. They are hired due to their access to politicians and civil servants and their knowledge of the political system. Lobbying is big business in the USA where there is estimated to be over 30 lobbyists for each member of Congress.

employment of professional **lobbyists**. The Royal Society for the Protection of Birds (RSPB) hired approximately 50 lobbyists in order to have a significant voice in the Wildlife and Countryside Act of 1981.

Importance in society

The more important a group is in society, the more likely the government is to hear its opinions. Its importance might be in terms of its professional credibility and standing in society or in the negative power it might wield.

The BMA is well respected in society and so has the ear of government. However, even this group has, at times, turned to public campaigns to make its point, particularly over the government's reforms of the National Health Service.

Respect

Trade unions have often commanded the government's attention because of the threat of strike action if their demands are not heard. Chief among these groups was the National Union of Mineworkers (NUM). However, the strike weapon, certainly for the NUM, lost some of its potency during the 1980s with new anti-trade-union laws and high levels of unemployment.

The nature of the government

The influence of an individual group does not depend solely on the nature of the group itself but also on the government it attempts to influence. The government is not a neutral force in pressure group activity and some governments will be more responsive to this type of activity than others.

Margaret Thatcher's administrations were generally unresponsive to pressure group overtures, believing that the government had been elected to govern in the national interest, not in the interests of pressure groups. Those governments that are responsive to pressure group activity are more likely to be amenable to approaches from groups that share their ideological perspectives than those that do not. Had the Labour party won the 1983 election, for example, it is likely that CND would have been more influential.

Targets of pressure group activity

The influence of pressure groups as a whole within a political system largely depends on the range and usefulness of targets for pressure group activity. These targets are known as **access points** and they are, in effect, holes in the political system through which pressure groups can gain access.

Access points

CLEARing the air

'*Few pressure groups have succeeded in routing the combined forces of the government and industry as decisively as the Campaign for Lead-Free Air (CLEAR), which began its fight in January 1982. Tom King, then the Environment Secretary, had announced the previous year that oil companies would have to cut the lead in petrol from 0.4 grams per litre to 0.15 grams by 1985. Mr King had compromised between environmental campaigners, who wanted a complete ban, and the petroleum industry, which wanted no change.*

CLEAR's media campaign highlighted mounting evidence that even small quantities of lead in the air could harm children. The oil companies countered that the dangers were exaggerated and that the cost of phasing out lead would be exorbitant. Godfrey Bradman, a property developer, gave CLEAR a boost by donating £100,000 and by then persuading Des Wilson, a ubiquitous pressure-group activist, to direct it. The decisions of the USA, Japan and Australia to phase out leaded petrol helped. But the coup de grace *came when CLEAR, two months after its launch, leaked a letter by Sir Henry Yellowlees, the government's chief medical officer, warning that the lead in petrol was "permanently reducing the IQ of many of our children".*

In April 1983, when the Royal Commission on Environmental Pollution published a report that confirmed the dangers to children and called for the banning of lead in petrol, Mr King gave in. He announced that the government would support the elimination of lead, that oil companies would have to provide lead-free petrol and that car manufacturers would have to make engines that could use it.

By 1990 lead emissions from car exhausts were 70 per cent lower than a decade earlier. In 1993 a European directive, requiring new cars to be equipped for lead-free petrol, came into force. Yet despite differential taxation that makes lead-free petrol cheaper, many older cars have not been converted to use it. Nearly half the petrol sold in Britain is still leaded. The oil industry does not expect all the British to stop buying the leaded sort until 2005. "You shouldn't get involved in group politics unless you realize that [success] may not happen in your lifetime," says Mr Wilson.'

Source: *The Economist*, 13 August 1994

Project

Choose an issue in which you have an interest and monitor the work of pressure groups in that area over the course of a year.

The availability of access points is determined by the structure of government, the power of political parties and the openness of government. The USA with its strong federal and state governments as well as strict separation of powers (see page 83) between the institutions of central government is riddled with access points. Britain, on the other hand, with its unitary state and limited separation of powers, is a much more closed political system and it is difficult for pressure groups to gain access.

Local government as a target

Local government in Britain is in a weak constitutional position. All power flows from the central government, and so local government is constitutionally dependent on the centre.

Since 1979 central government has taken advantage of its superior position to weaken still further the role of local government. The privatization of council housing, the marketization of local authority services and tighter central government control of local government financing have diminished the position of local government.

Nevertheless, local authorities do retain responsibility for the delivery of local services and for such important functions as local planning. Therefore, pressure groups concerned with issues such as local transport, land development or the provision of leisure facilities often turn their attention to local government.

In metropolitan areas, pressure groups face a simple unitary system, with a metropolitan district responsible for the delivery of services. However, in the shires groups must focus their activities on either the county councils or the district councils, depending on the issue concerned. (For a fuller discussion of the role of local government, see Chapter 10.)

Central government as a target

As we have seen, in a unitary state, power lies at the centre. Therefore, many pressure groups concentrate their activity on this level of government. Within central government the institutions do not share equal power, with Parliament being sovereign. However, the executive branch with a majority in the House of Commons and backed by strong party discipline is, in reality, in a very powerful position.

Parliament

Constitutionally, Parliament is sovereign, which means that it has the power to make any law and it controls finance (see page 90). Therefore, it might be imagined that pressure groups would spend a good deal of time and money lobbying the legislature. However, in reality, the number and usefulness of access points in Parliament are limited.

Although Parliament is bicameral, the upper house, the Lords, has lost much of its power during the twentieth century. It no longer has the power to veto legislation and it plays no role at all in financial matters. Therefore, the usefulness of the House of Lords, from a pressure group's point of view, may be minimal. However, the Lords does retain the ability to amend or delay legislation and, by so doing, can provoke important changes to a bill or at least gain some publicity for a cause. The huge size of government majorities in the 1980s prompted some observers to suggest that the only real opposition to government policies came from the Lords. Therefore, pressure groups may choose to lobby the upper house in certain situations, especially if issues concerning the countryside, the constitution or the elderly are involved.

Within Parliament, sovereignty has passed to the House of Commons and it presents an attractive target for pressure groups. However, the first-past-the-post electoral system usually gives the governing party a working majority, and as this is backed by

Unitary state

Weakened local government

Parliamentary sovereignty

House of Lords

House of Commons

Party discipline

strong party discipline, the government is often in a dominant position. In the 1950s and 1960s, the government's position was almost absolute, with party discipline only rarely breaking down. In the 1970s and 1980s, backbench revolts became more common. This gave pressure groups the opportunity to work on a group of government backbenchers in the hope of threatening government defeat.

Questions

Pressure groups also make use of MPs to ask oral and written questions of ministers, to suggest amendments to legislation, and even to put forward private members' bills. Questions can be helpful to gain information or to bring an issue to the attention of Parliament, the media and the public.

Private members' bills

Private members' bills (see page 89) can be very effective in promoting the aims of pressure groups. The most common method of introducing a bill is through the ballot by which half a dozen backbenchers are selected to put forward a bill of their choosing. The successful backbenchers are usually besieged by lobbyists immediately after the results of the ballot are known.

Free votes

Private members' bills are most likely to succeed when the government gives its tacit support to a piece of legislation. This is most common with matters of social morality which the government does not wish to make a partisan issue. Normally, under these

---

Pressure groups and Parliament

'The House of Commons has a reputation as the best club in London. One can see why. Not only does it have a wonderful clubhouse, but many of its members are paid by eager lobbyists to pursue their clients' interests ...

Following the lobbying industry's explosive growth in the 1980s, some MPs now seem to see their job more as peddling influence than pursuing the interests of their constituents. More than 200 MPs (out of 651) are employed as parliamentary consultants to lobbying companies and other commercial organizations. Their duties can range from mere advice on parliamentary procedure to supportive speeches, questions and lobbying of government ministers. The fees for such work can be considerable. A single parliamentary consultancy can pay £10,000 or more a year, a third of an MP's salary ...

The Public Relations Consultants Association and the Institute of Public Relations, which between them represent more than 150 companies and 5000 individual members, are jointly to set up a register of political lobbyists and establish a code of practice. This will require registered lobbyists to name MPs who work for them, and to give details of the clients to whom the service is provided, which goes a little further than the Commons' existing rule. But the lobbyists' new code will not require disclosure of what voters are entitled to know – how much is being paid and for what. The Association of Professional Political Lobbyists, a smaller group of lobbyists, has gone much further, in a bid to attract clients who want to look spotlessly clean. This group has ruled that none of its members may pay fees of any kind to MPs or employ them in any capacity ...

Source: *The Economist*, 24 September 1994

circumstances MPs are allowed a free vote (see page 94) and so the stranglehold of political parties is relieved. An example of successful pressure group activity behind a private members' bill includes that carried out by the Abortion Law Reform Association which campaigned for the liberalization of abortion law in 1967 and has successfully prevented any retreat from this position.

Pressure groups can also take advantage of the Select Committee system in the Commons (see page 100). These committees are permanent and scrutinize the work of most government departments. This allows pressure groups to build links with the members of the committees and to give evidence before the committee.

Committees

The executive

The government is responsible for initiating and implementing policy. Therefore, the greater part of policy-making takes place in the executive branch rather than in the legislature. The responsibility for this decision-making rests with ministers on the advice of civil servants.

It is not easy for pressure groups to gain access to ministers. They are at the apex of the governmental system and their time is precious. Groups such as the CBI and the TUC have been able to gain regular access to ministers at times, but most will attempt to build relationships with the civil service.

Civil servants are often willing to consult with pressure groups because they can be a source of information and cooperation. The former helps to give administrators a sound understanding of important issues. The latter is necessary to implement government policy effectively. Peter Middleton, a former permanent secretary to the Treasury, summed up the position of civil servants: 'If you want information, you've got to allow people to give you opinions too' (quoted in *The Economist*, 13 August 1994).

Civil servants

From a pressure group's point of view, civil servants can provide information and, most importantly, an indirect route to the minister. The two-way nature of these relationships is often referred to as **clientelism**. Insider groups that might claim to have such a relationship include the National Farmers Union with the Department of Agriculture and the Howard League for Penal Reform with the Home Office.

Clientelism

The judiciary

Although the power of the English courts is limited by the doctrine of parliamentary sovereignty, pressure groups can bring cases before the judiciary. Between 1989 and 1991, members of the Anti-Poll Tax movement adopted a policy of civil disobedience by refusing to pay the community charge. They were taken to court and imprisoned and, as a result, gained considerable publicity for their cause.

Courts

Political parties

We saw above how the strength of political parties in Britain reduces the opportunities for pressure group activity in the Commons. The reasons for their strength lie largely in their electoral role. They nominate candidates, organize and finance their campaigns, provide a manifesto and command voter loyalty. Therefore, MPs owe their

Strong parties

Grass-roots lobbying

positions in the Commons to their party rather than to their own personality or organizations. They are likely to pay more attention to the views of their party than to those of their constituents. This reduces the effectiveness of grass-roots lobbying.

Comparison

In the USA, members of Congress are keenly aware of their constituency interests and so are very susceptible to pressure group activity that might influence their chances of re-election. Campaigns to influence public opinion and the provision of election finance give pressure groups the opportunity to influence the views of members of Congress.

Perspectives on pressure group activity

Although pressure groups are now a well-established part of the political scene in democratic countries, there remains considerable disagreement over the desirability of pressure group activity. Broadly speaking, opinions can be divided into three perspectives:
- **pluralism**
- **sectionalism**
- **corporatism**.

Pluralism

Made popular in the 1950s and 1960s in Britain and the USA by political scientists such as Anthony Downs (*An Economic Theory of Democracy*, Harper and Row, 1957) and David Truman (*The American Governmental Process*, Alfred A Knopf, 1951), pluralism identifies pressure groups as the main means of participating within a political system and argues that, as such, they improve democracy.

Participation

There are three methods of participating in a political system:
- voting
- joining a political party
- joining a pressure group.

Postwar consensus

Pluralists consider voting to be of only irregular significance. General elections occur only periodically and individuals are asked to vote for packages of policies put together by political parties. Therefore, voters do not have an opportunity to wield influence on the specific issues that concern them. In addition, for much of postwar British political history, those packages of policies provided little choice for the electorate. The postwar political consensus meant that there was little difference between the Conservative and Labour parties, so the electorate was trapped in the political status quo.

Oligarchical parties

Joining a political party is also an inadequate form of participation because parties tend to be dominated by a few leaders at the top of the party hierarchy – parties are **oligarchical**. Therefore, individuals joining a party would have little influence and, once again, would have to support a whole range of policies without the opportunity to specialize in their area of interest.

Pressure groups, on the other hand, can be formed around any political issue. They can be long-term or short-term, and they give the individual the opportunity to have influence over specific issues. Pluralist theorists believe that democracy could be redefined in terms of groups rather than individuals. Groups would be free to form around any issue and they would compete freely with each other, with the government acting as a neutral referee and arbiter of their claims. The result would be the best possible outcome for society.

Group competition

This vision of pressure group competition can be compared to the perfect competition of economic theory and the free market doctrines of the eighteenth-century economist Adam Smith. According to this view, if each pressure group pursued its own self-interest, it would collectively determine the national interest and the country as a whole would benefit.

A criticism of pluralist theory is that all pressure groups are not equal and therefore the competition between groups is not free. Critics dispute the argument that pressure groups can form around any issue. Some issues are considered socially unacceptable and so it is difficult for groups to form. The unemployed do not have a pressure group to speak on their behalf partly because they are difficult to organize and to contact.

Unequal competition

Critics also point to the fact that pressure groups, like political parties, are hierarchical. Robert Michels, a German sociologist, in what he termed the 'Iron Law of Oligarchy', argued that all organizations become more bureaucratic and oligarchical as they grow in size (Robert Michels, *Political Parties*, The Free Press, 1949).

Oligarchical groups

Some pressure groups are much more powerful than others. They will be able to dominate the decision-making system, often influencing the outcome in their favour. Several pluralists have accepted this criticism and have absorbed it into a new theory of **elite pluralism**. According to this perspective, the government, as neutral referee, will act on behalf of the weaker groups in society, thus compensating for their disadvantaged position.

Elite pluralism

A final criticism can be levelled at both pluralism and elite pluralism: the government and the state are not neutral. The attitude of the government changes as the personnel of government change, even within the same party. Moreover, Marxists would argue that the state is not neutral. All states are run along the lines of an ideology. Britain is a liberal–capitalist state and is therefore dominated by a liberal ideology. Groups operating within this ideological framework will automatically be favoured by the system.

State bias

Sectionalism

The sectionalist perspective is largely an extension of the criticisms of pluralism. Sectionalism believes that the most powerful pressure groups are the interest groups. By definition, these groups are dedicated to furthering their self-interests. In so doing, they distort the national interest in their favour and can dominate the system to such an extent that they undermine democracy.

In Britain this view is most closely associated with the right of the Conservative party. The New Right argues that in the 1970s the trade union movement became too powerful. The trade union legislation of Edward Heath's government (1970–74) led to

New Right

strikes, a three-day working week and, eventually, an election fought on the question of who governs the country – the government or the unions. The Conservative party lost the election and the Labour party came to power, introducing an era of unprecedented consultation between trade unions and government. According to New Right analysis, the trade unions had exceeded the role of a pressure group and had been given too great a voice in the management of the country. They were not elected to take part in government decision-making and they were undermining the authority of those who had been elected to govern the country.

As a result, Margaret Thatcher's administrations between 1979 and 1990 were reluctant to involve pressure groups too closely in the consultation process – and trade unions were excluded completely.

Corporatism

Corporatism involves bringing pressure groups totally inside the governmental process. The pressure groups sacrifice their independence in return for the protection and patronage of the government. Traditional corporatism is often found in dictatorships such as Nazi Germany and Mussolini's Italy.

Tripartism · The theory of corporatism has been amended to explain the involvement of the TUC and the CBI in government decision-making in the 1970s. This is known as neo-corporatism. The tripartism of the social contract era (1974–79), in which the CBI and TUC were involved with the government in making economic policy, was an attempt to use the experience and information of the two leading industrial groups in an effort to bring down the level of inflation and to improve Britain's economic performance.

Such incorporation of pressure groups is common in many European countries, including Sweden and Germany. The philosophy is that pressure groups can bring information and cooperation to the governmental process, and thereby the quality of government decision-making will be improved.

Critics of such a philosophy argue that the government has been elected to govern and it should do so in a responsible manner. It should not allow unelected and unrepresentative pressure groups to have undue influence in this process.

Exercises

Short questions

1 a   Distinguish between political parties and pressure groups.
   b   Why is it sometimes difficult to distinguish between the two?
   (ULEAC, January 1995)

2 a   Distinguish between two types of pressure group.
   b   Explain, with examples, how this distinction is blurred.
   (ULEAC, January 1991)

3 Explain the continuing growth of promotional (i.e. cause) groups.
   (EdExcel, January 1996)

Essay questions

1 a Why is Parliament subjected to so much lobbying by pressure groups?
   b Should there be greater control over lobbying?
   (ULEAC, June 1992)

2 'We have elections and opinion polls, hence pressure groups are unnecessary.' Do you agree?
   Cambridge, June 1993)

3 What distinguishes successful from unsuccessful pressure groups in Britain?
   (Oxford & Cambridge, June 1994)

4 To what extent do pressure group politics pose a threat to democracy in Britain?
   (Oxford, June 1992)

5 a Why have pressure groups increasingly concentrated upon Parliament?
   b To what extent are their activities a cause for concern?
   (EdExcel, June 1996)

Data response question

Consider the fictitious press report printed below involving two pressure groups, Friends of the Earth (FoE) and the National Farmers Union (NFU), and suggest the tactics that would in your view probably be adopted by each group. Using your knowledge of pressure group behaviour and successes, suggest which group would be most likely to win, indicating any other factors that could be important influences on the final outcome.
(AEB, June 1992)

Friends become foes for farmers!

'*Plans to build a new reservoir at Applecombe Moor as part of a national water grid which were last week welcomed by the county NFU branch received a hefty "thumbs down" on Monday when leaders of the nationwide conservation body, Friends of the Earth, came out strongly against the proposal.*

Both the MPs for the county have been heavily lobbied by members of both organizations during the past week and it seems that both Margaret Winter (Appleton North) and Larry Havant (Appleton South) are still undecided, even though Mrs Winter has long been known as a member of FoE, and, as a farmer with 1000 acres adjacent to the moor, Mr Havant is a member of the NFU.

The County Council has indicated informally that it will support the water authority if, as now seems likely, the Minister feels it necessary to order a public inquiry into the proposal.

However, the reservoir idea seems likely to become a major issue at the next election. Prospective Green candidate, Polly Shaw, said this week that she will be organizing a county-wide petition and a water rates boycott against the plan. "This whole matter is too important for the NFU steamroller to crush the opposition of all of us who really care."'

Sources

Andrew Adonis, *Parliament Today*, Manchester University Press, 1993

Samuel Beer, *Modern British Politics*, Faber, 1969

Tony Benn, *Arguments for Democracy*, Penguin, 1979

BBC Television, *Thatcher, The Downing Street Years*, Fine Art Productions, 1993

Richard Crossman, 'Introduction', in Walter Bagehot, *The English Constitution*, Collins, 1964

A H Birch, *The British System of Government*, Allen & Unwin, 1980

Hugh Collins, *Marxism and Law*, Oxford University Press, 1987

Julian Critchley, *Heseltine, The Unauthorised Biography*, Coronet, 1988

Richard Crossman, *The Crossman Diaries* (condensed version), ed. Anthony Howard, Methuen, 1979

Robert Dahl, 'The concept of power', *Behavioural Science*, 1957

A V Dicey, *Introduction to the Study of the Law of the Constitution*, 1885

Anthony Downs, *An Economic Theory of Democracy*, Harper & Row, 1957

Patrick Dunleavy and Chris Husbands, *British Democracy at the Crossroads*, Longman, 1985

Government policy paper, 'The civil service: continuity and change', HMSO, 1994

Government white paper, 'Efficiency and effectiveness in the civil service', HMSO, 1982

Wyn Grant, *Pressure Groups, Politics and Democracy in Britain*, Philip Allen, 1989

John Griffith, *The Politics of the Judiciary*, Fontana, 1977

Alan Griffiths and John Wall, *Applied Economics*, Prentice Hall, 1986

John A Hall, *Liberalism*, Paladin, 1987

H L A Hart, *The Concept of Law*, Clarendon Press, 1961

Anthony Heath, Roger Jowell and John Curtice, *How Britain Votes*, Pergamon, 1985

Peter Hennessy, 'The throne behind the power', *The Economist*, 24 December 1994

Peter Hennessy, *Whitehall*, Secker & Warburg, 1989

Ivor Jennings, *Cabinet Government*, Cambridge University Press, 1958

Bill Jones et al., *Politics UK*, Prentice Hall, 1998

Dennis Kavanagh and Anthony Seldon (eds), *The Major Effect*, Macmillan, 1994

H C G Matthew, *Gladstone 1809–74*, Clarendon Press, 1986

Robert Michels, *Political Parties*, The Free Press; first published as *Zur Soziologie des Parteiwesens in der Modern Demokratie*, Leipzig, 1925

L Minkin, *The Labour Party Conference*, Manchester University Press, 1980

Philip Norton, *The Commons in Perspective*, Basil Blackwell, 1985

Philip Norton, 'The pattern of backbench dissent', *Parliament in the 1980s*, Basil Blackwell, 1985

David Pannick, *Judges*, Oxford University Press, 1987

Clive Ponting, *Whitehall: Tragedy and Farce*, Hamish Hamilton, 1986

James Prior, *A Balance of Power*, London, 1986

R A W Rhodes, 'Local government', in B Jones and L Robbins (eds), *Two Decades in British Politics*, Manchester University Press, 1992

Geoffrey Robertson, *Freedom, the Individual and the Law*, Penguin, 1993

Joshua Rozenberg, *The Search for Justice*, Hodder & Stoughton, 1994

George H Sabine, *A History of Political Theory*, Harrap, 1937

David Truman, *The Governmental Process*, Alfred A Knopf, 1951

Erik Ohlin Wright, *Class, Crisis and the State*, Verso, 1975

Hugo Young, *One of Us*, Macmillan, 1989

Hugo Young, *The Judges*, BBC Radio 4, 13 April 1988

Hugo Young and Anne Sloman, *No, Minister: an Inquiry into the Civil Service*, BBC, 1982

Index

access points, pressure
    groups, 229
acts, legislative process, 80–1,
    88–9, 100–2
additional member system
    (AMS), 28
adversarial politics
    definition, 15
    party system, 54
    stability, 32
advice, civil servants, 136–40,
    144–5
agenda, Cabinet, 118–19,
    127–8
agreement to differ, 107
alternative vote system, 28
amendments, Lords, 97
American Declaration of
    Independence, 70
Armstrong, Sir Robert, 119,
    152
assembly, control, 91
association, freedom of, 185,
    186, 188
Attorney-General, 174
Audit Commission, 203–4
authority, 3–4
    judiciary, 180–1
    monarchy, 166
    Parliament, 164

backbenchers, revolts, 95–6
backwoodsmen, 79
Bagehot, Walter, 13, 109,
    113, 114, 165
Banham Committee, 196–7
Beer, Samuel, 95
Benn, Tony, 147, 149, 150
bilateral meetings, Cabinet,
    125
bills, passage of, 88–9
bills of rights, 10, 15–17,
    165, 182, 185, 190–1
Birmingham Six, 175

Blair, Tony, 119–20
    Cabinet, 126
    civil service, 157
    European Union, 216–17
    mayors, 197
    personality, 127
BMA see British Medical
    Association
bottom-up parties, 59, 131
Boundaries Commission, 21,
    28
British Medical Association
    (BMA), 226, 228, 229
Britton, Leon, 138
Brixton riots, 180
budget, 90
bureaucracy, 145, 160, 218
Burke, Edmund, 23, 70, 71,
    86
Butler, Robin, 119
by-elections, 22
bylaws, 195

Cabinet, 106–13
    agenda, 118–19, 127–8
    collective responsibility,
        8–9, 106–8
    committees, 109, 110, 124
    composition, 116–17
    decision-making, 123–6
    kitchen, 125
    Prime Minister, 105–34
    reshuffles, 131
    role, 113
    wider system, 108, 111–12
Cabinet Secretariat, 118–20
Campaign for Lead-Free Air
    (CLEAR), 230
Campaign for Nuclear
    Disarmament (CND),
    226
CAP see Common
    Agricultural Policy
capping, 201, 205

Castle, Barbara, 145, 149,
    150
CBI see Confederation of
    British Industry
centralization, 199–200, 208
    Europe, 220
    local government power,
        200
Charles I, King of England,
    78
civil liberties, 15–16, 184–5
Civil List, 167
civil service, 135–62
    accountability, 158
    anonymity, 137, 144,
        147–8
    anti-radical, 150
    appointments, 117–18, 149
    background, 146–7
    bureaucracy, 160
    continuity, 136, 159
    Efficiency Unit, 153
    functions, 136–40
    higher civil servants,
        136–40
    neutrality need, 143–4,
        147, 149–50, 156–8
    New Labour, 158–9
    permanence, 141–2, 145–7,
        156
    policy implementation, 145
    politicization, 117–18,
        150–2, 156–7
    power, 144–9, 148
    pressure groups, 233
    Prime Minister's support,
        128
    recruitment, 142
    reform, 154–8
    scale, 147
    secrets trials, 152
    senior grades, 156
Civil War, 78, 164
Clarke, Alan, 187

class system
  definitions, 34–5
  monarchy, 166
  political parties, 51
  voting, 34–6
clientelism, 233
CND see Campaign for
  Nuclear Disarmament
coalition governments,
  29–32, 106, 129
coercion, 3
collective responsibility,
  ministers, 8–9, 106–8
collective rights, 185
committees
  see also select committees;
    standing committees
  Cabinet, 109, 110, 111–12,
    124
  councils, 195
  interdepartmental, 147
  Parliament, 90, 99–102
  political parties, 96–7
Common Agriculture Policy
  (CAP), 213
common law, 112, 176
Commonwealth, 166
community charge, 204
competitive tendering, 112,
  202, 202–3
Confederation of British
  Industry (CBI), 225,
  236
conferences, political parties,
  59, 60–2
consensus politics, 15, 53
consent, 4
  liberalism, 68
conservatism, 68, 70–3
Conservative Party
  1922 Committee, 56,
    96–7
  candidate nomination, 41
  Central Office, 58
  class voting, 34–6
  conference, 59
  dominance, 54
  European Union, 214,
    215–16, 220
  funding, 43
  government 1951-1955,
    73
  House of Lords, 79
  leadership election, 56, 57,
    58

organization, 55–9
policy provision, 47–8
reform, 40, 58
sectionalism, 235–6
shadow Cabinet
    appointments, 49
  structure, 131
  tendencies, 56
  voting patterns, 24–8
constituencies, 21–2
constituents, role of MPs, 86
constitution, 5–17
  Cabinet, 113–14
  civil service, 156
  conventions, 167
  devolution, 209
  evolution, 71
  history, 11–12
  judiciary, 171–3
  reform, 14–17
  types, 10–17
  written, 15–17
constitutional monarchy, 78,
  163–5
constraints, Prime Minister,
  127–31
control
  assembly, 91
  executive, 89
  financial, 90
  political parties, 83
conventions, 13
cooperation, socialism, 73–4
corporatism, 189, 199, 236
council tax, 205–6
councillors, 194–5
county councils, 196
Court of Appeal, 171, 179
Criminal Justice Act 1994,
  189
Critchell Down affair, 137–8
Cromwell, Oliver, 78
crossbenchers, 50, 79, 96
Crossman, Richard, 113–15,
  118, 146, 149, 150
currency, single European,
  215, 217

Dahl, Robert, 2
delegates, 23
  representation, 87
Delors, Jacques, 218
democracy, 19–20
  House of Lords, 79–80
  representative, 20, 86

Denning, Lord, 177
Deputy Prime Minister, 112
deviant voting, 34–6
devolution, 15, 63, 206,
  208–9
Dicey, A.V., 9, 10, 13, 82–3,
  172, 173
dissolution of Parliament,
  32–3
district councils, 196
divine right of kings, 164
dominant party system, 39
Donaldson, Lord, 174
Droop formula, 29
Duverger, Maurice, 52–3

ECHR see European Court of
  Human Rights
Ecology Party, 64
ECSC see European Coal and
  Steel Community
education, 69, 202
EEC see European Economic
  Community
Efficiency Unit, 86, 122
EFTA see European Free
  Trade Area
elections, 19–38
  1997, 26–7, 43, 52
  campaigns, 42–7
  candidates, 41–2
  funding, 43, 46
  local government, 194
  manifestos, 45–6, 47
  results, 25–8
  secret ballot, 21
  voters, 20, 21
elective dictatorship, 15
electoral reform, 80–1, 83
  see also reform issues
  constituents, 86–7
  political parties, 40
electoral systems, 20–33
  assessment, 22–3
Elizabeth II, Queen of
  England, 78, 166, 167
embourgeoisement, 34
EMS see European Monetary
  System
environment, issues, 64
equality concept, 69–70, 74,
  186
ERM see Exchange Rate
  Mechanism
EU see European Union

European Coal and Steel
    Community (ECSC), 213
European Commission, 218
European Convention on
    Human Rights, 13, 184,
    190
European Council, 218
European countries, Prime
    Minister, 116
European Court of Human
    Rights (ECHR), 190
European Court of Justice,
    219
European Economic
    Community (EEC), 213
    see also European Union
European Free Trade Area
    (EFTA), 214
European Monetary System
    (EMS), 215
European Parliament, 218–19
European Union (EU),
    212–23
    Council of Ministers,
        217–18
    critics, 220–2
    history, 212–17
    institutions, 217–19
    integration, 214–15
    judicial review, 182
    law, 112
    single internal market, 215
    social chapter, 215, 216,
        217
    sovereignty, 84–5, 220
evolutionary change, 70
Exchange Rate Mechanism
    (ERM), 215, 216
executive, 7–9
    civil service, 135–6
    control, 89
    councils, 195
    elective dictatorship, 15
    Lord Chancellor, 173
    parliamentary, 8
    power, 11–12
    pressure groups, 233
    sovereignty, 83
executive agencies, 111–12
expressive voting, 34

Fabians, 59
Factortame case, 85, 182,
    219
Fares Fair case, 181, 198

federalism, 7
    European Union issue, 221
financial control, 90
Financial Management
    Initiative (FMI), 153
first-past-the-post (FPTP)
    system, 22–8, 52, 91
floating voters, 46
FMI see Financial
    Management Initiative
foreign policy, 89
    leadership, 111
FPTP see first-past-the-post
    system
France, Cabinet system, 107
franchise, 20, 21, 81
free market, local
    government, 201
free votes, 94, 232–3
freedom, 69, 184, 186–8
Fulton Report 1969, 142
funding, elections, 43–6

GCHQ see Government
    Communications
    Headquarters
gender
    candidate selection, 41
    judiciary imbalance, 179
    local councillors, 194
    women MPs, 87, 98
Germany
    coalition government, 129
    electoral system, 28, 32
    Federal Constitutional
        Court, 183
Gillick case, 177
GLC see Greater London
    Council
Glorious Revolution, 78, 164
governance, 208
government
    Cabinet, 106–13
    central/local relationship,
        6–7, 197–9
    community model, 159–60
    election, 22
    functions, 7–10
    leadership, 110–11
    limited system, 9, 70
    local, 193–206
    members, 81
    Presidential, 91, 114
    Prime Ministerial, 113–23
    rule of law, 172–3

structure, 91–4
    types, 6–7
Government Communications
    Headquarters (GCHQ),
    188
Grant Related Expenditure
    Assessment (GREA), 200
GREA see Grant Related
    Expenditure Assessment
Greater London Council
    (GLC), 181, 195, 201
Green Party, 64
Griffith, Professor John,
    178–9
guillotine, Parliamentary
    motions, 92

Hailsham, Lord, 15, 174
Hansard, 93
Heath, Edward, 235
hereditary peers, 78
Heseltine, Michael, 138,
    147–8, 196, 205
High Court, 171
Hogg, Sarah, 122
hospital trusts, 204
House of Commons
    see also Parliament
    bills, 88
    composition, 8, 81, 231–4
    lobbyists 229
    origins of, 164
    political parties, 82
    power, 33
    reform, 97, 98, 99
House of Lords, 78–81
    see also Parliament
    bills, 88, 97
    composition, 78
    independence, 97
    Law Lords' decisions,
        175–6
    Lord Chancellor's role, 173
    origins of, 164
    political parties, 50, 97
    pressure groups, 231
    reform, 80
housing, 202
Howard, Michael, 157
human nature
    liberalism, 68
    socialism, 73–4
human rights, 184
hung parliament, 29
Hurd, Douglas, 181

Ibbs, Robin, 154, 155
ideologies, 67–76
individual responsibility,
    ministers, 9, 11–12, 137
individual rights, 185
individualism, 69
influence, 3
information, Parliament, 99
Ingham, Bernard, 121
insider groups, 226
institutions, 7–10, 71–2
    European Union, 217–19
instrumental voting, 36
internal market, 203
international agreements,
    12–13
investigation, Parliament, 89
Ireland see Irish Republic;
    Northern Ireland
Irish Republic, electoral
    system, 29
Irish Republican Army (IRA),
    226
Italy, government instability,
    32

James, Howell, 121
Jefferson, Thomas, 70
Jennings, Sir Ivor, 109
Jopling Report, 98
judicial inquiries, 180
judicial reviews, 85, 180–2,
    198
judiciary, 170–92
    appointments, 171, 174,
        184
    background, 178–9
    bill of rights, 190–1
    controversial laws, 179–80
    creativity, 175
    decision making process,
        175–7
    definition, 7
    gender, 179
    independence, 10, 171–2,
        173
    judicial/political decisions,
        172–3
    media, 178
    non-partisan, 171, 172
    policy making, 177
    politicization, 174, 184
    power, 182–4, 190
    pressure groups, 233
    race, 179

salaries, 171
written constitution, 16

Kilmuir rules, 172, 178
Kinnock, Neil, 152
kitchen Cabinet, 125

Labour Party, 59–62
    candidate nomination,
        41–2
    civil servants' opposition,
        149
    class voting, 34–6
    conference, 61–2
    discipline, 60
    European Union, 220
    formation, 40
    funding, 43–5
    government 1945-1951, 73
    groups within, 59–61
    headquarters, 63
    House of Lords, 79
    leadership elections, 60
    metropolitan authorities,
        194, 201
    National Executive
        Committee (NEC),
        61–2
    nationalization, 74–5
    New Labour, 74
    one member, one vote, 42,
        49, 61, 62
    organization, 59–63
    policy provision, 47–9
    reform of, 39–40, 48–9
    shadow Cabinet
        appointments, 49
    structure, 131
    voting patterns, 24–8
Labour Reform Group, 60
law
    see also statute law
    common law, 12, 176
    European, 84–5, 182
    rule of, 10, 70, 172–3
Law Lords, 174
leadership, government,
    109–11
legislation
    Parliamentary, 88–9, 97
    power of the Lords, 80
legislature, definition, 7
legitimacy, 4
legitimization, 91
Lewis, Derek, 157

Lib-Lab Pact, 30–1
Liberal Democrat Party, 63–4
    candidate nomination, 42
    development, 40
    organization, 63–4
    voting patterns, 24–7, 53–4
liberalism, 68–70
liberty, conservatism, 72–3
life peers, 78
limited government, 9, 69
lobby system, 121
lobbyists 229, 232
local authorities,
    Thatcherism, 69
local government, 193–206
    Banham committee, 196–7
    central government
        relationship, 6–7,
        197–9
    expenditure, 200–1
    free market, 201
    functions, 196
    politicization, 194
    pressure groups, 21
    structure, 195–7
    tier system, 195–6
Local Government Acts, 195,
    201
Locke, John, 68
Lord Chancellor, 171, 173–4

Maastricht Treaty, 96, 215,
    216
Mackay, Lord, 174, 178
Macmillan, Harold, 93
Magna Carta, 11, 163
Major, John
    backbench revolts, 96
    Cabinet, 125
    collective responsibility,
        107–8
    European Union, 216,
        221–2
    personality, 126–7
    Political Office, 121
    Press Office, 121
majority, Parliamentary, 128
mandarins, 137
mandate, electoral, 30
Manifesto Group, 60
manifestos, elections, 45–6,
    47
marital rape, judicial policy
    making, 177
market testing, 155–6

marketization, local government, 201, 202–3
Marxism, judiciary, 178–9
Master of the Rolls, 177
Matrix Churchill case 1992, 189
media
  election campaigns, 42
  judiciary, 178
  Prime Minister, 132
  Sinn Fein, 188
Members of the European Parliament (MEPs), 219
Members of Parliament (MPs), 81
  discipline, 95
  dissent, 95–6
  lobbyists, 232
  outside interests, 87, 97–8, 232
  promotion, 95, 116
  questions, 92–3, 232
  reform, 97, 98
  role, 86
  women, 41, 87, 98
  workload, 97
MEPs see Members of the European Parliament
meritocracy, 70
  civil service, 141–2
metropolitan authorities, 194, 196, 197, 201
Militant Tendency, 60
Mill, John Stuart, 68
ministers
  appointments, 49, 116–17
  Cabinet, 106–8
  civil servants, 145
  question time, 92–3
  resignations, 138–40
  responsibility
    collective, 8–9, 106–8
    individual, 9, 11–12, 137
  weakness, 148–9
minority government, 29–30, 33, 129
monarchy, 163–9
  authority, 16
  Bill of Rights (1689), 184, 185
  constitutional, 78
  dissolution of Parliament, 32–3
  non-partisan, 165, 167
  Parliament, 13, 78, 164–5

powers, 165–6
Monday Club, 56
Montesquieu, Baron, 7, 9, 171
motions, guillotine, 92
movement, freedom of, 188
MPs see Members of Parliament
multi-party system, 29–31, 39, 51–2
municipal socialism, 201

National Health Service, 204
national identity, 207
National Union of Conservative Associations, 59
nationalism, 51, 71–2
nationalization, 74–5
NATO see North Atlantic Treaty Organisation
neutrality, civil service, 143
Next Steps programme, 154–5
Nolan Committee, 87
North Atlantic Treaty Organisation (NATO), 13
Northcote-Trevelyan Report (1854), 117, 141
Northern Ireland, 7, 51, 208

Official Secrets Acts, 152, 179–80, 187
oligarchy, pressure groups, 235
ombudsmen, 199
one member, one vote (OMOV), 42, 49
One Nation Toryism, 55–6
one-party system, 54
opinion polls, 36
Opposition, the, 81, 92, 98
order, conservatism, 72
outsider groups, 226
overall majority, 8

Parliament, 77–104
  authority, 164
  civil rights, 185
  composition, 77–82
  dissolution of, 32–3
  functions, 85–90
  hung, 29
  interaction of functions, 90–1

judiciary, 171–2
local government relationship, 6–7, 197–9
no confidence vote, 92, 95, 96
origins of, 164–5
performance, 91–102
presssure groups, 231–3
Prime Ministerial constraints, 127–31
questions, 92–3, 232
sovereignty, 9, 11, 82–3, 231
staff, 99
Parliament Act 1911, 12, 21, 81
Parliamentary Private Secretary (PPS), 123
parliamentary system, 7–8
parties see political parties
patronage, 49, 116–17, 130–1, 204
peers, 78–9
Pergau Dam affair, 181
petit bourgeoisie, 35
Pickles, Judge, 178
Plaid Cymru, 51, 225
pluralism, pressure groups, 234–5
policy
  civil servants, 136, 150
  judiciary, 177, 183
  manifestos, 45–6
  political parties, 47–9
Policy Unit, 122
Political Office, 121
political parties, 39–64
  committees, 96–7
  control, 83
  development, 40
  discipline, 49–50, 95
  electoral role, 41–7
  functions, 40–50
  governing role, 40, 47–50
  House of Commons, 82
  House of Lords, 97
  leadership, 111
  organization, 55–64
  party identifiers, 35
  party systems, 50–5
  policy making, 47–9
  power, 115–17
  pressure groups, 224–5, 233–4

Prime Ministerial
  constraints, 127–31
  strength, 94–5
  structure, 55–64, 131
  whips, 50, 87, 94, 96
political rights, 185
politicization
  Cabinet secretariat, 119
  civil servants, 117–18,
    150–2
  judiciary, 175, 184
  local government, 194
politics, definition, 1–2
poll tax, 204–5
Ponting, Clive, 143, 152,
    187
power
  see also separation of
    powers
  definition, 2
  House of Commons, 33
  monarchy, 165–6
  political parties, 115–17
  pressure groups, 227–9
  Prime Minister, 33
  types, 3–4
PR see proportional
    representation
pragmatism, conservatism,
    70, 72
precedent, law making, 176
Presidential government, 9,
    91, 114
Press Office, 121
pressure groups, 224–37
  access points, 229
  corporatism, 236
  influence, 3
  Parliament, 231–3
  payments to MPs, 87
  pluralism, 234–5
  power, 227–9
  sectionalism, 235–6
  types, 225–7
Prevention of Terrorism Act
    1974, 15, 186
Prime Minister
  appointment of, 33
  Cabinet, 105–34
  constraints, 127–31
  Deputy, 12
  Lord Chancellor's
    appointment, 173
  media, 132
  origin of post, 165

patronage, 49, 116–17,
    130–1
personality, 126–7
popularity, 131–2
power, 33
question time, 93
staff, 120–3
Prime Ministerial
  government, 113–23
Prime Minister's Department,
    123
primus inter pares, 128
Prison Service, 157
private members' bills, 89,
    99, 232
Private Office, 120–1
privatization, 70, 202
Profumo Affair, 140
property, rights, 186
proportional representation
    (PR), 28–33, 209
public opinion, 24
public order, 4
public ownership, 74–5

quangos, 203–4
Queen-in-Parliament, 77–8
Queen's Speech, 88
question time, Parliament,
    92–3

racial imbalance, judiciary,
    179
rate capping, 201
rate support grant, 20
rating system, reform, 204–5
rational beings, 68
Rayner, Derek, 153
rebellion, backbench MPs, 95
Redcliffe-Maud Report, 195
referenda, 83–4, 214
Referendum Party, 221
Reform Acts, 21, 83
reform issues
  constituents, 86
  constitution, 14–17
  House of Commons, 99
  MPs, 97, 98
  parliamentary system, 94
  select committees, 102
regency approach, voting, 36
regional government, 206–9
religion, freedom of, 186
representation, 86–7
  coalitions, 31

representative democracy, 20,
    86
representatives, 23, 86
reselection, 42
'reserve' powers, 165, 167
reshuffles, Cabinet, 131
responsibility
  coalitions, 32
  electoral systems, 22–3,
    23–4
  ministerial
collective, 8–9, 106–8
individual, 9, 11–12, 137
revolution, conservative view,
    70
Rhodes, R. A. W., 199
rights
  see also bill of rights
  British citizens, 185–9
  civil, 185
  European Convention on
    Human Rights, 13
  liberalism, 68
  silence, 188–9
Royal Assent, 13, 88, 165
rule of law, 10, 70, 172–3

Scarman, Lord, 180
Scotland
  devolution issue, 63, 206,
    209
  political parties, 51
Scott Inquiry, 190
Scott, Lord Justice, 180
Scottish Nationalist Party, 51,
    225
SDP see Social Democratic
    Party
sectionalism, pressure groups,
    235–6
Seldon, Anthony, 119, 126
select committees, 90, 100–1,
    233
  composition, 101
separation of powers
  see also power
  control of assembly, 92
  definition, 9, 67
  judiciary, 171
  Lord Chancellor, 173, 174
services, local government
    tiers, 195–6
shadow Cabinets, 49
Shaftesbury, Lord, 79
silence, right to, 188–9

single transferable vote (STV), 29
Sinn Fein, 188
Smith, Adam, 68, 70
Smith, Chris, 98
social class, 34–6
    see also class system
Social Democratic Party (SDP), 63
    see also Liberal Democratic Party
socialism, 73–5, 201
socialization, voting, 34
sovereignty
    bill of rights, 182
    European Union, 84–5, 182, 214, 220
    executive, 15, 83
    illusion, 222
    Parliament, 9, 11, 82–3, 181, 231
    popular, 83
Soviet Union, Communist party, 40
Speaker, office of, 81
special advisers, Prime Minister, 122
speech, freedom of, 185, 186, 187–8
sponsorship, trade unions, 62
Spycatcher case, 119, 152, 187
staff, Prime Minister, 120–3
standing committees, 88, 99–100
state, definition, 6
statute law, 12
    judicial interpretations, 177
    judicial reviews, 180–2
    ultra vires, 15, 181, 198
Stormont, 208
STV see single transferable vote
supranational authority, 213

Tameside decision, 198
Taylor, Lord Justice, 180
TECs see Training and Enterprise Councils
Thatcher, Margaret
    Cabinet, 116, 119, 124–5
    civil service, 117, 137, 149, 153, 157
    conservatism, 70, 71

European Union, 215–16, 220–1
liberalism, 68–70
local government, 199–200
Official Secrets Act, 187
personality, 126–7, 132
Presidential government, 114
Press Office, 121
pressure groups, 236
reshuffles, 131
Thatcherism, 56, 69
    local government, 194
timetable
    Cabinet, 108
    Parliament, 97–8
Tisdall, Sarah, 152, 187
toleration, liberalism, 68
top-down parties, 59, 131
Trades Union Congress (TUC), 226, 227, 236
trades unions, 227
    Labour Party, 62
    rights, 188
Training and Enterprise Councils (TECs), 203
treaties, 12–13
Treaty of Rome, 12, 182, 213
Trevelyan, Charles, 137, 141
Tribune Group, 59
tripartism, 236
TUC see Trades Union Congress
two-party system, 39, 51, 52–4

UBR see Uniform Business Rate
Ulster Unionist Party, 225
ultra vires, 15, 181, 198
UN see United Nations
Uniform Business Rate (UBR), 205
unitary state, 6–7, 197, 207
United Nations (UN), 5, 13
United States of America (USA)
    allocation of office, 49
    Bill of Rights, 10, 185, 191
    Cabinet system, 107
    civil rights, 185
    civil service, 141, 143, 144
    election campaigns, 46
    executive agencies, 15
    federalism, 7, 198, 207

funding for campaigns, 44
House of Representatives, 99
judicial politicization, 184
limited government, 9
party power, 115
political appointees, 151
political parties, 40, 41, 47, 50, 53
Presidential government, 9, 91, 92, 114
President's staff, 120
separation of powers, 7, 93
Supreme Court, 14, 181, 183, 184
Vice-President, 112
USA see United States of America

voting
    behaviour, 33–6, 47, 51–2
    Liberal Democrat Party, 52, 54
    voters, 20, 21
    wasted, 27

Waldegrave, William, 152
Wales
    devolution issue, 63, 209
    political parties, 51
Walpole, Sir Robert, 165
Walters, Alan, 122–3
Ward, Judith, 175
wards, local government, 194
Weber, Max, 3–4, 145
Westland affair, 138
Wets, 56, 116
whip system, 50, 87, 94, 96
Wilson, Harold, 214
Wilson, Sir Richard, 118
winner-takes-all system, 24
women
    candidate selection, 41
    judiciary imbalance, 179
    local councillors, 194
    parliamentary representation, 87, 98
working peers, 79
workload
    Cabinet, 108
    MPs, 97
Wright, Peter, 187

Yeo, Tim, 138–9, 140